A New Dawn

A New Dawn

THE GENERAL ELECTION OF 1945

Norman Howard

POLITICO'S

First published in 2005
Politico's Publishing, an imprint of
Methuen Publishing Limited
11–12 Buckingham Gate
London SW1E 6LB

Printed and bound in Great Britain by St. Edmundsbury Press.

Methuen Publishing Limited Reg. No. 3543167

A CIP catalogue record for this book is available from the British Library

isbn 1 84275 137 9

AUTHOR'S NOTE

Numerous people have kindly provided me with living memories of their involvement in the 1945 General Election but I must particularly single out (Lord) James Callagahan, Michael Foot, Jim Cattermole, Leslie Hilliard and (Lord) Michael Young who freely gave of their time to answer my questions. I appreciate their generosity. I must also thank the staff of the London School of Economics, the National Archives and the British Library for their courtesy and practical help at all times.

Norman Howard
April 2005

CONTENTS

AN EXCITING DAY . . .

Lord Portal, who was Chairman of Great Western Railway, gave the family tea at Paddington, and presently I was told by the Prime Minister that he was resigning. A summons to the Palace followed.

My wife drove me there and waited outside for me. The King gave me his commission to form a Government. He always used to saythat I looked surprised, as indeed I certainly was at the extent of our success.

We went to a Victory Rally at Westminster Central Hall where I announced that I had been charged with the task of forming a Government, looked in at a Fabian Society gathering and then returned to Stanmore after an exciting day.

Clement Attlee, *As it Happened* published by William Heinemann Ltd 1954

CHAPTER ONE

The Surprise Result

In the broad span of British social and political life only a handful of General Elections have left their indelible mark in the annals of history. In 1832, 800,000 electors first became eligible to cast their vote and at the 2005 General Election more than 44 million were on the election register. Throughout this period the people of Britain made individual voting decisions in favour of one candidate or another on a local basis which, under our party system, collectively created new Parliaments. Some of these Parliaments were pedestrian, both in character and in the legislation they passed, whilst others were more profound and played a key role in determining the economic and social character of British society and its role in the world during the last century.

The 1906 General Election, which produced a Liberal Government with a majority of 243, was a major turning point in social reform and brought to a head many of the burning issues that emerged from Victorian Britain. Margaret Thatcher's victory in 1979 was the start of significant changes in the economic, industrial and social relationship within Great Britain, and Tony Blair's victory with New Labour in 1997 not only brought forward a new left-of-centre range of policies, which rejected traditional Labour attitudes, but saw the Tories on a gradual downward path of public support culminating in further electoral losses at the 2001 General Election.

But pride of place in this short list must surely be the 1945 General Election result, which not only surprised the two principal figures, Clement Attlee and Winston Churchill, but marked the transformation of British society with a raft of policies like the Welfare State and the National Health Service, which have survived the passage of time.

The 1945 General Election came at a crucial time in Britain's history with large tracts of Europe smouldering from the ravages of war, with the social fabric of society in tatters, with millions of people desperate for housing (nearly one in three homes were damaged or destroyed by enemy action), with the nation's finances in a parlous state and the defeated Axis countries reduced to abject poverty and degradation.

The 1945 General Election might seem a century away but its significance remains an essential part of post-war Britain. Whilst the Allied guns were still firing in the war against Japan the British electorate, in the charged atmosphere of peace in Europe, went to the polls in its usual quiet way and ejected the Prime Minister who had led the country through years of war and into victory. But this election was different and was the culmination of a trend that had first developed immediately after the previous General Election in 1935.

Today our elections are dominated by television, opinion polls and the media (it was the *Sun* wot won it!); by almost presidential campaigns with focus groups, policy groups, study groups, photo opportunities and all the paraphernalia of a modern marketing campaign whether it is selling a new toothpaste or promoting a pop group.

In 1945 it was all very different and was perhaps the last time in the twentieth century when the electorate made up its own mind without vibrant external pressures and all the bamboozle that we have come to expect with modern parliamentary elections including the management of news. There was no television; virtually no opinion polls; no slick marketing and publicity; radio provided free political broadcasts for the main parties but because of legal constraints virtually ignored the election in its scheduled programmes; newspapers were still affected by paper shortages and were often only four pages in size; the war against Japan in the Far East was still raging and, with post-war developments in Germany being major news, the election coverage was bound to be limited. In 1945 elections were somewhat simple. Except for the university parliamentary elections, there was no proportional representation, no postal voting (except for those in the services) – just a short list of candidates on a ballot paper which did not carry the party logo or even the name of the candidate's party. And all you had to do, using the stub of a pencil, was to put a cross against the name of your choice. A visit to the polling station was a simple act in democracy and an example of citizenship at its best.

So the electorate had to rely on its own judgement by listening to their local candidates at well-attended public meetings, hope their names were on the hastily created election register and take account of any views that might be held by any servicemen or servicewomen who were part of the family but away on active service. No one under the age of 31 had ever voted before in a General Election, so for a large section of the population voting and the exercise of democracy was something quite new and unique.

But the 1945 General Election will also be remembered as the surprise election when most people thought that Winston Churchill, having won the war, would coast to victory with the nation expressing its grateful thanks. The result was somewhat different from all the predictions made by the pundits, the press and politicians. And it happened because no one was able to measure the striking changes taking place in society, the effect the war had on social attitudes and people's beliefs, the long memories of the unemployed and the total failure of the Tories to challenge the growth of Fascism in the 1930s. Although significant signs of the swing of the political pendulum were evident, politicians, the press and opinion formers chose to ignore these trends.

Post-war television did not return until 1946 so at the 1945 General Election there were no party TV broadcasts. Today television is the dominant medium in any General Election, and local and national campaigns are fitted around the various political programmes and news coverage. Party leaders make national tours accompanied by a huge press corps but these are often in close proximity to regional television studios or satellite links, so they can hook into the national network and speak to millions of viewers 'live' from any part of the country. Neither Winston Churchill nor Clement Attlee had this to contend with when they campaigned around the country; indeed, it may well be argued, that their platform style and oratory would be incompatible with modern television programmes, as old newsreels clearly demonstrate.

For the BBC, the 1945 General Election posed problems too. Whereas today, with a multitude of channels, any programme can discuss political issues provided there is balance, in 1945 they were covered by archaic rules which in effect stifled discussion on issues that were to come before

Parliament in the immediate future. BBC news programmes were restricted to non-controversial factual statements and reports of speeches made by leading politicians.

All political parties were allocated broadcasts by the BBC, the two major parties had ten programmes each, and these had a major impact because there was very little else in the way of current affairs on the radio. Six nights a week for a month the dulcet tones of one politician or another could be heard, arguing his or her case. These broadcasts were simple statements of faith and were not slick productions with music and dramatic presentation. They consisted of politicians sitting before a microphone and reading a text. For one of his major radio broadcasts Attlee came into Labour Party headquarters, briefly discussed with a few colleagues the issues he should mention, then sat down and wrote his broadcast speech on a clean sheet of paper, folded it up, placed it in his coat pocket and left for the studio. It was neither typed up nor rehearsed. Today teams of writers would produce drafts and changes, and alterations to the script would be made right up until transmission.

In addition to Churchill, who spoke in four programmes, broadcasters included Anthony Eden, Sir John Anderson, Lord Woolton, Ernest Brown, Brendan Bracken and R. A. Butler – all leading members of the Coalition Government. The Labour team included Clem Attlee, Ernest Bevin, Herbert Morrison, A. V. Alexander, Stafford Cripps, Tom Johnston, Philip Noel-Baker, Ellen Wilkinson, James Griffiths and George Tomlinson. The Liberal Party had four broadcasts, the Common Wealth Party had one programme when they fielded their leader, Sir Richard Acland, and the Communist Party for their single broadcast used Harry Pollitt, their General Secretary, to spread the message.

Winston Churchill wrote some of his speeches at Chequers, the Prime Minister's country retreat, and some reports suggest that Lord Beaverbrook (owner of the *Daily Express*) and Brendan Bracken (a close friend and Minister of Information) had a hand in their production. Certainly the famous first Churchill election broadcast, in which he tried to suggest the Labour Party would need some kind of Gestapo to implement its policies, was the work of Churchill himself who, it must be remembered, started his working life as a journalist in the South African war.

No modern election would be complete without its fair share of opinion polls. Progressing from the simple head count based on a crude sample of the electorate, we now have exit polls, personality polls, individual constituency polls, issue polls, telephone polls, north/south polls and, in European elections, a poll to determine how each country is likely to vote.

Not content with taking our pulse and publishing their results, the pollsters want to do it on a daily basis so they can detect a trend with a swing away from the government to a swing in its favour. Taken together, the reader is able to make some kind of judgement as to whether the party he or she supports is going to win or lose and whether it is even worth turning out to vote. More experienced voters will use this information to vote in a tactical way and may even vote against the party they usually support merely to defeat a party they want to remove from office.

Polls are now an essential part of modern elections. They form a background to the election and may even influence the way electors vote, since some people always like to be on the winning side. Sometimes the polls are fairly accurate. Sometimes they get it wrong and then the pollsters call in the Statistical Society to analyse their figures to see where they made a mistake. Exit polls, which are a recent innovation, appear to be highly suspect since they depend on asking electors how they actually voted when they leave the polling station. There is firm evidence that some information provided by electors is not always accurate. The broadcasting media compete vigorously to make the first prediction as to the possible outcome of the result and there have been some classic examples where they have been hopelessly wrong.

At the 1945 General Election this was not a feature and most electors took little or no interest in the unsafe predictions of the *Daily Express* or the Gallup Polls published by the *News Chronicle*. Support for Gallup Polls declined when they made an incorrect calculation about the 1944 American presidential elections. Election polls were relatively new and were not part of normal election culture as they are today. It is doubtful if they played any significant part in determining the result of the 1945 election but newspapers had their own reasons for trying to anticipate the views of the electorate.

On 21 May 1945 the *Daily Express* predicted that 'out of 425 results so far forecast by the *Express* General Election ballot, 235 seats would go to the Tories and Labour would achieve only 160 seats'. How wrong can you get? At the final tally the Tories won 213 seats and Labour achieved 393. Did the

Daily Express get its calculations wrong or was it part of Lord Beaverbrook's hidden campaign to create a bandwagon effect?

Even the gamblers in the City of London got it wrong. The betting was 2–1 against Labour, with the prediction that the Tories would have a 100 seat majority over all parties.

On 14 June the *Daily Express* made another prediction. They suggested the Tories would win 55 per cent of the poll, Labour 39 per cent, Liberals 1 per cent. Their analysis showed that 87 per cent of Tories prophesied a Tory majority and of the Labour interviewees 21 per cent thought the Tories would win.

The following day the *Daily Express* made another forecast. They said the Tories would win 279 seats, Labour 185 and the Liberals 9. They went on to suggest that Labour would gain 49 seats and the Tories would lose 21. They were wrong on all counts.

They were not alone in making false predictions. The *New York Times* predicted the Tories would have a 100 majority. Because newspapers had so few pages and space was a premium, exact mathematical election polls were never a main feature in 1945 and therefore did not form part of the election folklore during public and private discussions which take place at work or in the pub. It could be argued that modern polls influence the elections, since everyone who believes them can assert to their friends and colleagues what the result is likely to be rather than make their own judgement.

In modern elections, candidates and their agents appear to swear by polls and listen with baited breath to the outcome of the latest count, and then make public statements that support a trend. In 1945 all leading politicians had to make their own judgement. They could not rely on polls – it was a gut reaction. That is why, when the result was announced on Thursday, 26 July 1945 that Labour had won with a huge majority, everyone was surprised – or at least most leading politicians got it wrong.

Despite all the straws in the wind, politicians and the press were unaware of the strong undercurrent that was sweeping across the country. The general opinion was that Winston Churchill was a dominant and powerful figure who was virtually impregnable. Wherever he went during the campaign, the crowds cheered in their thousands but on reflection it was just a simple British way in which the populace gave thanks to Churchill the war leader for his contribution to victory. They were not cheering him in his role as leader of the Tory Party.

After speaking to vast crowds in Edinburgh and Glasgow, Churchill turned to his private secretary, John Colville, and said, 'Nobody who had witnessed their enthusiasm could doubt the result of the election.' Even Churchill was carried away by his own enthusiasm – an impression that was far from the truth. He even transmitted his enthusiasm to King George and assured him there would be a Tory majority of between 30 and 80.

Ernest Bevin, who played a leading role in the Churchill wartime Coalition Government, was so confident that Labour would not win that he booked a cottage in the West Country for a summer and post election holiday. His wife had even packed the holiday suitcase. The day after the election he scrapped his holiday and was ensconced in the Foreign Secretary's chair, planning a trip with Clement Attlee to Potsdam for a crucial meeting with Joseph Stalin and Harry Truman, the new President of the United States of America.

Hugh Dalton, who was to become Chancellor of the Exchequer in the Labour Government, gained the impression that Labour would do well but never win the election. (Lord) Douglas Jay recalls in *Change and Fortune*: 'Dalton and I met once or twice privately during the election, both taking it for granted that the election would be an easy victory for Churchill.'

Herbert Morrison, Home Secretary in the Coalition Government during the war and a member of Labour's National Executive Committee, was always close to the Labour Party organisation both at the national and local level. He was optimistic about the result but never expressed the view that Labour would sweep into power.

Professor Harold Laski, Chairman of the Labour Party throughout the 1945 campaign, thought Labour would increase its representation in Parliament but not enough to win a majority.

Sir Stafford Cripps spent the period between polling day and the declaration of the result in the garden of his Gloucestershire home but was not confident of Labour winning. Since he had only rejoined the Labour Party in February 1945 after his expulsion in 1939, he may have been out of touch with attitudes at the grass roots.

A.J.P. Taylor, the famous historian, spent the election working for the Labour Party by campaigning for (Lord) Frank Pakenham at Oxford, and

Aidan Crawley in North Buckinghamshire. He claims, 'The audiences at the election meetings were not enthusiastic; they were merely determined. All the same I did not expect a Labour victory.' Neither did *The Times*. On 5 July 1945 it predicted, 'Labour landslide improbable'.

Tony Crosland, who hoped to be a Labour candidate and later became Foreign Secretary in the Callaghan government, was serving with the Army in Italy at the time the election result was declared. He wrote to his mother, 'What a day. Even I in my wildest dreams never expected a landslide like this.'

Barbara Castle, one of the new Labour candidates in Blackburn. said, 'Despite the euphoria of the campaign, no one in the Labour Party except Aneurin Bevan believed the Party could snatch victory from the wartime Prime Minister.' This view is substantiated by John Campbell who writes in his biography of Aneurin Bevan, 'Bevan was confident that Labour would win. His belief in progress, his Marxist sense of the unfolding of history and his consciousness, particularly as editor of *Tribune*, of the shift that had occurred in public expectations over the past five years reflected in the enthusiasm reported by Labour activists round the country, all told him that Labour must win.'

Chris Mayhew, who was connected with the Coleman's mustard family, fought South Norfolk for Labour and he too was confident that Labour would win. He recalls, 'I remember with pride forecasting a 120 clear majority.' These were isolated views, since almost all the experts were confident that Winston Churchill as the war leader would coast to victory.

Attlee himself was never confident of victory. At the Potsdam International Conference, which he attended as an observer in the period between polling day (5 July) and the announcement of the election result (26 July), Attlee was asked by Mr Molotov, the Russian Foreign Secretary, what the result would be. Attlee replied that it would be a close thing but privately according to (Lord) Francis Williams, his Press Secretary, he was less optimistic and fully expected the Tories to pull it off.

This attitude is further confirmed by Wing Commander Robert Grant-Ferris, the Tory MP who lost his seat at St Pancras North but came back to Parliament in 1955 as MP for Nantwich. He recalls, 'I remember that on the day that Parliament was actually dissolved I went into the Tea Room at the House of Commons and found myself sitting alone with Mr Attlee and I asked him how he thought the result would go. He said to me he thought it would go well but he didn't expect to win the election though he thought they would take a lot of seats away from us; he didn't see the people turning out Churchill at that stage. Those words I remember so very clearly.'

Individual candidates often had highly colourful views of their own campaigns. Lieutenant James Callaghan, after knocking on hundreds of doors in his Cardiff constituency, was confident he would win the seat but not quite so confident about the national result.

Major Woodrow Wyatt, who was contesting the Aston seat in Birmingham for Labour, put it in his own inimitable style when he reported, 'As the campaign went on, signs of hope began to appear. Canvass returns for Lozells, the posher part where there were lace curtains in the window and kippers for tea, were showing more support than expected. A few days before polling day reports came in of Labour stickers going up where they had never been seen before. The unimaginable started to be imaginable: the Tory majority of 12,000 might not be invulnerable.' Woodrow Wyatt was elected and became the second-youngest MP in the House of Commons.

Those connected with the armed services were also confident that Labour would win but this view did not percolate through to the press and campaign leaders. Leslie Hilliard, who was Dr Edith Summerskill's election agent in Fulham West, was a warrant officer in the Royal Electrical and Mechanical Engineers and was based in London where he was involved in current affairs lectures to officers of his regiment. As a pre-war Labour Party election agent he was released from the Army for the 1945 election campaign, which he conducted still in his warrant officer's uniform. He was quite emphatic. Within the Army there was a strong groundswell for change. Soldiers wanted to return to jobs, not unemployment, and many of them thought it was the Tories who had got them into the war. There was a clear and distinct mood change among servicemen.

Geoffrey Goodman, who later became assistant editor of the *Daily Mirror*, served in the Royal Air Force as a reconnaissance pilot in northern France whilst the General Election was being contested at home. Geoffrey recalls, 'We had our own mock election, organised by the officers and the men of our Mosquito squadron. By an overwhelming majority we elected a Labour MP.

The Liberal candidate came second though well down the running order, and a Communist candidate came close up on the Liberal. Way down among the stragglers was the Conservative candidate. He laughed it off and drank his beer. All over the RAF and Army bases something similar was happening – with similar results.' But this kind of activity and response never made it into the newspapers.

Rab Butler, the shrewd Tory politician who served in both the Chamberlain and Churchill governments and nearly became a Tory prime minister, appeared to be one of the few Tories who felt they would lose the election. Fighting to hold his seat in Saffron Walden in Essex, he expected a bad result, probably defeat for the Tories. Edward Pearce, his biographer, writes that Butler's 'judgement may have involved some shrewdness but it was a piece with Butler's temperament, at once non-resistant and attuned to the evolution of things.'

But underneath all these attitudes was a fundamental change taking place. Ellen Wilkinson, the former Chairman of the Labour Party, sensed that something was happening when she spoke at an Albert Hall rally organised by the *Daily Herald* during the election campaign. Speaking about her Jarrow seat she said, 'Something like a religious revival is taking place up there, but there is no noise; it is very quiet. There is a great seriousness, a feeling too deep to be very demonstrative.'

Even the results of the local elections in France had no effect in convincing the British public and its political leaders that a groundswell for change was on the move throughout Europe. In Paris, out of 70 seats the Communist Party won 27, the Socialists 12, the Resistance Group 8, the Radicals 6, the MRP 14 and various Conservatives 3.

Yet Churchill's nationwide tour convinced everyone that this popular wartime leader would be returned with a safe majority. The crowds turned out in their thousands to see and touch him, and he was overwhelmed by the warmth of their affection. This personal enthusiasm for Churchill washed off on to the press who were convinced he would win. But the press did not have the depth of understanding that was to be reflected on 5 July. They were unable to detect that Churchill was less popular with servicemen than with civilians and was suspected by many organised factory workers. True, he was popular with the middle and professional classes but they only formed part of the wider electorate.

As the election campaign moved closer to polling day the *Daily Express*, who championed Churchill, initially suggested he would have a majority of 60. The *Daily Mail* was somewhat more cautious and predicted there would be a Tory majority without specifying a figure. *The Times* said the Tories would hold 46 Midland seats, which appears to have been hopelessly wrong when the swing to Labour in Birmingham alone was 23 per cent.

The *Daily Herald* would have surprised the country if it had not come out in support of Labour. They said, 'Prospects for a Labour victory are good.' The *Newcastle Journal* clearly were out of their depth when they predicted that both Ernest Bevin and Herbert Morrison would lose their seats: both were elected with large majorities.

The more prosaic *Financial Times* said a 'Churchill victory certain' and *Reynolds News*, owned by the Cooperative Movement, claimed there would be a Labour victory in Scotland and the North.

The press became even more specific in their predictions. The *Daily Herald* said there would be 'victory for Labour in Scotland, London, Wales, Monmouth, Yorkshire, Essex, Durham, Derby, Leicester, Norfolk, Nottingham and Stafford' though how it arrived at these conclusions was not made clear. The *Daily Express* later thought there would be a Tory majority of 70 and the *Liverpool Post* suggested there would be a three-figure majority for the Tories. The *Glasgow Herald* was less confident: they predicted the Tories would have a majority of between 10 and 40 seats. Undaunted, the *Daily Express* decided to tackle the subject from another angle. Rather than asking 'how are you going to vote', they asked 'who do you think will win the election'. The answer they received was that 54 per cent of those asked thought the Tories would win and 38 per cent thought Labour would win.

The *News Chronicle* used the services of Dr Gallup in attempting to make a prediction, but this was tempered with a good dose of caution. In a survey covering the period 24 to 27 June 1945, they predicted that 47 per cent of the electorate would vote Labour, that 41 per cent would vote Tory and the Liberals would get 10 per cent of the vote. In fact, the *News Chronicle* came within 1 per cent of the actual result, though for obvious reasons their poll did not include service voters. Except for the *News Chronicle*, almost all of the predictions were wide of the mark.

So the 1945 General Election result was a surprise to the press, a surprise to the national political leaders, a surprise to the King, a surprise to the rest of Europe and probably a surprise to the electorate themselves. To see how this came about we need to examine the political actions that had taken place since the last General Election in 1935, the role of the Tory Party in the lead-up to the war and the social changes that occurred during the five years of military turmoil and warfare, not forgetting that with more than 400,000 killed on active service and 65,000 civilian deaths, the election and the causes of war would have been a major talking point in many households.

CHAPTER TWO

Pre-war Politics

Prior to the 1945 General Election, the last time the majority of the nation went to a polling station for a parliamentary election was on Thursday, 14 November 1935, when Prime Minister Stanley Baldwin was returned standing under a National Government banner. The Tories won 432 seats with 53 per cent of the poll, Labour came second with 154 seats and 37 per cent of the poll and the Liberals gained 21 seats with 6 per cent of the vote, and 9 others were returned under various titles. With a majority of 278, the Tories were in a comfortable position in Parliament and were unconcerned about winning every vote in the House of Commons. The Labour vote in 1935 was no higher than its vote in 1929, whereas the Liberal vote was 4 million down and the Tory vote was slightly down in 1935 compared with 1929. Although the 1924 and 1929 Labour Governments attracted some middle-class voters, the Labour Party was essentially still a working-class party.

The considered view of some political commentators was that Baldwin won the 1935 General Election because of his strong support for the League of Nations but the League had made some controversial decisions which led Sir Stafford Cripps, the Labour MP for Bristol East, to describe it as the 'International Burglars Union'.

The 1935–45 Parliament created a record by having three different prime ministers dealing with three different monarchs. In addition, the House of Commons sat in three different Chambers. The original Chamber was damaged during a blitz in May 1941 and MPs met some of the time in Church House Westminster and in the former Chamber of the House of Lords.

In 1935 the Second World War was barely four years away and dark clouds were looming over Europe. During those years, in Germany Hitler had consolidated his powerful position by marching into Austria, threats were issued to the Sudetenland, Mussolini had conquered Abyssinia (Ethiopia) and in Spain, Franco was rattling the sabres as he prepared for civil war.

All these important international issues, and the way the Baldwin Government reacted to them, were bound to have an effect on British public opinion and some of this remained in the minds of the electorate when they went to the polls in 1945.

By 28 May 1937 Stanley Baldwin left the centre stage of political life to make way for Neville Chamberlain, known to some as the 'umbrella man'. Coming from a famous Birmingham family steeped in local government, Chamberlain presided over a Cabinet in the crucial weeks and months that led up to the Second World War in September 1939. He was the only prime minister in the twentieth century not to face the electorate.

Neville Chamberlain had his critics. Robert Boothby, a radical Tory MP who was close to Churchill, described him as 'aloof, arrogant, obstinate and limited. He was a failure.' Iain Macleod, who entered Parliament in 1950 as a Tory MP, had other views. He believed Chamberlain was a great social reformer, a first-class municipal administrator and was 'the first prominent politician to grasp the power of the political machines in the modern age'.

Instead of taking a tough line with Hitler in a period of naked power politics, Chamberlain embarked on a policy of appeasement, which led to the biggest bluff known in history – Munich – and inevitably to war. The Tory MP Oliver Stanley held the view that Baldwin regarded Europe as a bore and that Chamberlain thought it was something like a larger Birmingham.

The Parliamentary Labour Party under Arthur Henderson supported the League of Nations though George Lansbury, who succeeded him in 1932, held strong pacifist views. In 1935 the Labour Party Conference voted against Mussolini's invasion of Abyssinia and shortly afterwards Lansbury resigned the leadership of the Parliamentary Labour Party. This led to the election of Clement Attlee who remained in office until 1955. In 1937 the pay of Ministers was reviewed and Attlee, as leader of Her Majesty's Opposition, received £2,000 per annum to run his office, undertake research and travel the country.

In the run-up period to the war several Tories flirted with Hitler. Archibald Ramsay, a Tory MP, was actually imprisoned during the war for his Nazi sympathies. He was not alone in extolling the virtues of the dictator. The *Daily Mail* wrote kind words about both Hitler and Mussolini, and the Prince of Wales (who later became King Edward VIII and abdicated) expressed his warmth towards the dictator by making a visit to Germany, and meeting Hitler and other leading Fascists.

Support for Germany was fairly widespread among certain powerful groups within British society. Sir Thomas Moore MP (Tory, Ayr Burghs) said, 'If I may judge from my personal knowledge of Herr Hitler, peace and justice are the key words of his policy.' He went on to suggest the German military machine could be strengthened if all the former German colonies were handed back. Some Tories and large companies formed the Anglo-German Fellowship, which replaced a similar organisation known as the Anglo-German Society. One report suggested the Anglo-German Fellowship membership consisted of 'distinguished representatives of British big business who claim Hitler has an unanswerable case and who plan to set up a club in London at which Nazi-ism can be preached and Ministers of National Socialism entertained.'

Many members of the Fellowship were guests of Hitler and Goering, and a whole series of leading Nazis came to London and were entertained by the Fellowship and provided with an opportunity to deliver their Fascist message. It would be wrong to assume that the pre-war Tory Party was entirely pro-German but nevertheless an important section of the Party and big business were prominent sympathisers of Hitler and this did not go unnoticed by the Labour Party and the public at large.

Perhaps the most surprising politician who was mesmerised by Hitler was the Liberal Leader, Lloyd-George. In September 1936 he went to Berchtesgaden – Hitler's Alpine retreat – and had two meetings with the Führer. Back at his hotel, Lloyd-George in a comment on Hitler said, 'He is a great man and wonderful leader. He is a man who can not only plan, but can put his plans into execution. He is the Saviour of Germany.' On his return to Britain, Lloyd-George wrote an article for the *Daily Express* in which he said,

> Hitler is a born leader of men. A magnetic, dynamic personality with a single-minded purpose. The old trust him and the young idolise him.

15

The idea of a Germany intimidating Europe with a threat that its irresistible army might march across frontiers forms no part in the new vision.

Just over a year later in December 1937, when Hitler gave practical support to Franco in the Spanish Civil War, Lloyd-George, whilst critical of this action, stated,

I have felt it to be my duty to criticise his [Hitler's] activities in Spain, I have never withdrawn one particle of the admiration which I personally felt for him and expressed on my return from Germany. I only wish we had a man of his supreme quality at the head of affairs in our country today.

It is doubtful whether this view of Hitler was shared by Liberals throughout the country but a strong and warm expression of support for Hitler by one of their own leaders must have had a serious effect on the Liberal Party in Parliament and at the grass roots.

Another keen supporter of Hitler was Churchill's cousin, the Marquess of Londonderry. He made a fortune out of the coalfields of Durham and was no friend of the miners, particularly during the 1926 General Strike. He urged friendship with Hitler's Germany and developed a close connection with Ribbentrop, and was jokingly referred to as the 'Londonderry Herr'. Even Churchill referred to his cousin as 'that halfwit Charlie Londonderry'.

These episodes were just part of the way that Britain's foreign policies were being developed and articulated in the 1930s with strong right-wing views accepted as the norm.

Meanwhile the high level of unemployment experienced in the early thirties was in slow decline as Britain prepared for war. The Jarrow protest march of October 1936, when 12,000 signatures were presented to Prime Minister Baldwin by the town's MP Ellen Wilkinson, emphasised the disparity between distressed areas and the rest of the country. Unemployment was to become a major issue at the 1945 General Election.

In the House of Commons the threatening situation in Europe was constantly on the agenda. Hugh Dalton, who was later to play key roles in the Churchill Coalition and the Attlee post-war governments, sought to have an independent and private inquiry into the state of our air defences. The Tories voted this down.

In 1938 we had the Munich crisis when Chamberlain flew in from Germany to Heston Airport near Heathrow, waving a piece of paper declaring there would be 'peace in our time'. The Labour leader Clem Attlee, the Liberal Leader Sir Archibald Sinclair and both Anthony Eden and Winston Churchill all incurred odium by saying that Britain had suffered unmitigated defeat at Munich. The Tories retorted by supporting Chamberlain with 366 votes to 144 in a House of Commons debate. And even when Chamberlain had taken us into war and was forced to face a confidence motion in Parliament in May 1940, he rallied 281 Tory MPs to his banner with 200 MPs from all parties voting against.

So the activities of the Tory Party in the crucial period before Britain declared war against Germany were bound to register in the minds of the electorate. It is difficult, even with hindsight, to see why so many Tory MPs supported Chamberlain. Chamberlain put his trust in Hitler, yet all the available evidence proved this was misplaced.

In 1933 Hitler declared, 'The German people have no thought of invading any country.' In 1935 he stated, 'Germany neither intends nor wishes to interfere in the internal affairs of Austria, to annex Austria or to conclude an *Anschluss*.' He said the same in 1936: 'We have no territorial demands to make in Europe.' Two years later Hitler gave an assurance that Germany had no hostile intentions against Czechoslovakia.

Despite this catalogue of mistruths, the Tories in Parliament continued to back their 69-year-old Prime Minister. But this did not go unrecorded and public opinion was becoming distinctly anti-Tory as Britain entered the war.

Opposition to the Chamberlain government and the international situation took off in many ways. Although there were vigorous debates in the House of Commons in which Winston Churchill played a key role, the policies of Chamberlain and appeasement continued with little change. But the public and political activists outside Parliament wanted to bring about a fundamental change in the government's approach to the problems of the Spanish Civil War and the growth of Fascism throughout Europe.

Chamberlain's support for General Franco by adopting a non-intervention policy towards the Spanish Civil War provided the background to the

17

creation of the International Brigade – a body of volunteers who offered to fight for the Republican side. Whilst Britain took no action to interfere in what Chamberlain described as a domestic issue, both Hitler and Mussolini provided active support in military and personnel terms. The Spanish government that Franco was trying to overthrow was in no way a Communist government but a coalition of left-wing interests. The International Brigade drew support from young people who were active in the wider Labour movement and from those who were united in their desire to safeguard freedom. Among them was Jack Jones, a young Liverpool trade unionist who later became the General Secretary of the Transport and General Workers Union and a campaigner for pensioners. Their courageous activities struck a chord with progressive people in Britain who organised relief operations and other help for the victims of war.

The Labour movement gave general support to the Republicans and in December 1937 Clement Attlee led a small delegation to Spain where they met leading personalities who were fighting Franco. As an ex-soldier from the First World War, Attlee had a ready understanding of their practical problems in tackling enemy forces. The defeat of the Republicans in Spain and the ascendancy of Franco created a distinct threat to the free world, with three aggressive dictators in strategic positions throughout Europe. It manifested itself in Britain by the growth of the Blackshirt movement under Sir Oswald Mosley, who paraded his anti-Semitic policies and nationalistic attitudes on the streets of London and elsewhere, and at police-protected meetings. It was estimated that Mosley attracted more than 40,000 supporters to his tarnished banner.

All these adverse political conditions created the desire among supporters on the left to form a popular front of opposition in which parties and organisations would concede their own plans in favour of a united opposition to the government and to the threat of war. The British Communist Party used this and other political activities in the 1930s to seek affiliation to the Labour Party but this was firmly rejected by the Labour Party Conference.

One of the early supporters of the Popular Front was the Sunday newspaper, *Reynolds News*, owned by the Cooperative Movement and they were followed later by the *News Chronicle*, the voice of liberalism in Fleet Street.

The view among left-wing political activists was that if only there was complete unison in opposing the Tory Government, the policies of opposition towards Hitler, Mussolini and Franco could be strengthened, challenged and transformed so that war could be avoided. This approach, if somewhat naïve, became fairly widespread throughout the Labour and trade union movements and among left-wing liberals. Various attempts to come together were floated but did not enjoy the full support of the diverse organisations in the field. Partly this was due to the Labour Party National Executive Committee, who believed they could not devolve their role as a political party to an untried and untested outside body.

One of the leading advocates of a united front was Sir Stafford Cripps, a wealthy lawyer who had been appointed Solicitor General in the final days of the Ramsay MacDonald Labour Government and who represented Bristol East for Labour in Parliament. He was active in the Socialist League, an organisation that brought together the Independent Labour Party, the Society of Socialist Enquiry, the National Guild League and other small groups. At one time Ernest Bevin, the General Secretary of the Transport and General Workers Union, expressed some interest in the League but essentially it was a collection of middle-class intellectuals.

The Labour Party reacted strongly to all these multifarious political activities and in March 1937 it declared that membership of the Socialist League was incompatible with membership of the Labour Party. The League quietly disbanded itself, stating that it did not wish 'to allow its continued separate existence to be made an excuse for further disunity in the ranks of the workers'. But the mood for a united effort to defeat the Tories continued.

The frustrated Sir Stafford Cripps was later the driving force in the creation of the United Front, which was another attempt to bring together left-wing organisations who were united in their opposition to Hitler, Mussolini and Franco and all the threats that flowed from their vicious policies. Without the financial support of Cripps it is doubtful if the concept could have made much progress, but there was always the underlying opposition of the Labour Party National Executive Committee who saw that total opposition to Chamberlain and the Tory Government should be through normal Labour Party activities both in the constituencies and in Parliament.

19

At the time of these political events, Cripps was a member of Labour's National Executive Committee and he drafted several reports setting out his beliefs. In a memorandum to the NEC he stated his 'alarm at the growth of the menace of the fascist powers, that the Labour Party had not increased in anything like the same proportion as the intensity of anti-government feeling and the growing desire of the country for some form of combined opposition to defeat the Chamberlain government at the next election'. He argued that it was unlikely the Labour Party could defeat the government single-handed and that it should enter into a wide popular front with all other anti-government groups.

The memorandum was sent to the Labour Party NEC, who debated it at some length in January 1939, but the proposals were rejected by seventeen votes to three. Undeterred, Cripps sent copies of his memorandum to all sections within the wider Labour movement and this action incurred the wrath of the Labour Party. They suggested Cripps should withdraw his memorandum, which he plainly refused to do, whereupon he was expelled from the Party. His own constituency in Bristol gave him full support and did not recognise his expulsion.

The action of the National Executive Committee was endorsed by the Annual Conference of the Labour Party later in the year. One of the strongest opponents of Cripps at the conference was a young delegate from St Albans who bore the name George Brown – the same George Brown who, in Harold Wilson's governments, was to play an important if not somewhat dramatic and erratic role. The Conference also rejected a motion for non-cooperation in defence measures by 1,670,000 to 286,000.

Although he became a Minister in Churchill's Coalition Government, Cripps remained outside the Labour Party until the early part of 1945, when he was readmitted to membership. Because of his expulsion, Cripps was able to develop his theories unrestricted by the limitation of Party membership and he became a national political figure overnight. His ideas did not settle any of the major issues facing the country, but he persisted in his campaign to win over public support. He argued that it was important to remove the Chamberlain government and replace it with one that could give practical aid to Spain, make an alliance with Russia against Germany and replace the policy of appeasement with one of stern opposition to aggression. Cripps decided to organise a nationwide petition and invited all electors to sign. This action drew support from many people within the Labour movement. Both Aneurin Bevan and George Strauss joined the petition committee and from the trade unions Will Lawther, the acting President of the Mineworkers Union, gave his full support. They were also supported by numerous parliamentary Labour candidates and local activists; as well as Lloyd-George, Bernard Shaw, J. B. Priestley, the Dean of Canterbury and John Maynard Keynes.

The petition covered six main points:

Defend Democracy
Plan for Plenty
Secure our Britain
Protest the People's interest
Defend the People
Build for Peace and Justice

Cripps described it succinctly as a 'petition to save Spain, to save China, to save democracy, to save civilisation and freedom for the British workers'. He told a Birmingham rally, 'We must have socialism, pure socialism, nothing but socialism. How are you to get socialism? Only through democracy and freedom and therefore first let us make sure of democracy and freedom so that we can win socialism.'

In addition to a series of meetings, 200 local petition committees were set up and, rather than adopt an anti-Labour stance, the public were invited to join the Labour Party and within five weeks more than 3,000 people signed up. Although the petition campaign had no immediate effect, it was one further political activity which highlighted the inadequacies of government policies and pushed the electorate towards the left. The culmination of all these extramural activities prompted the Labour Party National Executive Committee to take a strong line and they expelled Aneurin Bevan, George Strauss and Charles Trevelyan, though they were not long outside the Party.

In the period just before the war a new publishing venture had a strong impact on public opinion. The Left Book Club was launched by Victor Gollancz the publisher, who recruited John Strachey and Professor Harold

21

Laski. Strachey, who had been a Labour MP and associated with the *Spectator*, was an academic intellectual who flirted with Oswald Mosley before his Blackshirt days and straddled the political spectrum of the left, ending up as a Minister in Attlee's post-war government. In the 1930s John Strachey was pro-Soviet and wanted the Labour Party to accept the Communist Party into affiliation, but over the years his views mellowed so much so that during the war he became a Wing Commander in the RAF and made numerous patriotic broadcasts. His massive tome, *The Theory and Practice of Socialism*, was described by Denis Healey as 'exciting, convincing and thorough but written in schoolboy journalese'. It sold 41,000 copies with two further editions selling 2,385 and 5,801 copies.

Harold Laski was another intellectual who had lectured at McGill and Harvard Universities before coming to the London School of Economics. He played an active role within the Labour Party and served on its National Executive Committee from 1937 to 1949, and was a very popular lecturer with students queuing up to hear him expound his theories.

Victor Gollancz was a left-wing pacifist publisher who supported many good causes. The three became a selection committee in which they chose a suitable book which they published under the imprint of Left Book Club. The cost of each book was 2s. 6d which in decimal currency is 12½ pence. The book club idea came from America and there was a general feeling among the Left Book Club protagonists that a large audience existed within the general public for books on economics, history and the arts with a left-wing bias. Of the first six books published by the club, two were written by confirmed Communists, three by people who would be termed fellow travellers and only one by an author who was clearly non-Communist. In 1937 Clem Attlee published under the Left Book cover his important analysis of politics in the thirties – *The Labour Party in Perspective* – which spelt out a modern view on a wide range of subjects. More than 50,000 copies were sold. Many of Attlee's ideas for the 1945 government were raised in this volume.

The club attempted to involve the Labour Party but Labour wanted a strong voice on the book selection committee and this was never forthcoming. Indeed, the National Executive Committee of the Labour Party became concerned about the role of the club, particularly at constituency level where it competed for the minds and active support of its local members. The club was an overnight success and indicated that there was an unsatisfied demand among the public for a clear case advancing left-wing views.

In addition to publishing a book every month, the Left Book Club developed a local structure that held meetings and rallies. Local study groups were formed and a rally at the Albert Hall in London was so full, with 8,000 supporters, that an overflow meeting at the Queen's Hall had to be arranged. Similar meetings were held in Manchester, Birmingham, Cardiff, Glasgow and other major cities. These drew larger crowds than those organised by the Labour Party and this did not improve relations between the two bodies. The organisation produced a monthly newsletter – *Left News* – which brought all the activists together and provided a forum for organising anti-government propaganda.

The Left Book Club attracted into its membership and activity a wide cross-section of the public who were concerned about the drift towards war, the situation in Spain and the negative approach to international affairs first of Baldwin and secondly of Chamberlain. The club at its peak could claim 60,000 members organised into more than 1,300 groups – a formidable political force that had no electoral ambitions. Some groups adopted Spanish refugee children, others collected money for Republican causes and a series of regional rallies was organised. Later, summer schools and camps were held, and a separate group formed the Christian Book Club under the auspices of Hewlett Johnson, the left-wing (Red) Dean of Canterbury.

Inevitably, there were differences of opinion among the key activists. Gollancz was essentially a pacifist whereas Strachey was not opposed to war provided it was a just war. The Communist Party of Great Britain saw the Left Book Club as fertile ground for recruiting members and this brought them into conflict with Gollancz. The Labour Party was also concerned about the rapid growth of the club and its impact on politics. An attempt was made to start an alternative Social Democrat Book Club with a board including Walter Citrine from the TUC, R. H. Tawney, Hugh Dalton and the distinguished author G. D. H. Cole. This noble effort never succeeded.

The Left Book Club also acted as an umbrella for those who championed the Popular Front, a peace offensive by the Left which split the Labour Party and resulted in the expulsion of several key people including Sir Stafford Cripps. At the same time the Communist Party was seeking to affiliate to the

Labour Party, but this was overwhelmingly rejected by the latter's Annual Conference.

As the club became more active at a local level, the national agent of the Labour Party wrote to all constituency parties stating, 'If the club or its groups indulge in political propaganda in opposition to the Labour Party, very serious notice would be taken by the National Executive Committee.' This drew a strong reply by Gollancz and Strachey, who argued that the club 'was a bastion of civilisation, an organisation which could work well for the Labour Party and constituted the most promising contribution to left-wing politics for a generation'.

In the months before the outbreak of hostilities in 1939 the Left Book Club held another major rally in London and speakers included Lloyd-George, former Liberal Prime Minister, Harry Pollitt, the General Secretary of the Communist Party, and Sir Stafford Cripps, with Paul Robeson from America singing appropriate ballads.

Alongside the activities of the club, Gollancz continued to bring out left-wing publications and he commissioned John Strachey to write a pamphlet entitled 'Why you should be a Socialist'. It was a phenomenal success. It originally appeared as a 90-page pamphlet in 1938 and the first 100,000 copies were sold immediately, and further editions were printed. At the final count more than 304,000 copies were sold.

Another left-wing publication which saw the light of day in the 1930s was *Tribune*. Financed by the wealthy Sir Stafford Cripps, it provided a platform for his particular brand of politics and for the Socialist League, which attempted to create a united front of all those opposed to Chamberlain and his government's foreign policies. Among those drawn into the *Tribune* orbit were Aneurin Bevan, who later became its editor, Professor Harold Laski, George Strauss and George Lansbury, who at one time edited the *Daily Herald*. Despite the opposition of the Labour Party, *Tribune* was a staunch supporter of the Socialist League and set about organising joint campaigns with the Communist Party and the Independent Labour Party in an attempt to create an electoral alliance whereby government candidates would be defeated by the combined activity of all anti-government parties. In effect, this meant consolidating the anti-government vote behind one candidate rather than having an open field of candidates.

Harold Laski was among many leading politicians who signed the manifesto organised by the Socialist League – it was a loose alliance which never had the intention of becoming an integral part of the Labour Party. Although Laski had a great admiration for Cripps, he thought his Achilles' heel was his 'moral arrogance' and that he could not work as a partner within a team. Laski himself was a prolific lecturer and writer, and gained a strong reputation within the Roosevelt administration in the USA. He wrote numerous books ranging from, *Trade Unions in the New Society* to *Parliamentary Government in England.* In the absence of television and extensive radio programmes, the written word and the public platform were the two essential ingredients for communication with the general public.

During the war Victor Gollancz was also the driving force behind another publishing venture with a series of yellow-covered books dealing with post-war issues and written by well-known politicians in a strong and forceful style. In their original form the authors remained anonymous but as the years rolled by and new editions were published their names became public and included Michael Foot, Peter Howard, Emmanuel Shinwell, Aneurin Bevan and many others.

Tom Wintringham wrote 'Your MP', a devastating catalogue of the activities of Tory MPs, which sold more than 200,000 copies. Tom Wintringham was something of a political maverick. He joined the Common Wealth Party and was their candidate at Aldershot in 1945, when he was defeated by Tory Cabinet Minister Oliver Lyttelton in a contest for which the Labour Party did not enter a candidate. Under the name 'Cato', Michael Foot, Frank Owen and Peter Howard wrote 'Guilty Men', later described as the most famous British political pamphlet for a hundred years. It sold more than 250,000 copies. The pamphlets continued throughout the war and were passed around in army barracks, naval ships and air-raid shelters. Their impact was immediate and helped to crystallise public opinion, and they were an answer to the predominantly pro-government newspapers.

At the 1936 Labour Party Conference Hugh Dalton presented a report on distressed areas when the idea of the Team Valley Industrial Estate was first mooted and was seen as a practical step in the fight against unemployment. The Labour Party argued its case at conference, in Parliament and at public meetings throughout the country. But the only critical measure of public opinion and the real effect government policies were having on the electorate is when these policies were put to the test at parliamentary by-elections. These were fought against a background of child poverty, hunger marches, the Poor Law and the Means Test.

Although the 1935 General Election was won by the Tories on 14 November, by March the following year they lost Dunbartonshire to Labour. Two months later Labour won back Peckham. In July 1936 they won Derby and by November Labour had been returned for Greenock. The same voting pattern at a further series of by-elections took place in 1937 when Labour won Wandsworth Central and Islington North. In February 1937 an official Tory MP for the Oxford University seat was replaced by an Independent Tory and four months later in Cheltenham a similar exchange took place when a by-election occurred in this constituency. Again, in 1938 – the year of the Munich crisis – Labour was successful at a series of by-elections winning Ipswich, Fulham West, Lichfield and Dartford. Even in 1939, when the government was attempting to rally public opinion and was busy preparing for war, the electors continued this pattern of rejecting Tory candidates. Labour won Southwark North and Lambeth (Kennington) in May 1939 and in August they won Brecon and Radnor.

One seat that Labour failed to win was the famous Oxford by-election when the Tories fielded Quintin Hogg (Lord Hailsham). The selected Labour candidate was Patrick Gordon-Walker who developed an unlucky streak when it came to elections. He had fought and lost the 1935 General Election and in later life he lost two safe Labour seats. In August 1938 the sitting Tory, Captain Bourne, died and there were high hopes that Labour would win the ensuing by-election. Being a university town the local Labour Party had more than its fair share of academics and among the leading lights was the President of the Oxford Labour Party, Richard Crossman, who later became an MP for Coventry and a Secretary of State in Harold Wilson's governments. Crossman argued that both the Labour and the Liberal Parties should withdraw their candidates in favour of an Independent and he had in mind the distinguished Master of Balliol, A. D. Lindsay, who until recently had been the Vice-Chancellor of Oxford University. Although he would stand as an Independent, he was in fact a Labour Party supporter. With Chamberlain's sell-out on Czechoslovakia, Crossman believed that 'in six months if Chamberlain goes on there won't be anything to save. We must unite to beat Chamberlain.'

Crossman was in a powerful position to achieve his objectives since he was a local councillor and leader of the Labour group on Oxford City Council. Enormous pressure was brought upon Patrick Gordon-Walker to stand down. He was extremely reluctant to acquiesce to this pressure and sought support from Labour's National Executive Committee and the local Labour Party. He appears to have received less than his fair share of support from Labour Party leaders. But the tide of challenging the government in this unique way swept the country and eventually the Labour Party both nationally and locally conceded by agreeing they would not enter a candidate at this by-election, despite the fact that the concept of a Popular Front did not enjoy official Labour support. The Liberal Party also decided not to contest the seat.

On 30 September, Chamberlain flew back to Britain from Munich with his 'no war' agreement with Hitler and at the same time Civil Defence authorities in Oxford began distribution of 80,000 gas masks. It was against this background that A. D. Lindsay sought to win the support of Oxford's electors and by the same token hoped to challenge the policies of Chamberlain and the government.

In Quintin Hogg the Tories had a doughty fighter in what was a traditional safe Tory seat. A considerable amount of national interest was created in the by-election, with leading campaigners from all sides descending on the city of lost causes. Even Harold Macmillan, a Tory MP, gave his support to Lindsay but when the votes were counted on 27 October 1938, Quintin Hogg won the election with 15,797 votes to Lindsay's 12,363 votes – a swing against the government of 3.9 per cent. It would seem that as the rumbles of war began clearly to emerge the electorate were less than enthusiastic about adopting an anti-government attitude. Quintin Hogg was able to state that his success at the election was a vote for Neville Chamberlain and his policies. This was not entirely correct since the next by-election, held on 18 November at Bridgewater, was a Tory loss when Vernon Bartlett, an Independent candidate standing on a Popular Front ticket, swept into office with a swing against the government of 7.6 per cent. Vernon Bartlett was an international journalist with a strong League of Nations background and the Labour Party did not contest the seat.

Critics of the period have argued that it was foolish to run A. D. Lindsay as an Independent candidate at Oxford and concentrate purely on foreign affairs. He had little contact with the working-class vote and the absence of a Labour candidate made it confusing for the electors.

Meanwhile Patrick Gordon-Walker stood on the sidelines but despite his honourable approach to the election and the Labour Party he was not reselected to fight the seat at the 1945 General Election; instead the Labour Party chose Frank Pakenham. Gordon-Walker's bad luck with elections was to stick with him all his political life. In 1964, when Labour won the General Election after thirteen years of Tory rule, he lost Smethwick following a racialist campaign against him.

Despite the result, Harold Wilson appointed him Foreign Secretary, and shortly afterwards a by-election occurred in the safe East London seat of Leyton and Patrick Gordon-Walker became the Labour candidate. The electors of Leyton had other thoughts and in January 1965 he lost the seat by 205 votes and was forced to resign his office. He did not return again to Parliament until the following election.

The last by-election before the outbreak of war was in North Cornwall when the Liberals retained the seat with a majority of 1,164 for Mr T. Horabin. Labour did not contest the seat. Tom Horabin later left the Liberal Party and in 1947 took the Labour whip. The Tory candidate had a poster which claimed, 'You are reading this in peace because you live under a National Government.' Within weeks the poster became an historic relic.

Between the 1935 and 1945 General Elections there were 219 by-elections, many uncontested. The Tories lost 30 seats, almost all to Labour. These changes in political allegiance were reflected too in the House of Commons. In 1936 Harold Macmillan lost the Tory whip and sat as an Independent for a year. The Duchess of Atholl, a Tory with a sound knowledge of the Spanish Civil War, resigned the Tory whip on a question of principle and became an Independent but then decided to force a by-election to expound her views, only to lose the seat at Christmas 1938.

There were several changes when Liberals became Liberal Nationals and Liberal Nationals became Independent. In all, 22 MPs in the 1935–45 Parliament either changed their allegiance or had it thrust upon them when they were expelled from their own party.

Leslie Hore-Belisha was a Liberal National and in February 1942 became an Independent. However, by the time the 1945 General Election was announced he faced the electors of Devonport as a National candidate. It did not matter what his label was, Michael Foot converted a 14,000 majority for the inventor of the Belisha Beacon into a 2,000 majority for Labour.

One or two MPs made a double switch. Clement Davies, the MP for Montgomery, changed from being a Liberal National into an Independent and in 1942 decided to take the Liberal whip. Edgar Granville took a similar course but waited until just before the 1945 General Election before declaring his Liberal colours.

Only one Labour MP made a voluntary switch. Mr A. Maclean, the MP for Burslem, left the Labour Party in 1943 and sat as an Independent for the remainder of the Parliament. It did not help his political career because at the 1945 General Election he was bottom of the poll.

Between November 1935 and August 1939 there were 78 contested by-elections plus two where the candidates were returned unopposed. From 1939 to May 1945 there were 141 by-election contests plus 65 seats where there was no opposing candidate.

By September 1939, when war was declared, a strong body of public opinion was against the government. This was demonstrated not merely by the government losing important by-elections but by the public's opposition to the Spanish Civil War, about the threat from Germany and the failure of the government to challenge both Hitler and Mussolini. It was a weak government led by a weak prime minister. Many British families could see at first hand the expulsion of Jews from Germany and where possible provided comfort and care. In local parks, air-raid shelters were dug and plans were prepared to evacuate millions of children from London and the provinces.

The years from 1935 until the outbreak of war in September 1939 were a period in which there was a distinct political swing against the Tory Government. In April 1938 both the Labour Party and the Liberal Party voted against conscription in peacetime. The Labour Party, which was strongly opposed to the First World War, came away from its soft pacifist approach in 1935 when George Lansbury's policies were defeated at the Labour Party Conference. Bevin, Dalton and others moved Labour's foreign policy away from a pacifist approach to one of vigorous opposition to Hitler and Mussolini. It was also strongly in favour of collective international agreements and the League of Nations, and continually probed the government about its approach and the preparations for war. It could never be accused of being a warmongering party. It abhorred war but as a minority party it was in no position to change the realities of life. It reflected the public's concern and it attempted to clarify its own approaches to an international scene and a challenge to a civilised way of life.

The dramatic Jarrow Crusade was a case in point. As the marchers struggled to reach London, the mood of the people began to change. Ellen Wilkinson who led the campaign said, 'The march disturbed the middle classes, many becoming greatly aware of the madness of want amidst plenty and began to ask questions and for the first time veered towards socialism.'

In the spring of 1936 Attlee moved a vote of censure on the Government. Following the invasion of Abyssinia, international sanctions were imposed on Italy but it was Baldwin who proposed that the League of Nations should abolish these sanctions. Despite a vigorous debate, Attlee's vote of censure was defeated.

In 1937 the Labour Party Conference agreed to set up a Spanish campaign committee with Ellen Wilkinson as the joint secretary. This helped to co-ordinate and focus a range of humane activities that were being undertaken by disparate groups. Also in 1937 Attlee denounced Britain's failure to take strong measures against Japan for attacking China, which Mao Tse-tung strongly welcomed. The following year Hitler marched into Austria. The Labour Party in Parliament urged the government to safeguard Czechoslovakia and both Attlee and his deputy, Arthur Greenwood, met Chamberlain to discuss the European conflict.

As the nation edged towards war in 1939, the domestic scene changed, with millions of gas masks being issued to the general public and a new Civil Defence organisation was created to tackle air raids. Conscription into the armed services was also passed by Parliament. Early in 1939 Chamberlain recognised Franco and in March Hitler occupied Czechslovakia. Two lone voices in the political wilderness were Anthony Eden, who previously had resigned as Foreign Secretary because he disagreed with Chamberlain on foreign affairs, and Winston Churchill, who expressed his utmost fears about the impending war.

On the question of conscription the Labour Party's Methodist and anti-war voices exerted their powerfully held views in opposition to the government; many still had fresh memories of the First World War with the massacre of millions of troops on all fronts. Many years later, Attlee believed the decision of the Labour Party to oppose conscription was on reflection wrong.

In May 1939 the Labour Party Conference met in Southport but Attlee was struck down with acute prostate problems and was unable to play a significant role in public affairs for the remainder of the year. This inevitably led to a weaker opposition in Parliament with various members of the front bench attempting to jockey for position in the event of an election for a new leader. The Labour Party Conference confirmed its opposition to the United Front campaign.

Throughout the summer the world moved cautiously step by step to a state of war. On 24 August 1939 the Labour Party National Executive Committee rejected unanimously any idea of working with Chamberlain in a War Ministry and in the same month Hitler and Stalin signed a non-aggression pact, which increased tension throughout Europe, and this was followed on 1 September by Germany's invasion of Poland. The same day Parliament debated this serious turn of events, with Attlee still absent and convalescing in North Wales. His deputy, Arthur Greenwood, held the fort in his absence but always consulted his leader despite the physical difficulties caused by Attlee being accommodated in a farmhouse without a telephone. On 2 September – the day before war was declared – Greenwood went to see Chamberlain and told him that unless war was declared in the morning it would be impossible to hold the House.

On Sunday, 3 September, with millions of children evacuated from cities to the countryside, Chamberlain declared war on Germany and with it life in Britain was never the same. The social changes that had transformed Britain in the thirties took on a new pace as the nation turned its attention to fighting the common enemy. Germany was strong and confident.

It is doubtful whether the political activities of leading Labour Party personalities had any detrimental effect on the general opposition of the public towards the government's policies. For many families the First World War was too close. Their daily papers reported on the fighting in the Spanish

Civil War, on the refugees fleeing from Germany and the threats to Poland, Austria and Czechoslovakia. Political opinions are created in various ways: by personal contact and belief, by antagonism to war, by class background, by the activities of government and by the daily grind just to exist, earn a living and bring up a family.

The 1935–45 Parliament was thus a period of immense change. The mood of the electorate was undergoing a significant movement as it reflected on all that was happening. Likewise, total loyalty by MPs to their political parties was being stretched to the point of expulsion or merely crossing the floor of the House of Commons. And yet the political pundits and party leaders were unable to measure this movement or indeed to understand that it existed at all. We must now explore what happened from the time the sirens of war sounded on 3 September 1939 to when the bells of peace in Europe rang out on 8 May 1945, for this period had a distinct and significant impact on the result of the 1945 General Election.

CHAPTER THREE

The Electoral Truce

Although in 1940 he won a confidence vote in the House of Commons following the debacle in Norway, Chamberlain accepted the moral defeat and made way for Winston Churchill who became Prime Minister in a Coalition Government that was to include a strong contingent from the Labour Party, representatives from the Liberal Party and some from outside Parliament. Mr Lloyd-George, who played a leading role in the First World War, was asked to join Churchill's Coalition Government but he refused to serve alongside Chamberlain who retained a seat in the Cabinet.

Labour reached its decision to enter the Coalition Government in 1940 whilst the Party was in Annual Conference in Bournemouth. It was made against a background of a major offensive by the German Army when they invaded Belgium and Holland, and swept through France. Clem Attlee put two questions to Labour's National Executive Committee: (1) Would they enter a government under the present Prime Minister (Chamberlain)? and (2) Would they enter a Coalition under someone else? There was unanimous agreement to answer 'No' to the first question and 'Yes' to the second, whereupon Attlee telephoned the result through to Downing Street and caught a train back to the capital.

The crucial role that Labour played in the formation of the Coalition Government is not often fully appreciated, neither is adequate recognition given to the loyal service of Clem Attlee who served in the Coalition War Cabinet from 13 May 1940 until the end of the war in May 1945, when the Churchill Caretaker Government was formed. He brought with him into government Ernest Bevin, the General Secretary of the Transport and General Workers Union, Dr Hugh Dalton who had served in previous

Labour Governments, Herbert Morrison, the leader of Labour's London County Council, Arthur Greenwood, Sir Stafford Cripps, George Tomlinson, Tom Williams, A. V. Alexander, George Hall, Fred Montague, Ben Smith, Chuter Ede, Ernest Thurtle, the Earl of Listowel and Ellen Wilkinson. This team was supplemented by others during the war as government changes were made. Emmanuel Shinwell was offered a post as Junior Food Minister but he declined and remained on the backbenches, becoming a vocal critic of the Coalition Government.

Although this strong team was scattered around Whitehall in various Ministries, they were all dedicated to the prosecution of the government's war aims, but at the same time they were in a powerful position to influence the kind of Britain that should emerge in the post-war world. Within five months of coming to power, with the evidence of Dunkirk still in everyone's mind, with the Battle of Britain raging in the blue skies above, the government decided to plan for post-war reconstruction and Arthur Greenwood, the Labour MP for Wakefield and Deputy Leader of the Parliamentary Labour Party, was put in charge.

Meanwhile Bevin, who later became an MP, was made responsible for mobilising the nation's workforce, strengthening industry and the armed forces; Herbert Morrison became Minister of Supply and later Home Secretary, and was responsible for waging war on the home front and in industry; whilst Hugh Dalton became Minister for Economic Warfare, a new department which tackled on the high seas imports into Germany from neutral countries and where the Special Operations Executive was formed.

Notably absent from the initial War Cabinet was the Chancellor of the Exchequer. Today the Treasury's influence can be found in every government department casting its spell over policy initiatives and determining economic policy irrespective of which Party is in power. During the war the Treasury was subservient to other government departments whose primary aim was to win the war.

Clem Attlee's role was crucial in the work of the wartime Cabinet. He started out as Lord President of the Council but later became Deputy Prime Minister. In this role he took the chair at important subcommittees of the Cabinet. In effect, the Cabinet was divided into three areas of activity. First was the War Cabinet, which was presided over by Churchill, then the

Defence Committee and lastly the Lord President's Committee over which Attlee presided. But the common thread of all committees was Attlee, who was not only a member of each of the three committees but was Churchill's deputy in the War Cabinet and the Defence Committee.

Ellen Wilkinson, who was made a Minister at the Home Office, aptly described the contrast between Cabinet meetings presided over by Churchill and those by Attlee.

> The difference is this. When Attlee is presiding the Cabinet meets on time and works systematically through the agenda making the necessary decisions and then goes home after three or four hours. When Churchill presides we never reach the agenda and we decide nothing. But we go home at midnight conscious of being present at an historic occasion.

In May 1940 Clem Attlee's first task was to reorganise the government machine. He thought there were too many committees. The important Lord President's Committee over which he presided strangely did not include Churchill so the work of tackling the home front issues was left to Attlee. With Ernest Bevin at his side, Attlee was able to reach out to the wider trade union movement.

Within days of his appointment Bevin summoned a meeting of 2,000 executive members from more than 150 trade unions. Meeting in the Central Hall at Westminster, Bevin urged,

> I have to ask you to place yourselves at the disposal of the State. We are Socialists and this is the test of our Socialism.
>
> If our movement and our class rise with all their energy now and save the people of this country from disaster, the country will always turn with confidence to the people who saved them. They will pay more attention to an act of that kind than the theoretical arguments of any particular philosophy.

The delegates responded by promising their unreserved support for the government in winning the war.

Although the Coalition Government ran the war machine, Parliament was still operating and the Labour Party was still active in the House of

Commons. As a general rule Attlee was able to rely on the solidarity of the Parliamentary Labour Party but this did not include Aneurin Bevan and Emmanuel Shinwell, who from time to time voiced strong anti-government views.

In creating a Coalition, Churchill brought other people in from outside Parliament. Among the more famous of these was Lord Beaverbrook, owner of the *Daily Express*, an erratic schemer who soon ran into conflict with both Ernest Bevin and Clem Attlee. Eventually Beaverbrook left the government and always claimed it was due to Attlee's influence over Churchill.

The *Daily Express* was never a friend of the Labour Party and this became patently obvious not only at the 1945 General Election but in the post-war period when it unmercifully criticised the post-war Labour Governments for almost every trivial activity and exploited every post-war shortage. Attlee and Beaverbrook were never friends. Beaverbrook once described Attlee as a 'miserable little man' and Attlee refused to write an obituary of Beaverbook on his death, stating 'he was the only evil man I ever met.' So the attitude of the *Daily Express* towards the Labour Party was clearly defined and it never changed until Lord Hollick, a Labour peer, owned the paper for a short period when it became a strong supporter of Tony Blair's government in 1997 but changed back again to supporting the Tories when a new owner took over.

In Scotland a unique government structure was created by Tom Johnston, the Labour Secretary of State. He formed a Council of State for Scotland, which in effect was a Scottish Cabinet. It consisted of all former Secretaries of State for Scotland who were still active. It became a body with an expanding influence in Whitehall and Parliament. Whatever the Council of State agreed invariably was accepted.

Tom Johnston was a man of radical thoughts who used the Council of State to advance his ideas. He recalled,

Coming down Whitehall, I ticked off in my mind several of the things I was certain I could do even during the war. I could get an industrial Parliament to begin attracting industries north, face up to Whitehall Departments and stem the drift south of our Scots population. And I could have a jolly good try at a public corporation on a non-profit basis to harness Highland water power for electricity. And I would have a stab at teaching citizenship in the schools. And an attempt at altering the foolish rating system we had in Scotland – so foolish that as compared with England where the private builder between the years 1918 and 1939 had built 30 houses whereas our private builders had built only one . . .

I had ideas about hospitals and about afforestation and I might even try a Convention of Scottish MPs in Edinburgh and see what would emerge politically from that.

Despite the war, Tom Johnston achieved most of his objectives but in 1945 he decided he could no longer commute between Edinburgh and stay in London hotels which refused to serve real Scottish porridge and kippers! He remained in Scotland to mastermind the development of hydro-electric power.

Whilst the Coalition Government at ministerial level was dominated by the Tories, Labour's team was strongly represented in the War Cabinet. On a strictly numerical basis, Labour had a higher proportion of important offices in the Coalition Government compared with the number of seats it had in the House of Commons. The Liberal Party also held the key Minister for Air post. The public gave general support to this united war effort and this reflected itself throughout local government and in the important civil defence services. The press also gave general support to the Coalition Government, though at a later stage the Communist *Daily Worker* was banned and the *Daily Mirror* existed under threat of closure.

But the public were not docile. They had clear ideas as to how the war should be fought and were not afraid to express their opposition if they believed mistakes were being made. In true democratic style they made their views known at the ballot box.

With the creation of the Coalition Government came an electoral truce when it was agreed that if a by-election occurred no major party would oppose the party of the sitting member. In effect this meant that if a Tory MP died or left Parliament, the place was taken by another Tory and likewise, if a Labour MP departed from Westminster, the Local Labour Party was responsible for finding a successor. The intention was clear. There was a ferocious war being fought on all fronts and nothing should distract the nation from its determination to win the battle. But this was never as quite straightforward as the originators imagined.

Firstly it did not include those political parties who were outside the government. Secondly it did not include people of independent thought and thirdly it led eventually to the creation of other political parties merely as a means of challenging the government and expressing an opinion through the ballot box. The truce only related to by-elections. It did not mean that any other political activity was put into cold storage until after the war, though the immediate effect of the truce was that local political activity ceased. Constituency parties existed but did not undertake any publicity campaigns, the recruiting of new members or even contesting elections for the local council. Inevitably, the organisation and the machinery at local level eroded and with key personnel in the services there was a rapid decline in local party effectiveness.

Support for the electoral truce was not widespread and at the 1940 Labour Party Conference there was a mass of resolutions attacking the concept. Delegates learnt too that membership of the Labour Party had dropped from 409,000 in 1939 to 304,000 in 1940. This was a clear indication that organisation at the grass roots was in rapid decline as the nation concentrated its efforts on winning the war.

In 1942 the Labour Party Conference debated a proposition which sought to discourage Labour members from supporting anti-government candidates at by-elections. The motion was carried by 1,275,000 to 1,209,000 with the miners, engineers and railwaymen all voting against. The following year the Conference came back again to the electoral truce and debated whether the Labour Party should continue its support. More than 2 million voted in favour of maintaining the truce and 370,000 against.

The attitude of the Communist Party of Great Britain was somewhat different. Initially they obstructed the war effort, claiming that it was a capitalist war. They changed their views when Russia was attacked by Germany in 1941.

With the rapid growth in war industries, as factories turned over to manufacturing aircraft and weapons of war, there was an increase in membership of the trade union movement. Many Tories maintained that trade union branches became unofficial Labour Party branches, running campaigns for a Second Front and for various social policies that emerged during the Coalition Government.

Both the Tories and the Labour Party had a number of full-time political agents and organisers in the constituencies but with the advent of war this activity virtually ceased. If agents were over 30 years of age they were often recruited to the Ministry of Information with the task of explaining the war aims or running campaigns to assist the war effort. If they were under 30 they were recruited into the armed services.

But whilst the Coalition Government got into its stride grappling with the enormous problems of defending the country from possible invasion, organising aircraft resources for the Battle of Britain, fighting the war in the Middle and Far East or dealing with the aftermath of heavy bombing raids and the blitz, the political climate was changing too.

In 1940 two constituencies made a mild change when the Tory representing Cambridge University was replaced by an 'Independent Conservative' and a similar change took place in Newcastle North. Sir Oswald Mosley was a by-election candidate in May 1940 but his support was derisory. In 1941 there were no changes in party representation in the House of Commons but as the war progressed and some people could see a slight glimmer at the end of the tunnel, opposition to the government became more vocal.

In March 1942 at Grantham an interesting by-election occurred. Known later as the town that produced Margaret Thatcher, Grantham was a Tory seat and under the electoral truce they could expect to return another Tory to Westminster. But David Kendall had other ideas. At one time he was a member of the Labour Party but in 1942 he tried unsuccessfully to secure the Tory nomination for this by-election. He owned a local engineering company, which had a reputation for paying good wages and offering attractive benefits. He had powerful support among his employees and he campaigned for improved production within industry to win the war. The Grantham Labour Party decided not to use its membership to campaign on his behalf and we had the ludicrous situation of the Communist Party urging its supporters to vote for the Tory candidate, a retired Royal Air Force officer who had been active in the Middle East. On polling day, David Kendall, standing as an Independent, romped home, scoring more than 50 per cent of the poll. This was the first major loss for the Tories since the start of the war but on reflection it merely continued a trend that had commenced in 1936.

But Grantham was not a lone swallow. One month later there were two by-elections in Wallasey and Rugby – two seats that had returned Tories in 1935. Both of these were lost to the Tories as the electors returned Independent candidates.

At Rugby the Tories fielded Sir Claude Holbrook who had been Chairman of the Rugby Conservative Association for fifteen years but this had little effect. The Rugby Independent candidate was a complete maverick. At one time W. J. Brown had been a Labour MP in the 1929 Labour Government. He fell out with the Party and was attracted to Sir Oswald Mosley's New Party before Mosley became a Blackshirt and a Fascist friend of Hitler. By profession Mr Brown was General Secretary of the Civil Service Clerical Association, a union which, because of the 1927 Trades Dispute Act, could not affiliate to the Trades Union Congress or the Labour Party. Mr Brown became disenchanted with all political parties so he waged a campaign against all political organisations. During the campaign he gave full support to the war effort, he wanted the services to become democratised and expressed his concern about repression by the government. Looking forward to a peacetime situation, Mr Brown wanted a non-party approach to tackling the post-war problems and the abolition of unemployment. Mr Brown must have made a deep impression on the electors of Rugby since he reduced the Tory vote by 13 per cent. It is possible the electors just wanted an opportunity to vent their opposition to the Tory Party in general and the Tory candidate in particular.

Meanwhile in Wallasey an even larger swing against the Tories occurred. They fielded a local alderman who thought he was going to inherit the seat under the political truce. The scene was, however, disturbed by Mr Reakes, another maverick ex-Labour councillor who had disagreed with the Labour Party over policy issues in the immediate period before the war. He stood as an Independent and reduced the Tory vote by 35 per cent. One of the features of this campaign was the entry of Sir Richard Acland in support of the Independent campaign. He had been a Liberal MP for Barnstaple in 1935 but joined the Labour Party in 1936. He was a man of deep convictions who believed he should not contest his old seat at the 1945 General Election but should find a new seat now that he had changed his allegiance. He fought Putney in 1945 but was well down the poll and later rejoined the Labour

Party. He fought and won at Gravesend in a by-election in 1947 but left the Labour Party because of his disagreement over the H-bomb. He eventually left Parliament and spent the rest of his life lecturing at a university in the West Country. He inherited a very large estate outside Exeter in Devon, which he promptly gave away to the National Trust.

Another candidate at the Wallasey by-election was Leonard Cripps, the Tory brother of Sir Stafford Cripps, who stood as an Independent but lost his deposit. A strange feature of the by-election was that Ellen Wilkinson, a Labour Minister, spoke in support of the (Tory) government candidate.

The swing against the government or the Tory Party continued three months later when there was a by-election in Maldon in Essex. This had been a Tory seat but an Independent candidate emerged in the shape of Tom Driberg. He was then employed by Lord Beaverbrook on the *Daily Express* and wrote a gossip column under the name of 'William Hickey'.

Tom Driberg had the active support of the 1941 Committee, a group of intellectuals headed by J. B. Priestley, who wanted a range of radical policies adopted by the Government. He also had the support of Jack Boggis, Secretary of the Braintree Labour Party who resigned his post to run Driberg's campaign. The by-election occurred at a time when Britain's armies were losing vital positions in the Middle East, including Tobruk, and this may have had a decisive effect on the result. It was a high turnout and the Tory vote dropped by 22 per cent allowing Tom Driberg to be returned with a comfortable majority. He remained an Independent until just before the 1945 General Election when he became the official Labour candidate and retained the seat.

Tom Driberg became very active in left-wing politics and was elected to Labour's National Executive Committee and eventually was made the Party Chairman. He was a well known homosexual and had affairs with what was known as the rough end of the trade. He was a frequent visitor to public conveniences where people of similar ilk congregated. Many regarded him with disgust and believed his marriage was merely a cover for his covert sexual activities. He had a long association with Guy Burgess, the Foreign Office traitor who fled to Moscow when his KGB activities were rumbled. Strangely for someone with this background, Driberg was an active High Churchman. One story that did the rounds after his death was that he worked both for the Russian KGB and for British Intelligence. This view was disputed by Michael Foot who wrote,

> to suggest that any secret service – let alone our rabidly anti-red, anti-homosexual British contraption – would ever entrust him with one is richly comical. Tom would have enjoyed and exploited the joke. If the charge had ever been printed in his lifetime, he would have sued, and what a splendid array of witnesses or backers he could have summoned to his defence.

He died in 1976 as Lord Bradwell and had a Georgian mansion in Essex. In pre-war days Tom Driberg was a member of the Brighton Communist Party.

As for Rugby's Mr Brown, at the 1945 General Election he was returned with a majority of 1,566 when he defeated both the Labour and Tory Party candidates. In 1950 the seat was held for Labour with the small majority of 199. At the 1951 General Election Mr Brown fought as an Independent in Fulham West but was defeated. The Tory Party did not oppose him at this election. In Wallasey, Mr Reakes, the Independent MP, stood again in 1945 as an Independent but was defeated by Ernest Marples, the Tory candidate who went on to become a colourful character in Parliament. This was one of the few Tory gains at the 1945 General Election.

The immediate outcome of this string of by-elections was the creation of a new political party – the Common Wealth Party which was formed out of J. B. Priestley's 1941 Committee and other pressure groups that were active during the war. By 1943 the Common Wealth Party had scored its first electoral success. Distinctly left-wing in character, it afforded a safe home for Labour supporters and was attractive to other radicals in the country. It meant that opposition to the Tory Party could be more clearly focused and at the same time post-war policies could be developed.

Their first success came in April 1943 when they won Eddisbury and then in January 1944, just a few months before the D-Day invasion, they won Skipton in Yorkshire. Their next success was just before the 1945 General Election when they won Chelmsford in April 1945. A correspondent in the *Daily Telegraph* suggested the Common Wealth Party had been more successful because their publicity was better, the other candidates were mediocre, it was a wet evening and that Common Wealth supporters were the only ones to do any canvassing. Clearly the result had deeper implications and reflected the changing mood of the electorate.

The Common Wealth Party was never expected to be a long-term threat to either the Labour or Liberal Parties but it did capture the imagination of people who could see the end of the war on the horizon and with it the raising of the political temperature. It gathered behind it some wealthy sponsors like the millionaire Mr R. Mackay who later became a Labour MP at Reading. Peggy Duff, who spent most of her post-war life running the Campaign for Nuclear Disarmament, was particularly active. George Wigg, who later became a Minister in Harold Wilson's government, toyed with the idea of joining the Common Wealth Party but decided to stick with Labour. As mentioned above, Sir Richard Acland MP threw all his energy into campaigning for the Common Wealth Party but it never had a lasting effect. Another key person in its formation was Tom Sargant who later played a crucial role in the development of Justice – an organisation that campaigned against wrong decisions in court. He eventually rejoined the Labour Party and fought two parliamentary elections but was not successful.

Perhaps the Common Wealth Party's greatest success was at Chelmsford in April 1945 when they defeated the Tory candidate with a majority of 2,080 votes. The Labour Party did not contest the seat but the Common Wealth Party, in looking for a suitable candidate, remembered an RAF officer who used to attend their meetings. Wing Commander Millington was actively in charge of a heavy bomber squadron and reluctantly agreed to contest the seat, stating, 'I agree but there is not the slightest chance of winning.' He was wrong and proved the left-wing tide was on the move. During the campaign Wing Commander Millington argued 'that what is morally wrong cannot be politically right'. The electors of Chelmsford agreed. At the 1945 General Election the Common Wealth Party was only able to retain Chelmsford, whereupon the successful MP then joined the Labour Party.

The Common Wealth Party attracted several active members of the Labour Party into their ranks and some returned to the fold before the General Election was announced. One prominent member was Mr R. Mackay who returned to the Labour Party and was nominated as a parliamentary candidate for Hull North West. When his name was put to Labour's National Executive Committee for endorsement it was reported that Charles Jarman, Secretary of the National Union of Seamen, was likely to stand in opposition to Mr Mackay at the General Election and thus create a split vote. Despite reservations some might have had about advancing a former Common Wealth Party activist into Parliament as a Labour MP, it was agreed that Mr Jarman should be asked not to stand and after an exchange of correspondence he agreed.

Although the Common Wealth Party syphoned off the anti-government vote during the period of the electoral truce, the Tories also lost seats to other organisations. In Belfast, where a Unionist held the seat in 1935, a candidate from the Eire Labour Party was returned in February 1943.

In West Derbyshire a most unusual situation arose. Mention West Derbyshire and the name of the Duke of Devonshire comes to mind. The seat had almost been part of the family since 1885 except for two brief periods when the Liberal Party won it. But in 1944 the brother-in-law of the Duke of Devonshire, a certain Lieutenant-Colonel Hunloke, decided he should resign as MP for the constituency. Who should take his place? Well, the son of the Duke of Devonshire of course. The local Tory Party Association was summoned and quite by chance the Duke's son, Lord Hartington, happened to be home on leave from the services and without further ado he became the Tory candidate for the by-election.

The process of fixing a by-election date and triggering off the necessary electoral machinery is left to the chief whip of the appropriate party, in this case the Government Chief Whip. His name? James Stuart, another brother-in-law of the Duke of Devonshire. But the by-election was not quite that straightforward for Lord Hartington. In 1918 and 1922 the seat was won by Mr C. F> White on behalf of the Liberal Party. This time his son decided to stand as an Independent and this was the signal for people from various backgrounds to come to his aid. These included other Independents who had won by-elections, people from the Common Wealth Party and local Liberals. The Independent candidate won the by-election with a good majority. The sad part of the by-election was that Lord Hartington returned to his army unit and was later killed on active service. At the 1945 General Election Mr White stood as the official Labour candidate and held the seat with a majority of 156.

In Scotland Labour's premier position was damaged when the Labour candidate for Motherwell in April 1945 was defeated by Dr McIntyre from the Scottish National Party. The successful candidate had only a short time in Parliament because at the General Election three months later the Labour candidate was returned with a majority of 7,809.

Another change took place in Scotland when a seat held by the Tories for the Scottish Universities was lost to Sir John Boyd Orr, an expert on nutrition and Professor of Agriculture at Aberdeen who stood as an Independent candidate. He retained the seat at the subsequent General Election and eventually became a member of the House of Lords. Sir James Boyd Orr was the author of a report 'Food Health and Income' and in a section on slums he argued they, 'built up castles of misery with children who could only ever play on the stairs, who'd never seen the moon and hardly seen the sky'.

In May 1945 34-year-old Air Vice-Marshall D. C. Bennett was returned unopposed as the Liberal MP for Middlesbrough West. He was the youngest serving officer to hold this senior RAF rank. His stay in Parliament was very short. At the subsequent General Election he was opposed by Labour in the shape of a Battle of Britain pilot, Wing Commander Cooper, who achieved a majority of 2,613.

At one of the last by-elections of the 1935–45 Parliament held at Neath there were no changes in party representation. At Neath the Labour candidate romped home with a majority of 24,557 votes. There was no Tory or Liberal candidate but Jock Hastin took 1,700 votes for the Revolutionary Communist Party. He was the national organiser of the British Section of the Fourth International and was involved in industrial disputes with 'Bevin Boys' in the pits. His strong views made a rapid transformation after the war and by 1960 he was a member of the Labour Party.

The Independent Labour Party (ILP) also did well at wartime by-elections. Although it was a declining force it did not accept the political truce. One report suggested the maverick and mischievous Lord Beaverbrook offered the leader of the ILP, James Maxton, a donation to their election expenses of £500 for every by-election they contested. The ILP believed there should be a negotiated peace but there was little public support for this view. It fought eleven by-elections and lost its deposit at only one election (Bristol). At Bilston it came within an ace of winning when it was the only candidate against a Tory who won by 349 votes.

45

At the last by-election, held on 24 May 1945, the ILP lost Newport by 2,702 votes when they fielded Bob Edwards who was better known as the General Secretary of the Chemical Workers Union. Neither the Labour Party nor the Liberals fielded candidates. During the campaign Captain Somerset de Chair, speaking in support of the Tory candidate, said, 'Socialism went out of date 20 years ago. Socialism would mean the end of a free press, national newspapers would be nationalised.'

Following his victory the Tory candidate, Lieutenant Commander Bell, said, 'I won this election because the people of Newport stand solidly behind Mr Churchill and his Government.' Unfortunately for Commander Bell his time as an MP was very short. Within two months he lost the seat in the General Election when the Labour candidate secured a majority of more than 9,000.

Although throughout the war there had been a decisive swing against the Tories, the full effect and impact was never really understood by the political parties. Most people thought that by-elections were an opportunity when you merely change the party without changing the government, a luxury that would not change the world. Another important factor in these by-elections was the effect of the electoral truce. If a candidate of your own political persuasion is not standing, for whom do you cast your vote? Today, by-elections are fought vigorously and even prime ministers put in an appearance. In the wartime by-elections neither Churchill nor Attlee made personal visits and contented themselves by sending an extended letter of support to their own candidate.

Now that we can look back on the wartime by-elections with some clarity, there was a distinct leftward swing in the mood of the electorate despite the fact that thousands of potential voters were in the services, outside the country or evacuated and not on the election register. Social scientists hold more precise views. They believe the war broke down class barriers and that a community spirit was growing, which meant that people would work together for the common cause and not for private profit. This reflected itself in the electorate becoming less enthusiastic for the Tories, whom they saw as a barrier to a rising standard of living. They remembered the evils of pre-war Tory policies, which led to mass unemployment, malnutrition, the hunger marches and poor housing, and they wanted a change. A 1945 count of the homeless sleeping rough in London produced a figure of 603, whereas a figure for 1937 was more than 3,000. The war had produced quite dramatic changes in society. Sir John Mortimer, in his book *Murderers and Other Friends*, substantiates this general view.

> I don't think anyone who hasn't lived through the war years can understand how different they were from the divided and aimless Britain of today. There was an extraordinary feeling of unity, a common aim which was not only to win the war but to create a just society. Now no one can talk about a just society without first being asked how much it is going to cost and then greeted with almost universal derision!!

But the changes taking place in Britain were also reflected in Paris, which had recently been recaptured by the Allied forces. The French authorities decided to have early elections and in the capital out of 1,693 councillors elected, 359 were Socialist, 332 were Communists and 227 were Radicals. A straw in the wind that political pundits in Britain failed to recognise.

Churchill never took the by-election results seriously. Referring to Independent candidates, he said they were, 'little folk who frolic alongside the Juggernaut car of war to see what fun or notoriety they can extract from the proceedings'.

Whilst the electors were making their views known at the ballot box, those who were trying to change society and prepare for the post-war world were busy in the inner sanctums of Downing Street, Whitehall and Parliament, to where we must return.

CHAPTER FOUR

Post-war Reconstruction Plans

At the height of the Battle of Britain with dogfights over southern England and the English Channel, newspapers were inevitably dominated by the exploits of RAF fighter pilots. As the Coalition Government under Churchill got into its stride, the appointment of Arthur Greenwood MP, Deputy Leader of the Labour Party, as the person responsible for developing post-war reconstruction policies never quite hit the headlines. The announcement was possibly made to raise public morale. With the defeat of France and the Low Countries many must have thought an invasion by German forces was a distinct possibility. As the Home Guard was created and defences strengthened, the amount of effort by Arthur Greenwood and the resources available were limited, but at least the focus of attention was being directed to the future rather than raking over the ashes of the past.

Arthur Greenwood had served the Labour movement for many years and gave his name to housing legislation in previous Labour administrations. As Minister without Portfolio, he served from 11 May 1940 until 22 February 1942, when in a series of government changes he left office and became Leader of the Opposition.

But Arthur Greenwood was not alone in Whitehall in looking to the future. Lord Reith, who had left his clear imprint on British society as the first Director-General of the BBC, had been appointed Minister of Works by Churchill. In 1940 he set up a unit at the Ministry to look at post-war policies and since this government department was closely involved in rebuilding our bombed cities and towns, it naturally gave emphasis to housing and planning issues. Although Greenwood prepared the groundwork for developing post-war policies in Whitehall, the department did not become fully operational until William Jowitt became Minister for Reconstruction in 1942.

By 1943 the tide in the fortunes of war was on the change, with both Russia and the United States fully engaged and British troops regaining lost ground in the Middle East. This was the driving force to prepare plans for the post-war period A number of people thought that Lord Beaverbrook would be entrusted with this work, including Lord Beaverbrook himself, but Churchill decided otherwise. Responsibility for post-war reconstruction work moved around the corridors of Whitehall and each department had a unit looking at future policies, but it was the Minister's role to coordinate all the activities. Later in the war Lord Woolton, one of the Ministers brought in from outside Parliament as part of the Coalition Government, was put in charge of the Reconstruction Committee with Attlee, Bevin, Morrison, Anderson, Lyttelton and Butler as members. Lord Woolton brought a provincial approach to administrative matters, since in pre-war days he had run a Manchester department store. As a former Minister of Food he had considerable administrative experience and was in touch with the general public but the considered opinion was that he was not a success. After the war he became Chairman of the Tory Party.

With just a chink of light at the end of the corridor, the mood and attitude of the public were changing and it was essential for Whitehall and Parliament to develop appropriate policies for the post-war world. A simple flavour of part of the problem was illustrated by Ernest Bevin, who demonstrated the acute problem in housing where in the period 1939–43 there were more than 2 million marriages and only 10–12 per cent had a home. The development of post-war policies was encouraged by a feature in the 4 January 1941 issue of the popular *Picture Post*. At the height of the blitz, *Picture Post* published 'A Plan for Britain' under the names of J. B. Priestley, Julian Huxley, Thomas Balogh and A. D. Lindsay. The magazine claimed 'this is the time for thinking'.

At the same time the Church of England, meeting at Malvern College, began to move Church opinion towards the creation of a Welfare State. Led by William Temple, then the Archbishop of York, the evils of poverty and unemployment were seen as issues which the state should tackle. The Malvern Conference crystallised Church opinion and this was followed by the publication of a book by William Temple, *Christianity and the Social Order*, which sold more than 40,000 copies, no mean feat for a religious-based book. Following publication, William Temple toured the country and spoke at packed meetings in which he highlighted his social concerns and called for family allowances and better housing. Although he was later appointed Archbishop of Canterbury, he died before the 1945 General Election and was unable to see many of his ideas come to fruition. When he died the Labour Party passed a resolution which 'placed on record its sense of the great service he rendered to the Labour movement'. In her reply to a letter of condolence, Mrs Temple said the Archbishop, 'always had the cause of working people very much to his heart'.

The focus of the Labour Party's post-war policy thoughts was through a special Reconstruction Committee. As far back as December 1942 the committee had under consideration a wide range of topics including:

Public Health
Housing and Town Planning
Transport (Railways, Civil Aviation and Shipping)
Coal and Power
Land and Agriculture
International Affairs
Social and Economic Transformation of Great Britain
Education
Local Government
Finance
Scientific Research

The Fabian Society, which was affiliated to the Labour Party but did not contest elections, continued their work in developing left-wing policy ideas. Ellen Wilkinson MP, the academic G. D. H. Cole, Harold Laski from the London School of Economics, the writer and broadcaster J. B. Priestley and Harold Nicolson the diarist, all spoke at a well-attended series of meetings under the banner of two themes: 'Social Justice' and 'Socialism and the Future of Britain'.

In July 1943 the Labour Party Policy Committee agreed 'there should be intensive development of Party activity commencing in the autumn, consisting of Policy Conferences, Public Meetings and the promotion of study groups and discussion groups'. This was the signal for the Labour Party both in Parliament and in the constituencies to begin the task of preparing for the next election.

Later in 1943 the Labour Party National Executive Committee passed a resolution which stated, 'In view of the developments in the war situation, the NEC expresses its strong sense of the need for swift and decisive action by the Government in the field of reconstruction.' One of the key persons involved in this reconstruction policy work was Michael Young, a social scientist who at the time was Director of PEP, a research organisation that had been created in 1931. Before the war had commenced, Young drafted a Manpower Policy statement for Lord Perth, which was adopted by the government. Its key recommendation was to support conscription rather than rely on volunteers. Lord Perth was impressed by Michael Young and he was offered a post as his assistant, but MI5 found out that Young, like numerous other people, had flirted with the Communist Party so the offer was withdrawn.

Michael Young was a young man full of ideas and even when he reached the age of 80 was still developing new initiatives. We have to thank him for the Open University, a brilliant concept that produces more graduates than all the other universities put together. One of his original ideas was the development of *Which?* and the Consumers' Association. Another was the Institute of Social Entrepreneurs, a training scheme designed to ensure that the voluntary sector takes a practical approach to the management of socially desirable projects. He also started 'LanguageLine', a simple telephone scheme that enabled people from ethnic minorities to converse with doctors, housing departments and other agencies. It was an instant success and became a nationwide service. He later became a life peer, taking the title of Lord Young of Dartington and died in January 2002.

Like a number of politically active people in the thirties, Michael Young had developed his thoughts against a background of the Spanish Civil War in which he wanted to volunteer but was rejected for medical reasons. His company (PEP) won contracts to undertake basic research work over a wide range of social policies and this was to prove of immense value to the Labour Party at a later stage. As a result of his work for Whitehall, Young acquired vital information about developing policies that could be implemented in a post-war situation. The development of these policies, he claimed, was an integral part of the war effort. They were designed to raise morale among the troops and the public, and to prepare the country for the immense problems that would confront the nation after the war.

At this stage they were not official government policies, nor had Parliament given its blessing, but they were subjects that would have to be confronted at the cessation of hostilities. In 1944, armed with this valuable knowledge and experience, Michael Young was approached by Morgan Phillips, the recently appointed General Secretary of the Labour Party and invited to become its Research Officer. He accepted the offer and shortly afterwards started work in Transport House, Smith Square, Westminster. He was appointed on 23 January 1945 at a salary of £575 per annum plus a war bonus. He had difficulties in joining the Labour Party Superannuation Scheme for health reasons so the Labour Party created his own pension fund. He lived into his eighties. He had been a member of the Party for eleven years and was active in the St Pancras Labour Party. During the war he wrote three pamphlets:

Will War make us Poorer (Oxford pamphlet)
Civil Aviation
There's work for all

Michael Young came from Manchester and studied at the London School of Economics where he gained a degree in economics. He was later called to the Bar and during the early part of the war became a progress clerk at Marine Mountings in Swindon.

He played a key role in drafting Labour's election manifesto: 'Let Us Face the Future'. He gathered all the post-war policy issues that were being discussed in Whitehall, Parliament and the wider Labour movement, and brought them together as an omnibus policy document with a Socialist slant. Herbert Morrison's contribution to the contents was vital. The policy document was accepted by the Labour Party National Executive Committee and eventually the Labour Party Conference. Out of these issues was created the election manifesto. Despite the importance of the policy document some discussion took place about the actual title. Morrison wanted it to be called

'Let's Face the Future' with an apostrophe in 'Let's'. Michael Young argued for 'Let Us Face the Future'. In this case Young won the argument.

Throughout the war the Labour Party published every year up to 20 discussion pamphlets on topical policy issues. These ranged from 'Unemployment in the Distressed areas' to 'Labour's post-war water policy'. These small pamphlets, which sold for under sixpence (2½ pence), acted as the basis for discussions in community organisations, barrack rooms, trade union branches and schools. And so the debate on all these pressing post-war issues took off and helped to crystallise public thoughts and opinions about the kind of Britain that people wanted to see after the war.

Many of these important issues were discussed within the services and the Army Bureau of Current Affairs (ABCA) produced their own publications as a way of stimulating debate among servicemen and women. These debates and discussions were an essential part of raising morale within the services and occupied the spare time between training and active service. In the Middle East the services organised themselves around a miniature parliament in Cairo to put post-war issues into perspective and they held their own election. A report on these proceedings was sent to Labour Party headquarters by one of the organisers, Councillor Harry Soloman, who before his service days came from Stepney. At these 'parliamentary' meetings the Labour Party could muster 150 supporters and the result of their miniature General Election was:

Lance Corporal Hunt (Lab)	119 votes
(member of USDAW and correspondent for *Catholic Herald*)	
Flight Sergeant J. Taylor (Common Wealth)	55 votes
(Regular Airman)	
Flying Officer B. Goldstone (Liberal)	38 votes
(candidate for Petersfield and Hendon, 1934)	
Lieutenant W. Glen (Tory)	17 votes
(joined Army direct from university)	

In his report Councillor Soloman said that Lance Corporal Hunt went on to form a 'government' and that on the whole 'troops seemed to be tending towards the left and were neither Labour, Communist nor Independent Labour but still remained to be captured. The Labour Party, he wrote, was often attacked by the Communists and the Common Wealth Party seemed to attract those in the RAF.'

Some critics complained that ABCA was a left-wing tool and played a key role in swinging the service vote behind the Labour Party. This might have been the outcome of the debates and discussions within the services but it was also inevitable that once you put a problem on the agenda, the acceptable solution was likely to be radical and not reactionary.

In developing post-war policies, Whitehall had the results of various studies that were undertaken during the war by such organisations as Mass Observation and the British Institute of Public Opinion. These surveys monitored the changing attitudes of British public opinion and the effect the war was having on people's approach to society. It is interesting to note how a combination of wartime activities was gradually pushing the population in a leftwards direction rather than the opposite. The introduction of food rationing was a classic example of fair shares for all. The evacuation scheme, in which thousands of children were taken away from target bombing areas to places of relative safety, broke down class barriers and showed all those involved the other side of life. The creation of civil defences brought people together in a way that led inevitably towards community action and the whole spirit of comradeship that developed within the armed services created a new perspective on life and how society should be organised. There was a general mood of identifying the priority problems and putting them at the top of the agenda.

Michael Young once said that it was difficult to define what a classless society would be like but his nearest definition would be the kind of society that developed during the war. But whilst the population was being brought together either in the armed services, a munitions factory or in the general way of life, people began to identify the real reasons for the situation in which they found themselves. Why are we at war? Why did we have such high levels of unemployment in the thirties? Why cannot we have a real health service that meets the needs of the nation and not the variety of schemes like the panel doctors that were extremely limited? What are we going to do about the slums? These and other relevant questions became the current talking points and Labour members of the Coalition Government were in a powerful position to address these problems and in many cases had the answer.

The author Sir John Mortimer put it succinctly in a comment on the New York World Trade Center disaster of 11 September 2001 when he wrote,

> Looking back at the last war, when the bombs were falling and the disasters of the ruined World Trade Center towers were an almost nightly occurrence, I don't remember any suggestion that the inhabitants of this beleaguered island should be made to pass a test to prove that they had appropriate beliefs. I remember discussions as free in pacifist service units as they were in anti-aircraft bases and pubs shrouded in the blackout. Much of it was about a change of government after the war and there was considerable contempt for our pre–war institutions.

In addition to Attlee, Morrison and Bevin in the Cabinet, Labour Ministers were scattered throughout Whitehall. Chuter Ede, who had spent a lifetime in education, played a key role in developing education policy that culminated in the famous 1944 Education Act. In 1943 the Labour Party set out its views on education. Their proposals included:

a) raise the school leaving age to 15
b) reorganise secondary education
c) reduce class sizes to 30
d) assimilate public and boarding schools into local education committees
e) develop nursery schools
f) establish junior colleges
g) regulate juvenile employment
h) develop a school building programme
i) propose that teachers should be trained by universities

In other parts of Whitehall, Sir Stafford Cripps, the Minister for Aircraft Production and former ambassador to Russia, was able to introduce the relocation of industry, a key policy in tackling regional unemployment; Tom Williams was at the wartime Ministry of Agriculture and in the Attlee government transformed the farming industry and rural poverty; Tom

55

Johnston was Secretary of State at the Scottish Office in the Coalition Government and introduced a whole range of new policies that changed life north of the border; Hugh Dalton was at the Board of Trade, a department that had enormous powers in marshalling British industry for the benefit of the nation and the war effort; Wilfred Paling was at the Ministry of Pensions, which played a leading role in the development of the Beveridge proposals for social security; John Wilmot was at the Ministry of Supply, a key department in organising the material resources of the nation in a period of extreme shortages. George Tomlinson, who was to become Education Minister in the Attlee government, was Joint Parliamentary Secretary at the Ministry of Labour and was a member of the Post-war Settlement Committee.

Not only were Labour MPs in important Ministries, they were able to use their influence to adopt progressive policies and to demonstrate to the population their competence in running government. This should not be underestimated, because at the 1945 General Election Labour was able to show by practical example that it had the experience to run the country and fully understood the range of post-war problems that would confront the nation.

Not only was Whitehall active in developing reconstruction policies, all political parties created special subcommittees to determine their attitudes to post-war events. And inside Whitehall, too, there were a number of temporary civil servants in charge of key areas of activity. These included people like Douglas Jay, Harold Wilson and Hugh Gaitskell, all of whom were to play a vital role in post-war Labour Governments.

In 1943 Hugh Dalton prepared a paper, 'Post-war Aims of the Labour Party', which dealt mainly with foreign affairs – he argued that the major issue would be Anglo-American-Russian cooperation. But the public's attitude towards many issues was also changing. There was great sympathy towards Russia and the valiant fight they were undertaking to defend their country. They had lost 20 million people before the Allies had set foot in Normandy in 1944, including 6 million people who just starved to death. More than 3 million Russians were captured by the German Army before the Russians turned the tide. Despite the fact that Russia was a Communist country, which would normally have incurred the wrath of Britain's right-wing press, this never appeared to be a problem and public support and warmth towards Russia manifested itself in the enormous sums of money raised by Mrs Churchill for her Aid to Russia Fund.

The Labour Party attitude towards Russia was changing too. In 1943 the National Executive Committee of the Party congratulated Ivan Maisky on serving ten years as ambassador to Britain. Later, when he was appointed to another post in Russia, the NEC wanted to organise a reception for his departure but he had left before arrangements could be made.

Another example of the warmth towards Russia came in a May Day declaration issued by the Labour Party in 1944. This statement included a section which stated, 'We are wholly resolved too that alliance with the heroic peoples of the Soviet Union shall be preserved, strengthened and developed against any attempt to change it from the comradeship that it is today.'

In a more practical way of supporting the Russian people the wider Labour movement raised £762,811 for the 'Help for Russia Fund' and spent the sums raised on clothing, boots, medical supplies and tents. Most of the money came from the trade unions and Co-operative Societies, and from joint committees organised on a local basis. The movement also contributed £100,000 towards rebuilding the demolished hospital in Stalingrad.

The Labour Party clearly differentiated between support for the Russian Army and its people, and their Communist beliefs. At one point the National Council of British-Soviet Unity sought to affiliate to the Labour Party but they were 'deemed to be ineligible'.

The Communist Party of Great Britain under its General Secretary, Harry Pollitt, was always keen to affiliate to the Labour Party and all attempts were thoroughly rejected by Labour's National Executive Committee and the Annual Conference. The Labour Party argued that the Communist Party 'has a separate philosophy, programme and organisation and that the gulf between us has not been narrowed'. Although affiliation was rejected, the Communist Party came back again with a further attempt in 1946 and this too was thrown out. The Labour Party said, 'It only remains for the Communist Party to take the one rational course open to it – to admit failure, to disband its organisation and to advise its members to apply for individual membership of the Labour Party.'

In 1943 at the Kirkcaldy by-election the Labour Party complained that the Communist Party was interfering with the local Labour Party about the selection of a candidate. It was suggested that the local Communist Party 'have their supporters at work in the Trade Unions and Local Labour Party branches – some of them are so closely associated as to be suspected of being secret members of the Communist Party'. The National Executive Committee took a strong line. They quashed all the existing nominations and started the selection procedure again with a warning that 'any further interference would lead to the disqualification of candidates concerned.'

In the area of public ownership the barriers were coming down too. The train network came under government direction with little opposition from the private railway companies, most of which had been operating at a loss in the pre-war days. Using the railways for the national benefit made a lot of common sense as troops were carried around the country and vital war supplies were moved to production areas. In 1943 the Southern Railway chartered more than 700 trains under contract to the government.

Road transport was also reorganised to make the most efficient use of resources. Instead of a lorry taking a load from London to Manchester and then returning empty, the Ministry of War Transport organised the best use of available capacity, saving manpower and petrol in the process. It also made simple common sense.

The problems of the coal industry were plain to see. At its peak in 1919 more than 1 million people were employed in the pits. By 1941 it was down to 697,000. Production actually went down at various times of the war when miners could see higher rates of pay being paid in nearby munitions factories. Sir John Anderson, who became Chancellor of the Exchequer and was reputed to have enormous skills as a Whitehall administrator, produced a report on the industry. He argued, 'Nothing less than the reorganisation of an industry notoriously in need of modernisation would enable it to make an efficient use of its labour force and prevent still larger falls in production.' The *Sunday Pictorial* in August 1943 also argued for coal nationalisation.

The multitude of small pits (in Durham almost every village had a pit) were brought under the auspices of a National Coal Board scheme during the war and the next logical step was to bring them into public ownership. Although it was proposed by Gwilym Lloyd-George, the Liberal Minister of Fuel and Power, Churchill used his authority to stop this happening but nevertheless the simple fact that the mining industry should be serving the needs of the nation in a controlled form was accepted. The Miners' Federation had been in favour of coal nationalisation as far back as 1924 but this did not deter them from reaffirming this view when they met at Ayr in 1941 and voted for public ownership of the coalfields. It remained a cardinal point in their philosophy until the coal mines came into public ownership in 1947. Emmanuel Shinwell, as Minister of Fuel and Power, had the task of introducing the legislation and complained that whilst all kinds of organisations had been pressing for public ownership of the mines, there did not exist any up-to-date plans as to how this could be achieved. Throughout the war the *Daily Herald*, which supported the TUC and the Labour Party, argued strongly for nationalisation of coal. The coal owners proposed their alternative plan with some help by Robert Foot, a former BBC Director-General.

In 1942 the National Council of Labour came forward with a Coal Plan which advocated the requisition of all mines for the duration of the war, to be run by a tripartite national board consisting of owners, workers and the government. The Labour Party Conference unanimously accepted the proposal, though when the government came forward with a White Paper on the subject it carefully omitted the question of ownership.

Coal was a sensitive issue in the House of Commons. Hugh Dalton as President of the Board of Trade proposed a scheme for coal rationing but it drew considerable criticism from the Tories. Timing is all important when governments want to introduce new measures. In this case it was 1942 and Britain was at a low point in the war, and backbench members displayed their discontent by opposing the government's plans. The fact that pit owners, too, were also opposed to rationing, and the Tories' basic anti-miner approach which emerged, was all part of the combustible scene.

The early stages in the development of the Welfare State also flourished during the war. Houses were requisitioned by local authorities to provide homes for those who were bombed out. Others were acquired for refugees and national military needs. Although Labour representatives formed the driving force, support came from other political parties as well, who recognised the logic and the sheer common sense in working for the best needs of the nation at war.

The concept of public ownership was never far away from the Parliamentary Labour Party. As far back as December 1941 when Parliament was discussing the progress of the war, a group of Labour backbenchers moved an amendment which demanded

> that industries vital to the successful prosecution of the war and especially transport, coal mining and the manufacture of munitions should be brought under public ownership and control and that the necessary legislation should be brought in as soon as possible.

The amendment was fully debated and when the vote was taken some 40 Labour members voted for it and a third of the Parliamentary Party abstained. Ernest Bevin, who had advanced in Cabinet the argument for public ownership of the munitions industry, explained his approach and that of the government. He argued that the prime objective was to organise the nation's resources for the successful prosecution of the war and that must be a priority. If any industry failed the nation, the government would seriously consider any specific claim. Just a week after Parliament had debated the issue, the whole wartime scene changed. It was Pearl Harbor and the United States of America was fully at war.

At the 1942 Labour Party Conference Harold Laski introduced a report on 'Planned Economic Democracy'. The report committed Labour 'to a refusal to cooperate in any effort which seeks to preserve the main characteristics of the existing order'. Speaking to the delegates, Laski said,

> If we have foresight to see while there is still time, that wisdom in politics is the power to recognise the emerging future and to build towards it, we can transform a temporary alliance for war into a paramount alliance for peace. The age of competitive capitalism is over. A democracy means nothing less than a society of equals planning full production for community consumption.

Replying to the debate, Emmanuel Shinwell said,

> In this war, so far as the Government are concerned, they have been compelled by the changes in public opinion and the exigencies of war to accept many of the measures we had advocated for years. They have not gone as far as we want, perhaps because we have not wanted it strongly enough.

It was against this background that Parliament and the Cabinet created the machinery to develop post-war policies. Not all these policies were overwhelmingly accepted and the Parliamentary Labour Party took on the government and forced a vote on several occasions. Although Attlee was Deputy Prime Minister and Chairman of major Cabinet committees, his main area of activity was in the development of domestic policies covering housing, social insurance, employment, NHS, physical planning and the location of industry.

Perhaps the policy that created the widest discussion and provoked the most interest was the Beveridge Report on social security. Arthur Greenwood MP was the Minister in charge of post-war reconstruction at the time and his decision to invite Beveridge to prepare a report was to prove one of the most important and far-reaching acts by Parliament in the development of post-war policies. William Beveridge, who came from the London School of Economics, was given the task of reviewing the whole area of social security. He had already been working on manpower problems at the Ministry of Labour as a temporary civil servant but somehow he used to upset both Ernest Bevin as Minister of Labour and the permanent secretary at the department. Although his name will for ever be associated with this major study of pensions, health and social security, Beveridge's success in politics was virtually nil. In 1944 he was elected Liberal MP for Berwick-on-Tweed and at the 1945 General Election he sought re-election. Despite all the publicity his report secured and the personal publicity that he must have accrued, he lost this Liberal seat to the Tories, one of their few precious gains at the election.

The essential element of the Beveridge Report was the identification of what he described as the five giants, 'want', 'disease', 'ignorance', 'squalor' and 'idleness'. Beveridge argued that these immense social problems should be tackled by the introduction of a national health service, full employment and family allowances. The mere suggestion of these social changes set the bells ringing in Whitehall. Attempts were made to stifle the Beveridge Report but when it was published it became a best-seller with a sale of more than 500,000 copies. The publication of the report was scooped by Michael Foot, who at that time was editor of the *Evening Standard*. Sixty years later he rigorously stuck to his original confession that he obtained the information by strictly journalistic principles. The *Daily Telegraph* described the Beveridge Report as 'halfway along the road to Moscow' and the *Daily Mirror*, ever the watchdog for those in the services and their families, attacked the critics, declaring, 'Hands off the Beveridge Report.'

The Labour Party took the Beveridge Report extremely seriously. In every region they organised meetings to discuss the proposals and this was followed up with 45 area meetings where delegates from all wings of the Labour movement could consider in some detail the various elements. At the time the Labour Party did not have a clear policy on social security and related issues, so in one sense the publication of the Beveridge Report was most welcome since it was in line with the Labour Party's instincts and beliefs. In December 1942 the National Executive Committee decided to 'approve the principles laid down in the Beveridge Report' and thus it became an integral part of their post-war policy plans. At the same meeting the committee expressed the view 'that an essential part of reconstruction of the New Britain must be the provision of a Charter of Security'. At a later stage the National Executive Committee reaffirmed its belief in the Beveridge principles when it agreed, 'as a cardinal principle of its social policy, the maintenance of an adequate minimum standard of life for all should be the first charge on the nation's resources.'

The only time the Executive Committee of the Parliamentary Labour Party put down an amendment to Coalition business was on the Beveridge Report. It expressed dissatisfaction with the government's lukewarm attitude to the report and they pressed their amendment to a vote when 121 Labour MPs agreed with this view. Sir John Anderson, who spoke for the government, said he accepted three of Beveridge's proposals – family allowances, the NHS and full employment – but Labour MPs never felt the government had much enthusiasm behind their beliefs.

Although the Beveridge Report had the full support of the Labour Party both in Parliament and in the country, the Life Insurance Workers Union wanted to go a step further and bring part of the insurance business under public ownership. They sent a deputation to the Labour Party and argued 'the Parliamentary Labour Party was departing from their original position in favour of the nationalisation of industrial assurance and asked the

National Executive Committee for clarification'. The NEC responded that in 1943 the Annual Conference was in favour of creating an Industrial Assurance Board and the position remained the same. However, the question of bringing the insurance business into public ownership did not become an issue until 1949, when the Cooperative Movement succeeded in persuading the Labour Party that 'mutualisation of insurance' was to be preferred to 'nationalisation' and this became a essential element of the 1950 election manifesto.

The public reponse to the Beveridge Report clearly showed the nation was in the mood for a change in the way society was organised and it came at a time when the Allied forces were scoring victories on many battlefronts. This made it all relevant and drew suspicions from Churchill, who could see the country was drifting leftwards if not towards Socialism.

Clem Attlee, in a letter to Harold Laski who was a member of Labour's National Executive Committee, touched on the swing to Labour. He wrote, 'I find servicemen often of high rank and men in all walks of life who come to me and tell me they have been converted to socialism by what they have seen done in wartime.' In the background Attlee encouraged the development of these radical ideas. He argued that a modern social security system was an essential part of a Socialist society. But it did not stop with one policy. He said it should include the redistribution of industry, the development of new communities and the modernisation of our old industrial areas and rural slums. Attlee said,

> There must be adequate security against ill health, unemployment and old age, an adequate and steadily rising standard of living, a decent and well-equipped house in healthy surroundings for every family, full and equal education and complete medical care throughout life.

All these issues, suggested Attlee, should be tackled before the war was over. In a letter to Churchill he wrote,

> When you [Churchill] speak of men returning to their jobs as one of the essentials at the end of the war, I agree, but without planning there won't be the jobs. I am certain that unless the Government is prepared to be as

courageous in planning for peace as it has been in carrying on the war, there
is extreme danger of disaster when the war ends.

Churchill and the Tories were reluctant to see immense social legislation
introduced during the war. Churchill had little interest in the reform of social
security or economics in general. The chancellor of the exchequer said the
government could not make promises for post-war schemes. When the
Beveridge Report came before Parliament, Labour backbenchers urged that
it should be implemented forthwith and this drew some opposition from
those Labour Ministers in the government. Nevertheless the Labour Party
proposal was put to the vote and was defeated by 335 votes to 119. This was
a major revolt by the Labour Party in this Parliament. Only 23 Labour MPs
voted with the government and 22 of these were Ministers. This was a clear
expression of view by the Parliamentary Labour Party and was a further
indication of the radical development of policies that was sweeping through
the country. It was also an obvious sign that many people within the Labour
Party were becoming disenchanted with the Coalition Government and the
limiting role placed on Labour by the electoral truce.

Harold Laski, the academic from the London School of Economics, upset
his colleagues on the National Executive Committee of the Labour Party
when he wrote an article for an American publication in which he was critical
of Clement Attlee and the leadership of the trade union movement. In August
1943 the NEC disassociated themselves from Laski's remarks in a resolution
that was carried by fifteen votes to two. They then promptly issued a press
statement critical of Laski but this appears to have been a local dispute and
had no significant effect on the political situation except that it was additional
fodder for Laski's critics to store away for a future occasion.

Pensions and social security issues were always bubbling away beneath the
surface of wartime parliamentary co-operation. From time to time it
overflowed. When the government decided to increase old age pensions by
2s. 6d (12½ pence) a week, Labour backbenchers confronted Attlee who said
it was purely an interim increase and would they please await the Beveridge
proposals. Labour backbenchers were in no mood to accept this answer,
whereupon Ernest Bevin in his usual rumbustious style took them on to no
avail. Both sides lost their tempers and eventually the backbenchers voted

against the Coalition Government. Relations between Bevin and the Parliamentary Labour Party were strained to say the least.

In the same way that radical policies were being encouraged in the areas of social security, planning and associated issues were reviewed by the Ministry of Works now under a new Minister, Lord Portal. Perhaps the most radical policy to be advocated by the department through the Uthwatt Report was the suggestion that development rights in all undeveloped land should be nationalised. The report argued that if the state provides a range of services such as roads, railways and public utilities near undeveloped land, the value of the land will increase and this increase should be passed to the community. This proposal antagonised all those people who stoutly defended their article of faith about private ownership. The Labour Party went a step further. They argued that all development land should be nationalised for the benefit of society.

The question of land ownership has been tackled by various Parliaments but none has actually taken the dramatic step of putting it under public ownership. In the post-war Attlee government, both the Ministry of Agriculture and the Ministry of Local Government had their powers increased in relation to the compulsory purchase of land and John Silkin, son of Labour's post-war Minister of Planning, returned to the question with his Development Land Act in the Wilson government, which was promptly overturned by the Tories when they were returned to power.

But the mood of the Uthwatt report was to push back the frontiers of private ownership in favour of greater support for the public. This same approach emerged when Parliament looked at the provision of health services. The Tory Minister in charge of the Ministry of Health was Henry Willink and the range of ad hoc services around the country was clearly inadequate. If you were in the armed services then in effect you had a National Health Service. There was no question of a soldier trying to find a private doctor to deal with his injuries.

In some areas the local authority played a key role but many of the local hospitals were run as charities or trusts and depended on flag days for their resources. Most doctors ran private practices and some provided 'panel' services for the poor and needy. Even industry played a significant role and voluntary bodies provided services for the elderly and those without means, but these schemes often only covered employees and not their dependants. But the war forced all these services to change. If there were casualties in an air raid then victims were rushed off to hospital with no questions asked as to whether they could pay or were part of some hospital savings scheme. The Emergency Medical Service (EMS) was created and this was funded directly by the government. The centralising effect of the creation of EMS provided the essential ingredients for the post-war National Health Service.

The British Medical Association favoured a review of existing services and facilities but they were controlled by their doctor and consultant members and could only go so far. They wanted to preserve their distinct private role, though most of the doctors believed the system should be revised and that hospital administration should be coordinated. About as far as the BMA would go towards the creation of a National Health Service was their suggestion that a Medical Planning Commission should be established and that it should look at two areas. The first area they suggested should be some kind of regional health authority and this revealed instantly their antipathy towards a national organisation. The second area would be the creation of group practices operating out of health centres. The doctors said they were opposed to a salaried health service and also opposed any control by local authorities.

As the war progressed there was a build-up of new temporary hospitals by the services to meet the anticipated needs of the invasion of Europe. Many of these were in the South and adjacent to aerodromes so that casualties could be flown back to the UK for treatment. These hospitals were often equipped to high standards and after the war some were integrated into the National Health Service, whilst others were just demolished.

With the hospitals working to a central coordinated plan, no one could envisage quite what was to happen when the war was over. Clearly they could not return to a system where some hospitals were run by local authorities and some by private organisations. The trend was therefore to create some kind of National Health Service.

A key person in this discussion was Tom Johnston, the Labour Secretary of State for Scotland. He introduced into the Clyde basin the concept of civil defence hospitals, which provided free specialist examination and treatment for war workers. By April 1945 the scheme had wiped out the 34,000 waiting list from all the voluntary hospitals. Tom Johnston recalls,

After our civil defence hospitals had effectively drained off the waiting lists, we started a supplementary service to aid the general practitioner. We held meetings with GPs and before anyone could think up a hostile slogan we had the GPs enthusiastically sending their difficult cases of diagnosis to state specialists, and where thought necessary, to civil defence hospitals for treatment. Ten thousand patients were timorously treated that way. We got too the swagger hotel at Gleneagles converted into a fitness centre, first for colliers and then for war workers generally.

With progressive initiatives in public service like this, it is not surprising that Tom Johnston was described as one of the most outstanding administrative successes of the wartime Coalition Government. A graduate from Glasgow University, he was founder and editor of the Scottish Labour weekly *Forward* and was described as 'an inspired journalist, prohibitionist and scourge of landowners'.

Another keen advocate of a National Health Service was Dr Somerville Hastings, Chairman of the Socialist Medical Association who later became a Labour MP. He argued that doctors should be salaried and work together through health centres where a range of services would be available to the patient. The Labour Party embraced all these views in a pamphlet issued in 1943. Among other points it suggested that

(a) there should be a full time salaried and pensionable service
(b) the hospital services should have wide powers.

By 1944 the government was in a position to issue a White Paper on the future development of health services but this was first considered by the Reconstruction Committee on which sat the powerful voices of Labour Ministers. Attlee, Bevin and Morrison were all highly critical of different aspects of the paper which, compared with Aneurin Bevan's post-war National Health Service, was extremely mild. The paper was approved by the Cabinet but not before Lord Beaverbrook and Brendan Bracken had attempted to sabotage its recommendations. The BMA also continued its opposition to the basic concept of the service and some doctors even challenged the idea that the service should be available to all.

The Minister, Henry Willink, continued his discussions with various organisations on the creation of a health service and the Parliamentary Labour Party continued its opposition to the proposals in their existing form. They were looking for something more radical but had to wait until 1948 before the present-day National Health Service was born.

Despite opposition from the BMA and the Parliamentary Labour Party, the King's Speech in November 1944 included four Bills which were pale shadows of similar Bills introduced by the 1945 Labour Government. They were:

National Health Service Bill
Industrial Injuries Bill
National Insurance Bill
Family Allowance Bill

Although the emphasis among policy developers was about the challenge of post-war problems, this did not impede the Labour Party from exerting its influence on international affairs. In 1942, the massacre of the Jews in well-identified concentration camps became public knowledge. The wholesale movement of Jews throughout Europe to the gas chambers was not just an affront to human dignity – it bore out the worst fears of naked Fascism and galvanised people into further efforts to win the war. One million Jews were exterminated in the Auschwitz concentration camp. In an appeal to the United States of America and to all neutral countries, the Labour Party called for 'a solemn and memorable protest in the name of humanity'. The statement claimed the German crimes were 'amongst the bloodiest crimes in history.There is ample evidence that these crimes have been methodically carried out with such persistence and thoroughness that within a short time the Jewish people in Germany will have been exterminated.' The Labour Party asked the Pope to issue a statement and invited the Archbishop of Canterbury and the Chief Rabbi to address a public meeting. They also sent a deputation to see Anthony Eden regarding the serious food situation which had developed in occupied Belgium.

The conduct of the war was always top of the agenda. When the troops landed in Europe on D-Day the National Executive Committee of the Labour Party issued a clarion call. They urged,

> A solemn promise has been made by the Heads of Government (Britain, USA and Russia) that as each territory is cleared of the enemy its people shall be free to decide for themselves their future form of Government and the economic structure of their country.
>
> The NEC counts on the fulfilment of this promise and on the firm establishment when victory is won, of democracy and social justice in all liberated lands.

Another major theme of the Reconstruction Committee was the development of a coherent employment policy. Mass unemployment in the 1930s still dominated the Labour Party's thinking and it was determined that at the end of the war there should be a policy of full employment. This was a view shared by servicemen and women in all theatres of war and is best summed up by an interesting cameo involving Ernest Bevin as Minister of Labour and Churchill as Prime Minister. Just before D-Day, Churchill invited Bevin to accompany him to Portsmouth to say farewell to the troops who were about to embark on the great European crusade. Bevin recalled that as they moved among the soldiers, 'the one question they put to me was, Ernie, when we have done this job for you are we going back on the dole?' It was an incisive remark, which reached right to the heart of the development of post-war policies and Churchill was overcome by emotion. Bevin was fully aware of the problem. When he took over the Ministry of Labour in 1940 unemployment was still more than 1 million despite the fact that 1½ million people had been called up for military service.

In 1944 the Labour Party National Executive Committee created a Post-War Reconstruction Committee under the chairmanship of Emmanuel Shinwell. Other members included Dalton, Morrison, Attlee, Laski, Noel-Baker and Ellen Wilkinson. In a policy document presented to the Annual Conference of the Party, Harold Laski argued,

> We do not accept the view that the war on the one hand and reconstruction on the other can be regarded as two separate entities disconnected the one

with the other. [He warned delegates], this Party confronts grave dangers. There is the danger of fatigue at the end of the war and there is the danger of inertia and indifference. And there is the danger that is represented by the fact that privilege never forgets. Our task is to build institutions that are proportionate to the revolution in the minds of men and women of Great Britain and its Allies.

The arguments in the development of post-war employment policies were neatly divided between the forces of conservatism and the more progressive Keynesian thoughts. The Treasury argued that unemployment in the 1930s was largely due to the structure of industry, whereas the Keynesian theory was that you pumped money into capital projects and thus created employment. The pros and cons of each side were argued out vigorously in Whitehall and in Cabinet committees, and resulted in a Government White Paper published in 1944 which to some extent was a compromise between the competing ideas.

The paper had a mixed reception. It did not support the concept of stimulating consumer demand by use of budget policies and from the Labour Party point of view it was seen as a weak document. When it came to the House of Commons, Aneurin Bevan described the White Paper as a sham and proceeded to dismember it line by line. It did, however, have its supporters and some thought it went too far and that its aims and objectives could not be achieved. The left wing of the Tory Party welcomed the paper and in Parliament the Tories gave it their full support. Known as the Tory Reform Committee, 41 Tory members who signed an amendment to the resolution on the Beveridge Report constituted themselves into a permanent committee under the chairmanship of Viscount Hinchingbrooke. The group also included Quintin Hogg and from time to time they attempted to modernise the Tory Party in the development of post-war policies.

Quintin Hogg explained, 'We believe in the Party system and seek to work through the Conservative Party, of which, with its manifest faults, we are still loyal members, rather than to form a splinter party of our own.' The Tory Reform Committee's action followed four main lines. Firstly they criticised the Coalition Government 'wherever they felt that reactionary influences or internal discussions were preventing the adoption of reforms which were reasonable and beneficial'. Secondly they supported the government when they thought that opposition was both reactionary or irresponsible. Thirdly the group put down amendments to legislation where they thought the official proposals were unduly timid or ungenerous. Fourthly the Tory Reform Committee publicised its own policies if they thought the official Tory Party policies were reactionary or deficient.

The group's policies were brought together in a pamphlet 'Forward – by the Right', which was designed to lay the foundation of Tory post-war policies. Further pamphlets were published on Industrial assurance, workmen's compensation, civil aviation, agriculture, the coal industry and land utilisation. The views expounded by the group represented the kind of policies that were developed by the Tory Party in the post-war era when they were in opposition but during the war they represented only a small part of the Tory Party in Parliament, which was largely attached to pre-war policies.

Ellen Wilkinson, the leader of the Jarrow Crusade, became Chairman of the Labour Party when the incumbent George Ridley died. She was a doughty fighter for the Party and articulate in presenting its programmes, though she had frequent periods of bad health. In her usual radical tone she argued,

> Tinkering around with the social system was not good enough. The planning machine built up during the war must not be scrapped in the interests of freedom and plenty. If we do we shall only present the speculators and monopolists with the freedom to exploit the community for private profit and make a third world war certain.

The issue of unemployment was a major subject for the wider general public. Some could recall the period after the First World War when levels of unemployment were high and the 1930s which generated such campaigns as the Jarrow Crusade when the prospects for work were almost non–existent and where unemployment benefits were at poverty level.

But the Labour Party had other ideas about employment policies and the National Executive Committee, encouraged by Hugh Dalton, committed the Party to a policy of full support for a Keynesian approach to economics. Many of Hugh Dalton's prodigies like Hugh Gaitskell, Douglas Jay, Evan

71

Durban and others were beavering away behind the scenes in Whitehall where they were temporary civil servants, promoting progressive ideas and policies. In April 1944, the Labour Party National Executive Committee issued a full employment policy statement, which floated the idea of a National Investment Board. It also proposed,

1 Bank of England must become a section of the Treasury under the direction of the Chancellor and the Cabinet.
2 Export of capital strictly controlled.
3 Key to the maintenance of full employment is the maintenance of the total purchasing power of the community. Both inflation and deflation are disastrous.
4 Price control essential – balance budget year by year.
5 Large development programme.
6 Direct light industries to development areas.
7 Vast housing programme.
8 National Development Plan.
9 No return to the Gold Standard.
10 Set up International Development Board.
11 Reduce tariffs to encourage world trade.
12 Increase exports by at least 50%.

Hugh Dalton, who introduced the agreed document, was not popular in all quarters. Churchill once said, 'Keep that man away from me, I can't stand his booming voice and shifting eyes.' Dalton was violently anti-German and no doubt his experiences in the trenches during the First World War had a profound influence on his beliefs. Nevertheless, he had real practical experience in running a government department and the development of policies. He played a key role in the formation of the Special Operations Executive (SOE) which undertook clandestine operations throughout Europe. It was generally expected that he would become Foreign Secretary if Labour won the 1945 General Election but instead he was appointed Chancellor of the Exchequer.

He adopted progressive financial policies (interest rates were as low as 2½ per cent) but resigned after a simple indiscretion with the political correspondent of the London evening newspaper, the *Star*. Whilst walking into the House of Commons Chamber on Budget Day he briefly mentioned one or two points about his plans and these became evening newspaper headlines before Dalton had completed his budget statement. He later came back as Minister for Planning.

Three other key people in the development of Labour's post-war policies were Ernest Bevin, Stafford Cripps and Herbert Morrison. Bevin was brought into the Coalition Government by Churchill to run the Ministry of Labour. As the former General Secretary of the Transport and General Workers Union he had no direct parliamentary experience, had never stood for Parliament and started work at the age of thirteen in a Bristol brewery. But he was a shrewd and powerful organiser, and his immediate impact as a Minister meant that within six months of taking office Churchill brought him into the War Cabinet.

Bevin's first task was to mobilise the nation's human resources both for the armed services and for all the demands of industry in producing weapons of war. In January 1939 there were 480,000 people in the services – by January 1940 this had risen to 2,218,000. When he took over the Ministry of Labour, Britain had neither the arms nor the manpower to conduct a full-scale offensive. Within three years he completely transformed the situation and the nation achieved an unequalled position both in the production of armaments and the essential mobilisation of our manpower.

In 1941 Bevin proposed the conscription of single women between the ages of 19 and 24 into the services. It was a controversial move but it was the beginning of a different understanding about the role of women in society. Women not only joined the services but industry too. Light industry and agriculture were two popular areas and 45 per cent of civil servants were women and the number in commerce doubled. The immediate effect was that opposition to equal pay declined and the bar on married women being employed in certain jobs evaporated. To put it into perspective, when the war was over there were half a million women in the three fighting services and many who went into industry had a taste for industrial life and wished to continue.

Bevin was a keen committee man and in his early days in office he formed a Manpower Requirements Committee to ascertain precisely how many people the services would need, how many skilled engineers would be required by industry to produce aircraft, ships and munitions. The Secretary of the committee was a young economist from Oxford who was given the task of producing the report on which Bevin, the Cabinet and Parliament could make meaningful decisions. His name was Harold Wilson – a name that was to dominate British politics from the 1940s to the 1970s. Indeed, the *News Chronicle* wrote, 'He is only 29, but is regarded by the Whitehall high ups as one of the great discoveries of the war.'

Bevin's background in the trade union movement and his close contact with industry throughout the war enabled him to take a progressive view on the problems facing society and how they should be resolved. He constantly toured the country, visiting docks, shipyards, munitions factories, and kept his ear very close to the ground. He had plenty of ideas as to how the problems should be tackled and his practical experience of mobilising the nation's war effort put him in a unique position from which he could speak with authority. During his tour of the country he lectured on 'war and peace'. On housing he argued for a national housing credit which could make money available for house purchase at 2 per cent compared with the 4 per cent charged by the building societies. The immediate effect of the war on British manpower was that the working class made substantial gains. Because of the shortage of labour and the need for government to secure their full support and co-operation, working people saw increases in their take-home pay. Average weekly earning in 1938 amounted to 53s. 3d and by 1945 had risen 80 per cent to 96s. 1d, whereas the cost of living had only risen by 31 per cent. The influence of Bevin was clear to see.

Professor (Lord) Alan Bullock, in his masterly biography of Bevin, describes what he believes were the essential elements of Bevin's post-war attitude to society and politics. He suggested there were six areas which dominated Bevin's thoughts:

> First was action by the state to maintain full employment and secure the use of economic resources for social purposes, not simply individual profit. Among the forms which this might take were those recommended by Keynes for keeping up employment, the nationalisation of a number of key industries and services and control over the location of industry.

Second was action by the State to maintain the wartime policy of 'fair shares' wherever anything was in short supply – including physical controls, rationing, food and housing subsidies.

Third was a need for a social service that would provide all citizens as a right with assistance in case of need, poverty and sickness.

Fourthly was an extension of the State's provision of education to create greater equality of opportunity – for instance by raising the school leaving age to sixteen and providing better technical education and industrial training.

Fifthly was a new conception of industrial relations beginning with better wages and conditions (to be secured by joint negotiation) and extending to something approaching a partnership on equal terms between management and workers.

Finally was the extension of joint consultation with the unions and the employers to the whole range of government economic and social policy.

These were the essential ingredients in Ernest Bevin's mind and almost all these ideas found a place in Labour's manifesto, 'Let us face the future'. Alan Bullock argued that 'it was the concern for ordinary men and women running like a scarlet thread through everything he [Bevin] touched, which more than any economic or political theory inspired his ideas about the sort of world he wanted to see after the war.'

Among Bevin's main objectives was the reconstruction of industry. In a speech to the cotton manufacturers he suggested the industry 'needed to re-discover the radical innovatory tempo which had made it a leader of the earlier industrial revolution'. He argued for more research into the coal and steel industries and he wanted full employment to be an overriding object of state policy. He believed the government should have control of location and development of industry in accordance with the social needs of the nation. In January 1945 Bevin introduced the Wages Council Bill, which he described as 'one of the most far-reaching political documents of our time'. It eliminated sweated labour and established a new national wages structure. Many Tory backbenchers were opposed to his proposals but Churchill backed them. The Bill went down well with the TUC and organised workers.

Ernest Bevin has often been accused of being a right-wing trade union leader but his record demonstrates that he had a fertile mind with plenty of radical ideas. In May 1944 he was critical of the Labour Party for not being too Socialist in the views it was advancing. In a letter to Clem Attlee he expressed his concern about the future of civil aviation:

> The Prime Minister has taken the line that he will not agree to nationalise anything during the war. It looks as if Beaverbrook and all the forces associated with him are attempting to denationalise what we have got and I think there has got to be a pretty strong Labour view about the question of civil aviation.
>
> On transport the [railway] General Managers left me in no doubt that the railways are just going to be handed back. I plead for a clear lead and if we have to stand up to it then we must. The Party must make its position clear and keep its hands clean for the election; in the Uthwatt report on redevelopment land, public ownership and transport, denationalisation of air services, there is a clear cut division and I really think we ought to face it.

Bevin was an assiduous member of the Cabinet's Reconstruction Committee. It met 98 times and Bevin only missed six meetings.

Sir Stafford Cripps was also a great thinker with a keen desire to change society. Married into the Eno's Fruit Salts family, some might say Cripps was naïve in his approach but he was articulate in spelling out the evils of society and his answer to the problems. The first indication we had of his approach to post-war problems came in September 1942 when he resigned as Leader of the House of Commons and a seat in the Cabinet to become Minister of Aircraft Production.

Cripps was restless about the conduct of the war in the days immediately prior to the Battle of El Alamein. In a statement to the House of Commons about his resignation from the Cabinet, Cripps 'made clear his strong belief that great social changes must follow the war and that the Government simply because it was a Coalition, could not avoid the duty of framing a programme of post war reconstruction in advance'. Churchill was instinctively opposed to turning his mind to post-war problems and believed he should concentrate his efforts on the immediate problem of winning the war. This view was shared by other Ministers though some in Parliament thought a balance should be maintained between the war effort and plans for peace.

Although Cripps made a positive contribution towards the development of reconstruction policies, he was not entirely convinced about arguments for public ownership. As Minister of Aircraft Production with direct contact to large parts of industry, he believed it was enough to control industry and not necessarily own it. He did, however, argue that the coal industry was obsolete.

Another key player in the construction of Labour's manifesto was Herbert Morrison, who was Home Secretary during the war and was Chairman of Labour's special Campaign Committee. In the concluding months of the war, Morrison engaged in a series of public meetings in various parts of the country when he attempted to spell out the problems the nation would confront. Although he was careful in what he said, his critics suggested they were political speeches and this was not appropriate for a wartime Cabinet Minister. Churchill agreed and at a Cabinet meeting said, 'Herbert, I ask you to stop.'

Morrison replied, 'I cannot stop. Somebody must prepare the minds of the people without being politically provocative, and I don't consider I have been.' Nevertheless he did refrain from making further 'political' speeches until the 1945 election date became public.

Morrison believed 'the government was being half hearted about the way to prepare for post war problems' and 'Churchill was not going to tolerate any possible division within the Tory party because of alleged pressure by the Labour Party to prepare schemes of reform to be put into operation when the war was over.' He suggested that 'constructive planning of a kind which was bound to be politically controversial was almost impossible – an inherent weakness of a coalition.'

Morrison's enthusiasm for developing post-war policies was an example of his shrewd approach to politics. As far back as April 1941 he suggested to Labour's National Executive Committee that a special committee should be formed, which should include outside experts, to prepare economic and social policies. The results of their efforts culminated in a policy document being considered by the 1943 Annual Conference of the Labour Party. The policy statement made a strong reference to public ownership and this was echoed by Morrison in his speech to the conference. He said,

We must have the public ownership of the natural monopolies; we must have the public ownership of common services, of industries like transport and mining, which are at the service of all other industries; we must have the socialisation or the regulation of those restrictive monopolies of capitalism which themselves are based upon the economics of scarcity; and we must have control of the essential agency of the banking system, the Bank of England, that ought to become the agency of State policy and not the agent of private policy.

For the next twelve months Morrison did not play any official role in determining the Labour Party's attitude to post-war policies since he had resigned as a constituency representative on the NEC in the hope that he could be elected the Treasurer of the Party. He made a mistake and was not elected but duly came back again the following year when he played a key role in preparing the election manifesto for ultimate endorsement by the Annual Conference.

As Home Secretary, Morrison was often involved in civil liberty issues and Laski warmly endorsed his approach in preserving as much freedom as possible. Despite his liberal and tolerant views, Morrison was forced to suppress the *Daily Worker* – the voice of the Communist Party of Great Britain. In 1943 he decided to release from prison the Fascist leader Sir Oswald Mosley and his wife, but this led to strong opposition from the TUC and all parts of the wider Labour movement. The National Council of Labour – an organisation which embraced the Labour Party, the Trades Union Congress and the Cooperative Movement – passed a resolution 'disassociating itself from the actions of the Government' over Mosley. Sam Watson, the leader of the Durham miners, said there was deep concern among coal workers and urged the National Executive Committee of the Labour Party to put Mosley and his wife back in prison.

Ellen Wilkinson, who was a Junior Minister at the Ministry of Home Security, came to the defence of Herbert Morrison. She argued that the decision to release the Mosleys was based on a health report and that from a technical point of view they were still under 'house arrest'. Morrison's decision, she said, 'was judicial and not political in character'. Her defence of Morrison had no effect and despite the widespread dismay at his decision to release the Mosleys, Morrison ignored the opposition. Some libertarians argued that Mosley should not have been imprisoned in the first place.

Perhaps the most advanced political prophet at this time was Aneurin Bevan, who throughout the war sat on the backbenches and was a thorn in the side of the establishment. In 1944, when Allied troops were advancing throughout Europe and the outcome of the war was still unclear, he wrote an article in *Tribune* setting out his views on the structure of post-war Europe:

> An organic confederation of the Western European nations like France, Holland, Belgium, the Scandinavian nations and Italy, Spain, a sane Germany and Austria and a progressive Britain, is the only solution likely to lay the foundations for peace and prosperity in Europe. It is in this solution that Russia, because of her fears, cannot initiate and that America and Britain with their present policy of reaction will be unable to bring about. It remains, therefore for British Labour to show the way.

Here were the bare bones for the future European Union laid out by someone who within four years introduced the National Health Service and who was a dominant figure in the wider International Labour Movement. His views on Europe took somewhat longer to realise.

Life in the Labour movement with Aneurin Bevan was never smooth. In May 1944 an unusual joint meeting of the Parliamentary Labour Party and the National Executive Committee was held to discuss Bevan's conduct in the House of Commons, particularly over the issue of Regulation 1 AA which restrained people from instigating 'or make any other person to take part . . . in the furtherance of any strike or lock out'. The issue was hotly debated within the trade union movement. The Scottish TUC was opposed to the order and so were the South Wales miners. Inside the Labour Party Harold Laski was against and added to the confusion was that only 56 Labour MPs out of a total of 165 had cast their vote in favour of the regulation. It had all the ingredients of a first-class split. Sam Watson, the leader of the Durham miners at the joint meeting, proposed

> that we deplore the activities of Bevan in deliberately flouting the decision of the Parliamentary Labour Party and thereby causing disunity in its ranks. It

calls upon Bevan to give specific assurances in writing within 7 days that he will in future loyally accept and abide by the Standing Orders of the Parliamentary Labour Party. In the absence of such assurances the joint meeting recommends to the National Executive Committee the exclusion of Bevan from membership of the Labour Party.

The proposition was carried and after some soul searching Bevan complied with the instructions though he described them as both 'malignant and vindictive'.

This critical issue by Aneurin Bevan was a further example of the difficulties in maintaining support for the Coalition Government during the latter days of the war. It demonstrated the frustration that some MPs found when they were asked to support the government, knowing they were fundamentally opposed in principle to what was being proposed. They argued it was stretching loyalty too far. But Bevan also had his opponents within the trade union movement. The Miners Federation (of which he was a member) deplored his critical approach to trade unions. They argued, 'we do not expect from Labour MPs vituperation and invective.' Bevan was defended by Shinwell, who claimed that Bevan's remarks were an isolated incident.

The Labour Party's whole approach to post-war reconstruction was brought together in a statement that received widespread publicity.

It said,

Military victory followed by failure in peace would be a defeat. We regard post-war changes as the continuation of that great contemporary march of humanity of which the war itself is but one crucial phase.

On the one side is social strife and decay, on the other social cooperation and growth. The outstanding lesson of the Second World War is that there can be no security for nations against aggression, no security for individuals against poverty, no protection for the growth of democracy and freedom unless the keys of economic power and the essential means of production are brought under public ownership or control. Unless the keys of military power are brought under effective control by political authority of world wide scope . . . civilisation will not escape yet another disaster.

Capitalist enterprise has had its opportunity to build a society worthy of our people. The Labour Party calls upon its fellow citizens, regardless of class or creed, to demand that the foundations be laid for the transition to the socialist Commonwealth built by common consent. This is one of the supreme turning points of history.

We have the knowledge, we have the intelligence, we have the desire to embark upon the necessary steps. If we have the courage whilst there is still time, we may open a great epoch in the history of mankind.

Clearly, the Labour Party was in an emotional mood and some of their beliefs and approaches washed off on to the public. The Labour Party also involved rank-and-file members in the discussion and held policy conferences on health, pensions, education, housing and post-war planning issues in 33 towns throughout the country. Furthermore, they agreed to hold a weekend conference on reconstruction, which clearly was seen as a major topic.

The Communist Party, ever active, wrote to the Labour Party seeking a meeting to discuss 'a campaign of all working-class organisations to secure mass enrolment of trade unionists for the payment of the political levy'. The Labour Party chose to ignore this appeal.

Although the official Tory Party was preparing its policy approach to the 1945 General Election in a pedestrian manner with Churchill in the dominant position as leader of the Party, the Tory Reform group was attempting to change attitudes and approaches and address itself to the problems the nation would face at the end of the war. Their views were brought together in a pamphlet, *Forward – by the Right* which attempted to lay the foundation principles of Tory post-war policy. They followed up this publication with other statements covering insurance, workmen's compensation, civil aviation, agriculture and land utilisation. Some Tories even advocated more state controls to boost exports. The Tory Party's Achilles' heel was that the Coalition Government had not produced a White Paper on housing, a subject that was top of the agenda for servicemen and women.

Whilst these efforts were useful in clarifying Tory ideas on important subjects they had little or no effect on mainstream Tory thought, which was very much controlled by the party machine that surrounded Churchill.

However, these policies came into their own again after 1945 when the Tory Party was in a mood to reform itself following their sweeping defeat.

By the time the war in Europe was over the Coalition Government had in place a whole series of domestic policies which clearly had the strong imprint of Labour Ministers. Many of these policies were only in outline stage and were a catalogue of hopes and aspirations. But in two areas there was a clear line of action which had the backing of Parliament. First was the Education Act of 1944 known as the Butler Act and second was the introduction of family allowances, a cardinal point in the Beveridge Report.

The Butler Act was the culmination of a whole series of reforms that had been discussed widely throughout the education field and were the subject of separate reports before the war. Churchill was generally opposed to any new legislation on education during the war but Butler persisted and won through with the help of his deputy, Chuter Ede, a Labour Minister. His Bill sailed through the House of Commons with all-party support but ran into problems when an amendment to introduce equal pay for men and women teachers was passed with the government in opposition. Churchill regarded this as a question of confidence and a short time later the decision was reversed.

On family allowances, the proposal was that every family would be paid 5s. (25 pence) a week for the second child under school-leaving age. This was a major step forward and was driven by the vigorous campaigning of Eleanor Rathbone, an Independent MP. There was some opposition to this proposal from the TUC and from the trade union members of the Parliamentary Labour Party, who were more concerned about general wage levels and thought that family allowances would undermine the trade unions' negotiating ability.

But Parliament was not merely concerned with home issues. The daunting challenge of post-war Europe had to be faced and the Labour Party played an active role in developing practical policies that took account of the strong anti-German feeling among the population and the need to rebuild the war-stricken areas that had been demolished by bombs and shellfire.

In 1945 leaders of the free world met in San Francisco to create the United Nations Organisation. Britain's team included Anthony Eden, Clement Attlee and Ellen Wilkinson, and members of the Parliamentary Labour Party were outraged when it was learned that Eden would be leading the delegation rather then Attlee who was Deputy Prime Minister. The TUC were also upset when it emerged they had little or no role to play.

When the Allied troops landed in Normandy in June 1944, the Labour Party issued a strong declaration of solidarity with all the service personnel who with courage took the battle against Fascism to new heights. It said,

> The Labour Party salutes the brave soldiers, sailors and airmen of the United Nations who in this decisive stage of the war in Europe, are successfully engaging the common enemy in the West, the South and the East. It pays tribute to all those responsible for the skilfully planned and carefully organised preparations for this offensive and for the tremendous stream of essential supplies of all kinds which have sustained them. The National Executive of the Labour Party salutes with equal pride the brave men and women of the Resistance Movement.

The immediate effect of the invasion on politics was a sharp decline in activities as the public was anxious to learn about the latest stage in the battle for Europe and the concern about casualties. Members of Parliament were reluctant to accept speaking engagements that involved travelling long distances.

The Labour Party posponed its 1944 Annual Conference from May to December partly because of D-Day but also because of rockets and flying bombs that were landing in London where the conference was due to take place. When it was held the agenda included all the major wartime and post-war policy issues. An application by a Labour pacifist group for facilities to display their literature was refused. Among the debates was one on Greece, which was of some concern to the Parliamentary Labour Party. It was replied to by Ernest Bevin and few realised that he was to play such a dominant role in foreign affairs in the post-war government. An emergency resolution was passed, which called for an armistice in the civil war in Greece and the establishment of a provisional government.

The 1944 Labour Party Conference adopted a resolution which urged 'that Jews should be allowed to become the majority in Palestine – let the Arabs be encouraged to move out as the Jews move in'.

The conference agreed a policy statement on Germany which provided for:

total disarmament of Germany

military occupation of Germany

destruction of Germany's industrial power

international economic control

reduction in war potential

punishment of war criminals

controlled system of reparation and restitution

review of frontiers

standard of living to be basic and would improve as the rest of Europe progressed.

Behind the production of this policy statement was the clear imprint of Clement Attlee. One of the Cabinet's subcommittees was the Armistice and Post-War Committee chaired by Attlee and included among its members Ernest Bevin. The committee took a strong line on Germany and its war criminals, and the Cabinet generally accepted the views advanced by Labour members.

Attlee has often been accused of being a politician without colour and charisma but in the work of the Cabinet he clearly excelled. He was a good chairman, knew how to develop policies and to win over his opponents. Some say he was adroit but others might suggest that he had a calculating streak of ruthlessness. Whichever view you accept, Attlee had a clear vision of the way that post-war problems should be tackled and the detailed policies that were necessary for their success. His view prevailed in Parliament, in Labour's National Executive Committee and eventually the Labour Party Conference.

There were, of course, critics. *Tribune*, which was influenced by Aneurin Bevan, suggested that Labour's policy towards Germany 'would drive the German people to unite behind their Nazi masters'. The *New Statesman* was critical too and in Parliament Richard Stokes, the Labour MP for Ipswich, revived his Parliamentary Peace Aims Group, which attempted to draft a different policy statement. Aneurin Bevan's opposition to the NEC statement upset the Parliamentary Labour Party and the Trades Union Congress but this appears to have had no effect on the delegates to the 1944 Labour Party Conference who re-elected him with the fourth-highest vote in the National Executive Committee's election.

Right up to the Yalta Conference, attended by all the Allied leaders in February 1945, it was Labour Ministers who continued to play a significant role as chief protagonists on Germany. All the major decisions about post-war policies on manpower and troops in Europe were made by Attlee and his Cabinet subcommittee. In a long letter to Harold Laski, sent on 1 May 1944, Attlee set out his approach to the development of post-war policies.

I am sure you are under no illusion as to the press of problems which will face us at the end of the war or as to the difficult economic position of the country. Nor am I sure are you indifferent to the political and economic problems in the international sphere. Whatever Government is in power in the immediate post-war period will have a very difficult task. It is entitled to find that preparations have been made for the post-war period. Some of these it will no doubt want to alter in accordance with its political make up, but a greater number of matters must be settled now and will not be susceptible to much alteration because action will have to be taken immediately. Whether the post-war Government is Conservative or Labour it will inevitably have to work a mixed economy. If it is a Labour Government it will be a mixed economy developing towards Socialism. If it is a Conservative Government it will be an economy seeking to retain as much as possible of private enterprise, but both Governments will have to work with the world and the country as it exists. There are limits to the extent to which the clock can be put forward or back.

Attlee's approach was both practical and realistic and was an example of his wise attitude to politics and the post-war world. Many of the policy documents floating around Whitehall were strongly influenced by the presence of Labour Ministers in the Cabinet but more importantly on the Cabinet subcommittees where the detailed discussions took place. And the chairman of these committees was invariably Clement Attlee who skilfully adopted a progressive agenda and at the same time managed to suppress the natural opposition of Churchill who in many respects was out of touch on domestic affairs.

These progressive ideas also formed the background to the development of policies by the National Executive Committee of the Labour Party. The Annual Conference of the Labour Party had by resolution expressed its clear approach to post-war problems and the only slight difference of opinion between the floor and the platform was on the policy of public ownership. The Executive was in favour of a cautious approach and delegates wanted a full commitment. The delegates won.

The leading delegate who advanced the cause for public ownership was from Reading – Ian Mikardo – and he was supported by Evelyn Dennington. Ian Mikardo went on to become MP for Reading and a strong supporter of the left of the Labour Party, whilst Evelyn Dennington spent a lifetime in local government becoming Chairman of Stevenage New Town Development Corporation, Chairman of the Greater London Council and a baroness in the House of Lords. She freely confessed that she preferred local government to life in the House of Lords, which she said somehow never actually achieved anything.

When Michael Young died in 2002, Roy Hattersley suggested that Young and Mikardo had come together at the 1945 Labour Party Conference to secure the passage of the resolution that strengthened the Party's policy on public ownership. In a long discussion with the author about his role in the 1945 General Election, Michael Young did not reveal anything which might have led anyone to believe that he had undertaken any personal lobbying. He may have forgotten. As a service to delegates and as Research Officer of the Party he may have helped draft a resolution that complied with the Standing Orders of the Conference but it is doubtful, despite his general sympathy for its objectives, that he took an active role in promoting the resolution. But no doubt Roy Hattersley is correct.

Ian Mikardo's resolution urged the NEC in developing the manifesto policies to make clear,

> transfer to public ownership of the land, large scale buildings, heavy industry and all forms of banking, transport and fuel and power.
>
> Appropriate legislation to ensure that all national assets, services and industries shall be democratically controlled and operated in the national interest with representation of the workers engaged therein and of the consumers.

The conference approved the resolution with a side remark by Morrison – 'this has cost us the election.'

Much of the thinking behind Labour's programme was developed between 1934 and 1937 when policies for a centralised planned economy and public ownership were devised. The war brought all these policies into new and sharper focus, and recognised the important role the state played in winning the war and how essential it was that this machinery should now be switched to winning the peace.

But it was not the practice of the Labour Party merely to talk to itself about future policies. Despite the war and blackout restrictions, the Party embarked on a series of regional rallies where it spelled out to a wider audience the Labour Party approach to war and to the reconstruction of the nation after the war. In Newcastle more than 1,200 people attended a lively rally and a similar number turned out in Birmingham. Other rallies were held in Nottingham, Edinburgh and Leeds. The accepted view was that the spirit of the audiences was excellent. Despite wartime restrictions on travel and extensive long hours in industry, the Labour Party could fill the 8,000 seats at the Albert Hall for a rally in February 1944 at which the two Labour Prime Ministers from New Zealand and Australia spoke.

Once 1945 arrived, the prospects of victory against Germany were clear for all to see and this made the electoral truce extremely fragile. The National Executive Committee of the Labour Party held the view that the Coalition Government should continue 'just as long as Annual Conference believes it necessary in the national interest'. In a statement the Labour Party argued,

The Parliament elected in 1935 has long outlived its natural life. As soon as possible, having regard to the international situation and to the need for giving electors especially those who are in the fighting services a full and fair opportunity not only of voting but of appreciating the issues involved, a General Election must take place.

Without detracting from the war effort, preparation must be made now. That election will be fraught with great consequences for our country and for the world. It is the duty of every member and of every constituent element of the Labour Party to make sure that they choose as Candidates men and women who are fitted by character and ability to contribute effectively to the solution of the tremendous problems which will face a Government in the period after the war.

The tensions which existed within the Parliamentary Labour Party towards the end of the war were put to the test in December 1944 when the question of Britain's involvement in the Greek civil war was debated in Parliament. The resistance organisations within Greece who were provided with arms by the Allies were divided on almost strict political grounds, with one side favouring the monarchy and the other side which had the support of the workers and the trade union movement. The Russian government also attempted to influence the outcome since it saw Greece in an important strategic position in the southern Balkans. Churchill sent in British troops to support the King of Greece and when the issue was debated in Parliament, 118 Labour MPs failed to support the government by abstaining.

At the same time Sir Walter Citrine, General Secretary of the Trades Union Congress, led a delegation to Greece since it was assumed he would have some rapport with the Greek trade union movement who were heavily involved. The delegation included G. H. Bagnall, G. Benstead and G. Chester – all members of the TUC General Council. In his report Citrine said that he had met the Regent of Greece, ambassadors and all the key players in the dispute. At a meeting with EAM (the anti-monarchy group) Citrine confronted them with a series of challenges. 'What is your purpose? You want to improve the standard of living for the Greek people. How can you do that? Do you think you can do it by Greek killing Greek? That's no solution. People need food, clothes and shelter. These things have to be supplied by somebody and from somewhere. How can you make things in destroyed factories? How can you transport goods without ships and bridges, railway engines and vehicles? When all the fighting is done with, you will still have these problems to solve.'

The issue continued to be a major cause of dispute within the Labour movement and was debated at the Annual Conference when the Executive put forward a resolution calling for an armistice, something all sides could agree upon. The problem became so high on Churchill's agenda that he flew out to Athens to negotiate a settlement. But the problems in Greece were symptomatic of similar issues throughout the Balkans. All the royal families departed in haste when the people of these various countries had other ideas as to how they should be governed in post-war days.

The Greek issue clearly demonstrated that when passions are aroused, then backbench Members of Parliament have difficulty in maintaining a Coalition Government. William Whiteley, the Labour MP who was Chief Whip, had the task of securing the support of backbenchers for the government's policies. He appealed to the Labour Party 'for greater unity of action in future by-elections'. But Churchill did not always have a united backbench team. In February 1945, following the Yalta Conference, 21 right-wing Tories challenged the decisions made on Polish boundaries. It even led to the resignation of a junior Minister.

The Labour Party was always keen on maintaining its international links and in 1944 created an International Advisory Committee whose membership included Evan Durban, Hugh Gaitskell, Douglas Jay and Ivor Thomas MP. The NEC was anxious to send a delegation to Russia and embarked on correspondence with Anthony Eden, the Foreign Secretary. They also expressed a view about the return of the Spanish monarchy but Eden said he had no view on the subject and that it should be left to Spain to decide. In London, many of the émigrés from war-stricken Europe were accommodated and they maintained links with Whitehall, in some cases they were fully fledged governments in waiting, in other cases they were groups of people who were brought together for the common cause. The Labour Party maintained contacts with these bodies whilst always recognising that the Communist Party was fairly active behind the scenes. In some secret way these groups were able to keep in touch with the underground resistance movements in Europe.

In December 1944 the Continental Labour Parties who were based in London met to exchange reports on the position of their respective countries. They all agreed that 'no peace would be stable unless it was based upon the will of the peoples'.

The Labour Party International Sub Committee expressed its views on the possible post-war situation when it adopted a resolution that captured the mood of the public, which 'expressed horror at the terrible brutalities and wanton destruction perpetrated by German and Japanese forces'. It argued 'that no enduring peace could be achieved without cooperation with the USSR, USA and the Commonwealth'. Despite its traditional international outlook, the Labour Party did not allow aliens to become members.

As the Russian Army swept westwards, the citizens of Warsaw organised an uprising to hasten defeat of the German occupation army. But for some reason the Russians held back before capturing Warsaw and this presented the Poles with severe problems. The underground movement was short of arms and the German Army proved more difficult to dislodge as it fought back to recapture lost ground. Both the Labour Party and the Trades Union Congress were perturbed about this critical situation and jointly met the Russian ambassador in London. They urged the Russians to work with Britain and America in dispatching munitions and arms to the beleaguered Poles. The Russians even denied both British and American planes the opportunity to land. This sorry episode ended with most of the Polish fighters either being killed or captured by the Germans and deported to prison camps in Germany.

One post-war issue looming up on the horizon was the question of conscription. During the war it was accepted that young people would be recruited for the services and for industry but what kind of policy was needed in peacetime? With service people all over the world carrying out essential duties and anxious to return home to be demobilised, the question that arose was how to replace conscripted service personnel in all theatres of war with a purely voluntary force. This was a problem that confronted Ernest Bevin, who was responsible for both the demobilisation programme and general manpower issues. In an unusual step a joint meeting took place between the Trades Union Congress, the National Executive Committee of the Labour Party and representatives of the Parliamentary Labour Party in May 1945. Bevin argued that 'there must be no faltering in our war effort and there must be no faltering in our peace efforts'. He said that if the nation continued with National Service and if the school-leaving age went up to fifteen, then industry would be short of more than 1 million people.

Bevin went on, 'The Army had been built up in the past mainly from the unemployed. It would be a terrible state of affairs if the defence of the country had to depend on the unemployed. If social services were to be made universal and if there was to be full employment, the question arose as to whether the defence should become a social obligation. Collective security could not be made effective unless each nation had agreed to put its troops into a pool to stop aggression. It was no good joining an International Security

Organisation,' he continued, 'without being quite prepared to face the implication of what that involved. Conscription should be agreed by the Coalition Government and not become a party controversy.' Bevin pointed out that it took three to five years to build up the Army and it was only a military force that could deal with weapons such as the V1 and V2 rockets.

In the ensuing debate Herbert Morrison agreed with Bevin. He said, 'The rise and fall of the influence of Britain in foreign affairs would be according to its military powers. Diplomacy is weakened if a nation is unable to make a material contribution on the land, sea and in the air.' Morrison argued that 'the quality of officers during the war was far higher than in peacetime when the officer sector was made up mainly of men who desired to make the Army their career. It was the duty of the Labour Movement to urge the right thing in the interests of the country and not to be dominated by narrow political issues.'

Aneurin Bevan advanced a contrary view. Speaking on conscription he said, 'Organised strength was no substitute for a wise international policy. If the Labour Movement agreed to the principle of conscription, they would be making a present to the Tory Party at the election.'

The TUC view was advanced by George Benstead who said 'that no one liked military or industrial conscription but it was necessary to consider what was the right thing to do for the security of the country'.

Ellis Smith MP suggested the 'world had not finished with fascism and that was the challenge to all that was best in life and to the Labour Movement'.

Winding up the debate, Bevin said that he had grounds to believe that the public would be with him if he announced conscription up to the age of 30 but he would not be party to putting the country under long-term national service. He stated, 'The Labour Movement would be wise to agree to the provision of national service and keep the matter under Parliamentary control.' He wanted one year's service and five years on the reserve. Peacetime conscription therefore became a part of the Labour Party's post-war policy, though Bevin's hope for a one-year service was overtaken by the international situation when two years in uniform became the norm.

In December 1944 a conference was organised by the Working Women's Organisation, which had strong links to the Labour Party and the TUC.

Their discussions and debates ranged over every possible post-war issue and were an indication of what women were talking about in the munitions factories, in education and in the food queues. Here is just a flavour of the issues which concerned women:

Infant mortality	Children's homes
Wartime nurseries	Domestic help
Public welfare	Corporal punishment
Premature births	Nutrition
Milk in schools	Price regulations
Social security	Maternity child welfare
School buildings	Community centres
Nurses' salaries	Home helps
Juvenile delinquency	Foster parents
Tuberculosis services	Funding for doctors in Abyssinia

All these important points were to become part of the post-war Labour Government's agenda and were also debated at a Conference for Labour Party Women's Sections held at Friends House in Euston Road in 1944.

The pace of political activity was clearly on the move. In October 1944 the National Executive Committee of the Labour Party met at the Howard Hotel in Norfolk Street, London to discuss the General Election policies and organisation. Detailed plans and drafts were considered and agreed. As if they were forecasting their own defeat, the meeting concluded, 'It was generally agreed that it was highly desirable that as much legislation as possible should be placed upon the Statute Book before the Parliamentary dissolution.'

Side by side with policy developments and the preparation of post-war policies, the Labour Party embarked on a campaign to revive the organisation at grass roots level. In a joint letter to all local parties, Harold Laski and Ellen Wilkinson stated,

> The NEC have decided that the time has now arrived, without detriment or injury to the national war effort, [when] the party should undertake special efforts to revive its inner life and to build up party membership. This is a prime necessity.

The campaign was launched in February 1944 and had five elements:

progressive enrolment of people who can be absorbed into the active life
   of the party
quality in membership as well as quantity by selected methods
encouragement of businesslike methods in the conduct of party meetings
each constituency party to form a Development Committee
recruit from among *Daily Herald* readers.

In addition, a letter was sent to all local authority Labour groups asking all councillors to take a lead in a recruitment drive. The letter suggested that 'earnest and intelligent people are often more susceptible to a direct personal appeal from someone they respect than to a mass invitation.' This move was fully supported by Attlee who urged, 'For more than four years our Party has put everything into the war effort . . . it is to this great adventure of democracy that the Labour Party calls all men and women of goodwill.'

The action of the Labour Party National Executive Committee in stimulating a membership drive and more contact with the general public appears to have proved successful. In 1944 individual membership of the Labour Party was 313,750 and in 1945 they could justly boast that membership had risen to 537,661.

Despite its enthusiasm for increased membership, from time to time the Labour Party was always wary about people who they thought had links with the Communist Party. In London Mr Krishna Menon, an Indian politician and diplomat, tried to join the Party but the National Executive Committee rejected his application because they thought he was too close to the Communist Party. Krishna Menon was a former Secretary of the India League and the spokesman for Indian nationalism in Britain. When India gained its freedom he became high commissioner in London and later led the Indian delegation to the United Nations.

But fighting elections costs money and the estimate was that the election would cost the Labour Party somewhere in the region of £150,000. Because there had not been an election since 1935, the coffers were reasonably well placed but they anticipated a greater degree of activity which would mean increased expenditure. The war too had forced up prices and wages so when the Miners Federation made a donation of £20,000 it set the election fund off to a good start. The National Union of Railwaymen soon followed with an initial donation of £10,000 plus a target to raise at least one shilling per member. The by-election fund, which had been created to meet the costs of Labour candidates at parliamentary by-elections, was in a healthy position because of the electoral truce, so £10,000 was transferred to the election fund.

In making arrangements for the coming General Election the Labour Party recognised there were many problems to overcome, not least the huge dispersal of the population away from their traditional homes. Behind their thoughts were issues such as:

it was ten years since the last election
complete lack of political education during the war
a wide range of policies to debate
the organisation was run-down
the electorate had increased
problems of the forces vote
election costs would be higher
printing staffs were depleted
advertising cost were up 100 per cent.

The general view among officers of the Labour Party was the need to concentrate their preparations on major lines of election services in order to achieve the most effective results. In other words to focus their activities on essentials and not be sidetracked into irrelevant issues.

The driving force within the Party in the development of political philosophies and better organisation was Morgan Phillips. At its meeting in November 1943 the Labour Party National Executive Committee decided to appoint a new General Secretary when Jim Middleton retired. There was extensive interest in the vacant post and the Party received a large number of applications. Among those applying was the National Agent of the Labour Party and its liaison officer at the *Daily Herald*. After a series of three ballots, Morgan Phillips was appointed at a salary of £1,000 per annum rising to £1,250. He brought to the post an extensive range of qualifications including a period of study at the Labour College in Earls Court, Research Officer of the Labour Party and Head of Propaganda, plus experience in organisation at the grass roots in East Anglia. As a former Welsh miner he had direct links to the trade union movement.

Although Parliament and the Parties discussed future policies, they did so against a background of dislocated social life caused by the war. The fact that family life was under strain, with large numbers of people in the services, bombed homes, evacuation and all the restrictions, inevitably led to serious problems on the home front. London's population dropped by nearly 2 million to 6,908,000 and the blitz throughout the country demolished 2 million homes. There was a general increase of 57 per cent in crime, a large black market flourished and there was a general blurring of what was and was not crime. More than 20,000 deserters from the services found comfort in London where they had no ration book or work. One estimate suggested that in January 1945 there were more than 18,000 United States deserters in the United Kingdom. The war was an engine for change and it changed people's attitude towards the general ethical code which society had come to accept. The divorce rate had risen from 9,970 in 1938 to 24,857 in 1945. The mere separation of a soldier from his family for anything up to five years was the cause of many marriage break-ups. Even Quintin Hogg returned home to find his wife ensconced with a young French officer. He described the scene: 'My life was in ruins.'

An interesting sideshow to the war and the home front was the activities of William Joyce (Lord Haw Haw) on German propaganda radio. In 1940 it was estimated that two thirds of the population had tuned into his *Jairmany Calling* at least occasionally to hear him gloat about German victories and British defeats. Joyce had been an enthusiastic supporter of Mosley before the war but the two fell out and hours before the outbreak of war Joyce escaped to Germany. Although technically he was Irish, this did not stop the British authorities arresting him in 1945, putting him on trial and carrying out the death sentence. It is doubtful whether Lord Haw Haw had any long-term effect on British morale but his rantings were a talking point in public circles more often in jocular terms.

The war was also a great leveller. If you are sharing a dugout or cooped up together in a small ship, the classic differences between the classes becomes somewhat eroded. Because of rationing and wartime legislation everyone was treated the same and this tended to bring down the existing class barriers despite the black market and the creation of 'spivs' and 'drones'.

But the politicians and the press failed to measure the political impact these social changes would have on the General Election. Very little research work was being undertaken by the universities to monitor the transformation of society since the war effort was the major task that confronted the nation.

Towards the end of the war support for the Coalition Government was grudgingly conceded by the Parliamentary Labour Party and leading members outside Parliament. Harold Laski believed that Labour Ministers were subservient to Churchill and he blamed Attlee for putting the Labour Party in an invidious position. The distinguished economist R. H. Tawney expressed similar views. In a letter to Beatrice Webb, a leading socialist thinker, he wrote,

> As far as I can see the Labour Party has temporarily ceased not only to count but to believe in itself. In May 1940 a Coalition was inevitable or desirable – that depends on the war and the price gets heavier and heavier. I am inclined to think that it should come out of the Government as soon as victory is in sight. But if it is to do that it should be preparing its plans now . . . the leaders are too immersed in day to day duties.

The official attitude of the Labour Party was incorporated in a statement issued by the National Executive Committee:

> Nothing must be allowed to conflict in any way with the paramount necessity of bringing the war to a speedy and successful conclusion. In the view of the NEC, Labour's participation in the Coalition Government should continue just so long as in the opinion of the Party Conference it is necessary in the national interest and for fulfilling the purposes for which the Government was called into being.

In a further statement the Labour Party reaffirmed its position about the General Election, announcing that it would 'seek a Parliamentary majority and as such does not desire to participate in a Coalition'.

The Tories in their propaganda accused the Labour Party of 'breaking up the Coalition and continuing to put party and class before country'.

As victory in Europe came within the grasp of the Allied forces, the public became more interested in peace and the climate of opinion began to change. A large section still expected the Coalition Government to produce an agreed list of measures for the future but Churchill was reluctant to agree post-war solutions.

Early in 1945 the Parties began the process of reviving their local organisations, started fund-raising and embarking on the all-important task of selecting candidates. By 14 February 1945 the Labour Party still had 155 constituencies without a candidate and the position was not helped when for a variety of reasons selected candidates withdrew, as happened in Watford, Liverpool Kirkdale, Manchester Blackley, Chorley, Royton, Melton, Holland-with-Boston, Lambeth Norwood, Bilston, Wednesbury, Middlesborough West, Crewe, Maldon, Waterloo, Withington and Rutland and Stamford.

The Labour Party also came out with some original thoughts on election procedures. They suggested that voters should vote in the constituency wherever they happened to be on Proclamation Day – the day the election is officially announced. The intention was that electors would go along to a polling station, show their wartime identity card and sign a declaration before voting. The idea of absent voters voting by post on a wide scale was also floated. One of the reasons for these suggestions was that, because of the large-scale movement of the population that was anticipated on the cessation of hostilities, it was estimated that it would take at least four weeks to compile an election register by normal methods. None of these ideas was acted upon.

Because of the state of their organisation, the Liberal Party favoured an autumn election in 1945 and Churchill toyed with the idea of having a plebiscite in which the public would be invited to support a continuation of some kind of Coalition Government. This was formalised when Churchill wrote to Attlee and the Liberal Party in May 1945 stating that the Coalition Government should continue until the Japanese war was over.

Attlee generally favoured an autumn election, though he could understand the arguments for Labour continuing in a Coalition until the end of the war with Japan. He argued that an autumn election would enable a more accurate election register to be produced; servicemen and women would have more time to consider the issues and become better acquainted with the candidates. Bevin and Dalton supported Attlee but strongly opposed Churchill's idea of having a referendum. It was argued in some quarters that Labour leaders favoured an October election because they were pessimistic about the results of an election in July.

The Coalition Government creaked on but victory in Europe was about to change the situation. Attlee was in San Francisco helping to create the United Nations Organisation and Churchill had promised him that no announcement about a General Election would be made whilst he was out of the country. The pace of political change moved a few steps faster but instead of Parliament being the critical forum where all these important issues were debated we must now return to the Labour Party Conference by the seaside.

CHAPTER FIVE

Preparing for Victory

A parliamentary election within two months of the end of the war in Europe could be described as being another 'khaki' election similar to the one held after the Boer War or the 'Coupon Election' after the First World War. On 1 May 1945, Churchill organised a dinner at Downing Street for all the leaders of the Tory Party to discuss their election strategy. Their discussion had only just commenced when news came in that Hitler had committed suicide in a Berlin bunker, so for the remainder of the evening the discussion revolved around Hitler and not the election. The end of the war in Europe was but days away and on 8 May 1945 the nation celebrated its victory over Fascism and the Hitler war machine.

Almost immediately the possibility of a General Election became top of the political agenda and whilst Attlee was in San Francisco helping to create the United Nations Organisation, Herbert Morrison and Ernest Bevin went to see Churchill. The view held by the two Labour leaders, following discussions with the National Executive Committee of the Labour Party, was that a General Election should be held in October since this would allow the production of the election register to be more accurate, give time for the electorate to consider the issues and enable parties to select candidates and organise themselves.

Winston Churchill's view was that possibly the Coalition Government could remain in place until the war with Japan was over and, whilst both Attlee and Bevin had some sympathy for this approach, Morrison, who was closely linked to the Labour Party organisation, could not agree. In precise terms, Parliament should have been dissolved in 1940 but it was kept alive by an annual resolution of Parliament and this was due to expire in November

1945. To the Labour Party the most reasonable step would be to allow this Parliament to continue until the autumn, then have a General Election.

When he came back from San Francisco, Attlee had a meeting with Churchill and both held the view that the Coalition should continue until the war with Japan was over. At this stage knowledge of the atomic bomb was highly restricted and though Churchill knew about its development, Attlee was very much unaware that it existed and certainly had no knowledge that it would be dropped on Japan and bring the war to a rapid conclusion. But both had to win the support of their political friends. The Tories were keen to have an early election so that they could extract the maximum benefit from Churchill's glory and Labour still believed that an autumn election would be best. Churchill was determined to 'secure full backing for his policy of full prosecution of the war against Japan and the completion of urgent domestic legislation'.

The Liberal Party replied to Churchill by saying they were prepared to stay in the Coalition until the autumn, whereas the Liberal Nationals fully supported Churchill in all he proposed.

With the nation still in high spirits following the end of the war, more than 1,100 Labour Party delegates made their way to the Empress Ballroom in Blackpool on 21 May – just under two weeks after VE-Day – for what turned out to be a momentous Annual Conference. Among those attending were 200 candidates, many of them still in their service uniforms. The atmosphere was described by one observer as 'electric'.

The Conference concentrated on two issues. First was the whole relationship of the Labour Party to the Coalition Government and second was the election manifesto, 'Let Us Face the Future'. The debate on Labour's continued participation in the Coalition Government was held at a private session, though like many private sessions the contents soon became public. The debate in Conference was preceded by a meeting of the National Executive Committee at which Attlee reported on his discussions with Churchill and in the general discussion he was supported by Bevin and Dalton. The Chief Whip of the Parliamentary Labour Party expressed the view that his colleagues in Parliament would support an autumn election, and this approach had the support of Morrison, Bevan and a majority of other members of the Executive.

At the secret session, Conference delegates debated two questions. The first asked, 'Are you in favour of continuing in the Government until the end of the war in Japan?' The second question posed was, 'Are you in favour of the National Executive's attitude towards the Prime Minister's proposals?' The view of delegates was clear and unequivocal. Only 2 out of 1,100 voted 'Yes' to the first question and 'No' to the second.

This decision was relayed to Churchill in a letter by Attlee in which he wrote,

> It has been the view of the Labour Party, which I think you share, that a rush election like that of 1918, before the electorate and especially those serving overseas have had a fair opportunity of considering candidates and policies, would be utterly wrong and would gravely weaken the authority of any Government resulting from such an election at a time when public confidence would be especially necessary . . . An autumn [election] would provide a more complete and effective [election] register than that now in force and would give the Service electors the opportunity of more fully acquainting themselves with the candidates' standing and the issues involved in the election than would be available in July.

Churchill rejected this approach and immediately went to Buckingham Palace and resigned, thus putting an end to the Coalition Government to be followed by the creation of a Caretaker Government under Churchill.

With the break-up of the Coalition Government, the scene was set for both Labour and the Tories to win the hearts and votes of the general public and the servicemen and women scattered throughout the world. The view of most people was that Churchill would win because he had brought Britain through six years of war in Europe and that he should continue to lead the country in the remaining battle against Japan. But the nation was able to separate, Churchill the war leader from Churchill the Tory Party leader. They cheered and revered the war leader but would not trust him and the Tory Party to deliver the hopes and aspirations of the ordinary British elector who wanted to embark on a new adventure for peace and prosperity.

It was against this background that Labour Party delegates debated the contents of their election manifesto. The developing political situation had the effect of concentrating their minds and deliberations without the luxury of being diverted into extraneous issues. Ellen Wilkinson, who was chairing the Conference, gave a lead to delegates when she argued,

> A Britain without unemployment cannot be built on the shifting foundations of monopoly capitalism. The whole resources of the country must be efficiently organised in the interests of the community. Socialists wanted millions of homes, jobs for all, social security, educational opportunities and a state health service. These must be obtained and paid for by a highly efficient industry and properly planned agriculture. There must be no illusions. The Labour Party does not offer a short cut to paradise. We know that peace, like war, must be won but we will fight and fight for power.

With the General Election only weeks away the Labour Party National Executive Committee was able to report to the Conference that plans had been carefully prepared. More than 40 policy conferences had been organised throughout the country and some 900 speakers had been provided for local public meetings and, interestingly, for Army Education Corps events. To run the elections at a local level the Labour Party had embarked on an extensive training programme for potential election agents and more than 200 passed through the course. The Executive reported, 'The suspension of electoral activity caused by the war not only rusted the knowledge and experience of past workers but deprived younger members of attaining electoral experience.'

The Chief Women's Officer, Mary Sutherland, was able to report that 1,000 Labour women attended a rally in Leeds and more than 800 women had attended similar events in Durham and South Wales. The finances of the Labour Party appeared to be in a sound state too. Individual membership showed an increase of 30,262 in one year – and affiliation fees from trade unions were almost £50,000. But it was the contents of the manifesto that delegates were keen to debate.

Herbert Morrison, who had played a key role in the development of various policy strands, introduced the debate on the manifesto, which ranged over three days. Morrison always had the public interest at heart. He used to ask himself – 'what is best for the public?' and this approach clearly emerged in the policy drafts as delegates debated the manifesto section by section. Describing 'Let Us Face the Future' as Labour's Five Year Plan, he said,

> The real controversy and the real fight between the Labour Party and its Tory opponents will be as regards economic and industrial policy, the future of British industry, the ensuring of full employment, the control of financial and credit institutions, agriculture and housing.
>
> In our electoral arguments it is no good saying that we are going to socialise electricity, fuel and power or transport. The electorate will expect a case to be made as to why we want to do it and how public interest is to be advantaged by it.

In a warning to candidates about their election speeches he stated,

> I ask Candidates not to make unauthorised promises outside the Party programme. I hate the position of 'vote for me' and see what you will get out of it. First it is mass bribery at the public expense; secondly, I do not believe it elicits a healthy response from the great mass of working people, who are as public spirited as anybody else; thirdly it is contrary to the public interest because it is tying up too specifically concerning money affairs.

Herbert Morrison's antenna was not merely linked to policy developments, he was an election strategist too, no doubt based on his long experience at the London County Council. Addressing the delegates he said,

> We must win more industrial seats. We have got to win the suburbs and the so called middle-class areas. Why not? Those people work, they are employed people and are liable to the 'sack'. It is a matter of talking to them in their own language, not a matter of diluting our principles at all.

In a five-hour debate on the first day of Conference 30 speakers made their views known. Ian Mikardo who was the endorsed candidate for Reading argued, 'Although nothing but complete socialism could ever be their final goal, they could reach that goal more quickly by marching their political enthusiasm and their technical resources always in step.'

Appearing in army uniform, Captain Victor Mischon (now Lord Mischon and a distinguished lawyer) regretted that the policy statement did not show a sufficient sense of urgency and it did not make special reference to servicemen's problems.

Sir Stafford Cripps, who had recently been allowed back into the Labour Party, was warmly applauded and commented that he thought the atmosphere in Blackpool was more congenial than at Southport where he had been expelled in 1939.

The manifesto received widespread support from all sides. Lieutenant Hughes, the candidate for Wolverhampton West, said, 'It is the most vigorous statement of immediate socialist policy that has been before the Party for a long time. It is a fighting document on which we can win the election.'

Another military person introduced as a 'Desert Rat' was Major John Freeman, the candidate for Watford. He asked, 'Who wants a Labour Government?' He answered his own question by saying, 'The masses of people all over ravaged Europe, the workers by hand and by brain who have suffered even more than the people of this country in their fight for freedom – men and women who have been in constant danger and above all those poor tortured people in the concentration camps. These are the people who hand in hand with us, are capable of building up in Europe a secure and just and prosperous peace.'

The response from delegates was extremely enthusiastic and though they could sense victory and were optimistic, this was often due to the rousing speeches that for most were something quite new.

Clement Attlee was more thoughtful in his approach. He concentrated his speech to delegates on the difficult situation that would confront Britain in the world of international diplomacy and the maintenance of peace. Having just returned from San Francisco where the United Nations was created, he could speak with some experience:

> The problems of peace can only be solved by building up an international organisation. We want a World organisation with the will and power to prevent aggression. It must be armed with power. If we advocate the rule of law in the world, we must be prepared to make our contribution. That is inescapable. All of us in this movement are idealists but we are realists too.

Mr Attlee explained the difficulties that would arise in Europe with the cessation of armed conflict and the need to rebuild countries against a background of severe food shortages and a lack of both human and material resources. The picture he painted was grim and the challenge enormous. He also dealt with the problems of India, a subject that was close to his heart, and the need for Russia, the United States of America and Britain to work together for worldwide peace.

He was followed to the rostrum by another candidate in army uniform, Major Denis Healey. Few realised that his Conference debut would lead to more than 60 years of solid political activity for the Labour Party and international politics. Developing his arguments, Denis Healey said,

> Labour should have a clear foreign policy of its own which is completely distinct from that of the Tory Party. The socialist revolution has already begun in Europe and is already firmly established in many countries in Eastern and Southern Europe. The crucial principle of our own foreign policy should be to protect, assist, encourage and aid in every way the socialist revolution wherever it appears.
>
> The upper classes in every country are selfish, depraved, dissolute and decadent. These upper classes in every country look to the British Army and the British people to protect them against the just wrath of the people who have been fighting underground against them for the past 4 years. Unless we are very careful, we shall find ourselves running with the Red Flag in front of the armoured cars of Tory imperialism and counter revolution.

Throughout the Coalition Government the Welsh voice of Aneurin Bevan was heard from the backbenches. He had been critical of Churchill and sometimes he could not support the Labour members of the Coalition. But at Labour Party Conferences he had a different audience. Bevan had the knack of arguing his case in carefully thought-out phrases, which had the effect of winning the support of the mass of delegates. Speaking on behalf of the National Executive Committee he stated,

We believe it is the function of the State to intervene in the economic process, day by day, week by week, year by year in order to maintain the standards of the people and thereby the employment of the people.

With heavy industries it is impossible to conceive of an expansionist policy if at the same time you are going to leave those industries in private hands. We submit to the nation that circumstances have now arisen where the basic industries of our country can only attract finance, can only be properly equipped and adopt an expansionist policy on the basis of nationalised ownership.

Only a society on the verge of bankruptcy could produce a situation that we have in this nation at the moment and had before the war. This island is almost made of coal and surrounded by fish. Only an organising genius could produce a shortage of coal and fish in Great Britain at the same time . . . What is lacking is that power lies in the wrong hands and the will to do it is not there.

We are the natural custodians of the interests of those young men and women in the services abroad. We are the builders. We have been the dreamers, we have been the sufferers. We want the complete extinction of the Tory Party and 25 years of a Labour Government.

The same theme was picked up by Emmanuel Shinwell, who had also been a critic of the Coalition Government. He argued that 'if it had not been for the intervention of the State in industry, it is doubtful if we would have reached the position of being able to secure from the enemy, unconditional surrender. The war could not have been won by private enterprise. Let us not confuse private enterprise with individual enterprise.'

Replying to the debate on foreign affairs Ernest Bevin who at that time was more concerned with industrial issues and the demobilisation programme.

The Conference approved the manifesto and delegates left Blackpool buoyed up with enthusiasm but not before giving a standing ovation to a vote of gratitude to the armed forces and launching a £250,000 election fund. After the rendering of the 'Internationale', the 'Red Flag' and 'Auld Lang Syne', the final message came from the Labour Party Chairman, Ellen Wilkinson, who said, 'We are fighting the Party of big business, the Party that controls the great industries, the cartels and very largely the press. Those are our enemies.' The next objective was to translate this enthusiasm into the practical task of winning elections. But the press continued to convey the story that it would be Churchill who would win.

Although the Conference atmosphere enthused the delegates' hopes for victory at the polls, Ellen Wilkinson was still concerned about Clement Attlee being leader of the Labour Party. She thought he should stand down and let Morrison take his place. Ellen and Morrison had a very close attachment and although she had the support of Harold Laski in her endeavours, she made little or no progress. Hugh Dalton said it 'was out of the question. Apart from everything else the timing was quite impossible.'

The plan to oust Attlee moved a stage further when Morrison wrote to him saying he intended to stand for the leadership. He suggested that if Labour won the election and the King asked him to form a government he should defer a decision until the Parliamentary Labour Party had met and elected a leader. Attlee responded by stating, 'If invited by the King to form a Government, you do not say that you cannot reply for another 48 hours. You accept the commission and you either bring it off or you don't.'

Ernest Bevin, no friend of Herbert Morrison, on hearing of these moves phoned Morrison and said, 'If you go on mucking about like this you won't be in the b****y Government at all.' Leah Manning, an old friend of Ellen Wilkinson who was later elected MP for Epping, said, 'I was very fond of Ellen but to challenge Clement Attlee's leadership seemed a dirty bit of chicanery – and I told her so.'

With Labour out of the Coalition Government, Churchill did not take very long to create a Tory Caretaker Government and pave the way for a General Election. At the time Parliament was dissolved the state of the Parties was:

Tories	351
Labour	169
Liberal Nationals	25
Sinclair Liberals	19
National Labour	5
Ulster Unionists	9
Independents	16
Irish Nationalists	2

Scottish Nationalists	1
Nationalists	5
Independent Nationalists	2
Common Wealth	4
Independent Unionists	1
Communist Party	1

The National Labour Party – a throwback from the Ramsay MacDonald period – dissolved itself just before the election. Some nineteen Members of Parliament lost their lives during the war.

At the time Parliament was dissolved the Parliamentary Labour Party consisted of the following:

Trade Union General Secretaries	4
Ex Trade Union General Secretaries	7
Trade Union officers	10
Miners	37
Clerical Workers	7
Railway employees	9
Printing Trades	2
Farmers	2
Engineers	6
Woodworkers	5
Clergy	3
Professional	8
Legal	12
Educationists	4
Journalists	4
Navy	1
Medicine	4
Commercial trades	9
Politics	8
Miscellaneous trades	13
Cooperative Society officers	8
Housewives	2

The stage was therefore being set for a momentous General Election. The war had a direct effect on both the social and political conditions of the nation as it emerged from the conflict. It had stimulated industries in a positive way. Technical industries like aircraft manufacture, machine tools, plastics and electronics made rapid strides compared with pre-war days where they had dragged behind. In social terms, many of the existing institutions were under challenge as participation by the under-privileged in community work developed. Women's membership of trade unions doubled during the war, rising to 2,200,000 in 1944, or just over a quarter of women workers. The health of the nation was better too. The provision of cod liver oil and orange juice and extra vitamins, coupled with a more healthy diet and an active way of life, gave a new sense of purpose. Working-class self-confidence was on the move. All this aroused a strong moral feeling that post-war Britain must be better. It was, however, a secret that the nation kept to itself, at least until polling day. The silent revolution was about to explode.

The debate moved from Parliament and the Conference chamber to towns and villages throughout the country, to army camps scattered throughout the world, to Royal Navy ships on the high seas, to factories, village halls and the doorstep. Candidates had the task of expounding their views and policies to all who would listen, not realising that the tide of progress was about to engulf them, for it seemed the British public had made up their minds though the Party leaders and the national press were completely ignorant as to what was happening to the country after six years of war. This was confirmed by the pollsters, who showed that support for Labour had risen from 38 per cent in 1943 to 45 per cent in 1945 when over the same period support for the Tories had fluctuated from 23 per cent (1944) to 32 per cent in 1945. All Parties entered the 1945 General Election on the assumption that Churchill would be returned. The power of the opinion polls failed to register. It was against this background that a new Parliament would be elected and the contestants came from all walks of life, as we shall now see.

109

CHAPTER SIX

Facing the Hustings

More than 1,600 candidates contested the 1945 election for 640 seats with a third coming from the armed services. Seeking re-election were 130 sitting MPs and 30 Labour MPs decided not to stand again. The 1935–45 Parliament lost nineteen MPs who were killed in action during the war. The new House of Commons was therefore bound to have a majority of new members to face the challenges of peacetime Britain. Since the last election was in 1935 many of the existing MPs had been in Parliament for at least ten years and were creeping up to retirement age. At this stage in the development of parliamentary representation, no pensions were paid to Members of Parliament and this may have had an effect on the decision to stand again for some MPs, particularly those with no outside income, which was generally the case for Labour MPs.

In the days before reselection of candidates was ever dreamt of, a Member of Parliament just carried on unless the electors thought otherwise. In some respects they were free agents, loyal to their Party and behaving themselves according to the desires of the Chief Whip. At the time of a General Election they would consult with the local party chairman and an adoption meeting would be arranged to launch the campaign. The idea that an MP would submit himself or herself to some kind of local scrutiny was never considered. MPs were held in awe and respect, and the thought of challenging their retention of the seat was unthinkable. In the rare event of any disagreement within the local party, which might happen at the selection stage, the person offended (often a losing nominee) might resign from the Party and stand as an Independent. But once a person had been elected an MP they remained in office or as a candidate until they themselves decided they did not wish to continue.

Of the 1,682 candidates, the Liberal Party fielded 306, the Labour Party 604 and the Tories 624. In addition, the Common Wealth Party fielded 23 candidates and the Communist Party 21. Among the other 104 were candidates for the nationalist parties in Scotland, Wales and Northern Ireland, plus the Independent Labour Party and 25 candidates who fought the University seats.

Various attempts were made to persuade the Labour Party to widen its appeal to the electorate and discussions took place about creating an electoral pact. The Common Wealth Party suggested the Labour Party should withdraw their candidates in those constituencies where the Common Wealth Party had one. They were hoping for some kind of electoral agreement in 40 constituencies. The Labour Party declined to agree. But such is the way in General Elections that a local view prevails. The Labour Party did not field a candidate in Chelmsford or in Petersfield. In Chelmsford the Common Wealth candidate was elected and in Petersfield he came bottom of the poll.

The Amalgamated Engineering Union (AEU) also proposed there should be 'Left' Unity candidates, which was clearly a way of allowing Communist Party members to become official Labour candidates. The Communist Party was extremely active in the AEU but the Labour Party did not bow to their request, instead agreeing to 'enter the next General Election as an independent organisation to secure a majority'. This did not extend towards the Independent Labour Party where there had been close links for many years. Though there was no official agreement, both in Bridgetown and Camlachie – two Glasgow seats – the Labour Party did not field a candidate but left the seats open to the Independent Labour Party who won both seats.

The Liberal Party complained that because the election was held in July and not later in the year, they were unable to field a larger number of candidates.

How, then, do you become a candidate? All parties have different procedures but in the case of the Labour Party the individual is either a member of List A or List B of available candidates. Those on List A would be those who are sponsored by a trade union or the Cooperative Party, in which case a large proportion of the election expenses would be met by the

111

sponsoring body. This was all laid down by the Labour Party in the Hastings agreement, which spelt out the maximum amount that a sponsoring body could contribute both for the election and for the run-up period.

The Committee on Public Standards has taken a close interest in the question of election expenses in an attempt to gain some control over the amount of money spent both locally and nationally on campaigns and the Election Commission was created and is expected to have a strong influence in the way elections are conducted. But in 1945 the position was more simple. The Labour Party depended on donations from trade unions, the Cooperative Party, from individuals and by door-to-door collections where the local parties were organised. The Tories depended on donations from private companies and from well-off supporters. The elections were conducted by local returning officers operating under various Representation of the Peoples Acts.

Likely candidates who wanted to gain access to the Labour Party's List B of available candidates were usually nominated by someone else within the Labour Party, or a local branch could be the nominating body. This does not mean that if you are not on List B you cannot become a candidate but if you are on the list then local parties and their affiliated units have access to the individual's biographical details. In some constituencies a person may be sufficiently well known and liked to receive a nomination without being entered on List B but if you live in one part of the country and are interested in contesting a seat in another, then List B opens all the doors.

At the 1945 General Election the practice of canvassing a constituency would have been frowned upon but today it is quite common for aspiring candidates to descend upon the constituency and hawk their wares around the area in the hope they can pick up a nomination from a unit within the Party. In some cases the constituency invites expressions of interest and then informs the nominating units about the details of the likely candidates. It is now possible to nominate yourself, just like applying for an advertised job.

Because of the war and the general state of political organisation, many candidates were selected without going through the normal process. Often the selection meetings were arranged in a somewhat hurried fashion and in one or two cases the wrong person was selected as later political activity revealed. In Birmingham, Jim Cattermole was appointed the City Organiser of the Labour Party and took up his employment on 1 January 1945. His job was to run the General Election in twelve Birmingham seats, all of which were held by the Tories. He recalls that his first task was to revive the moribund organisation and create a structure to select parliamentary candidates. In some cases there were active city councillors who had visions of reaching Westminster and most local people knew about their activities and achievements. For this the selection process was straightforward with local people competing with one another to become the candidate.

But the end of the war brought a large influx of service people who wanted to become candidates. Jim Cattermole recalls that several servicemen just came into Birmingham looking for possible seats and these included Woodrow Wyatt, Roy Jenkins and Raymond Blackburn. There was never any real scrutiny of their background and qualifications. They were servicemen, still in their officer's uniforms and no doubt cutting a dash at the selection meetings. These meetings usually consisted of about 20–25 people with a representative of the regional Labour Party present to see fair play and that all the rules were obeyed. Their simple task was to secure the adoption of another Labour candidate and close scrutiny of the candidate was a luxury.

It must be remembered that the war in Germany was not over until 8 May 1945 and the General Election was held on 5 July 1945. In that period, if they had not already selected a candidate, each political party in every constituency had to make a decision as to whether they were going to contest the seat and how they would select their candidate. The role of the national party organisation was to revive the local party and set in train these procedures. In some cases it was straightforward since the sitting MP was standing again. But in many areas the local party organisation did not exist or, if it did, it was just a list of names which somehow sprang to life and out of it emerged a group of enthusiasts who became active. In some areas there would be heated discussions about fighting the seat. Several seats were uncontested by the Labour Party and where there was a

Common Wealth MP, who enjoyed tacit Labour support there would be difficulties.

The Tory Party was not without its problems. Mr Ashe Lincoln, who fought Harrow East as a Tory candidate, recalls his selection process.

In 1945 I was still on active service for the Royal Navy and one day I was sitting in the Admiralty and received a message instructing me to go to No. 10. I thought, what have I done now? I went over to 10 Downing Street and when I was on the doorstep there was another Commander, namely Peter Scott and he said he had been summoned in a similar fashion. We were ushered inside by Brigadier Harvie-Watt, who was the personal assistant to Winston Churchill. He said, 'the old man wants to see you' so we were ushered into the presence of the All Highest who said to us, 'Gentlemen, there is going to be a General Election and I want to tell you gentlemen that I have every constituency filled with support for me except two and I want you gentlemen to take them over.' That was that. We had to decide there and then. I chose Harrow East because I thought that Harrow sounded as if we had a better chance than anywhere else and Peter Scott took Wembley North. In the result we were both defeated but that's by the way.

Viscount Lambton, who fought Chester-le-Street for the Tories, emerged because of his family connections. His father wrote to Lord Londonderry, the President of the northern area Tories, who put him in touch with the constituency Chairman, Sir Cuthbert Headlam MP. They had lunch together when it was agreed that Lord Lambton would become the Tory candidate for Chester-le-Street. He said that a similar arrangement was made at Seaham for Maurice Macmillan, son of Harold Macmillan. Viscount Lambton said, 'Our selections may sound old-fashioned but Tory Central Office had great difficulty in finding candidates to fight in hopeless Labour seats in Durham; both our constituencies had been Labour strongholds for fifty years. Also we said we would pay our election expenses. A popular gesture as the Tory Party was broke at the time and local party leaders did not enjoy contributing to a lost cause.'

The Liberal Party had problems too. Their organisation was thin on the ground and they only contested 306 seats, receiving 9 per cent of the total vote. With such a scattered system there was little or no organisation in hundreds of constituencies. John Junor, who later became editor of the *Sunday Express*, was a lieutenant in the Fleet Air Arm and desperately wanted to became the Liberal MP for Aberdeen and Kincardineshire. He writes,

> I had fallen in love with the place and wrote to the local constituency association. The Chairman was a Blacksmith in Glassel, a remote village miles from anywhere. In my Fleet Air Arm pilot's uniform I travelled to Aberdeen and I took a bus to meet the Chairman who was still in his Blacksmith's apron. He was a wonderful man. Blacksmiths and fishermen are the salt of the earth and I think he rather liked the cut of this youngster of twenty three arriving in pilot's uniform and saying 'please, I want to be a candidate.' A couple of months later I was called up to a meeting in Aberdeen and selected and that was it. The Chairman was one of the greatest men in my life. It is always the simple men who are the greatest upholders of democracy and decency.

In the case of Jim Callaghan it is interesting to recall how he became a candidate for Cardiff when he was living in Lewisham. In 1937 he was a young trade union officer working for the Inland Revenue Staffs Association. Being a Civil Service union, they settled all their disputes by means of arbitration, which meant that both sides would have to present their case to an independent panel. The panel would usually consist of three people with a barrister in the chair and each side was allowed to nominate an assessor. In the case of the Inland Revenue Staffs Association they suggested that Professor Harold Laski from the London School of Economics (LSE) should be their assessor and it was Jim Callaghan's task to present the union's case.

He must either have had a good case or was particularly effective (possibly both), because he made a deep impression on Professor Laski who, in addition to his work at the LSE, was a member of Labour's National Executive Committee. Professor Laski suggested that Jim Callaghan should become a student at LSE but Callaghan's reaction was that he was convinced a war between capitalism and Communism was imminent so he declined the invitation. He did, however, accept the offer of a library ticket and this gave Callaghan access to the LSE library. A warm and close relationship developed between the two and when Callaghan was away in the services they used to correspond. It was Professor Laski who suggested that Jim Callaghan should become a candidate and proposed his name to Labour Party headquarters, and he was supported in this move by John Parker, the MP for Dagenham who was General Secretary of the Fabian Society and keen to secure a spread of young candidates throughout the country.

After being proposed by Professor Laski, Jim Callaghan was interviewed by the Labour Party Assistant National Agent, Dick Windle, and his name was confirmed at the next meeting of the National Executive Committee and was entered on List B. Although he was an officer of the Inland Revenue Staffs Federation (IRSF) there was no way in which the union could play an active role in promoting Jim Callaghan. Under the 1927 Trades Dispute Act all Civil Service trade unions were prohibited from affiliating to the Labour Party or the Trades Union Congress. This restriction was removed by the incoming Labour Government.

On the Executive Council of the IRSF was a Mr D. Kneath who was active in the Labour Party in South Wales and he suggested to Callaghan that there was a vacancy at Cardiff in which he might be interested. A meeting was duly arranged at the home of Bill Headon, the Secretary of the Cardiff South Constituency Party. Mrs Headon was also present at the meeting and she quickly wanted to know from Jim Callaghan whether he was Irish and a Catholic. Jim was able to assure Mrs Headon he was neither Irish nor a Catholic but in fact was a Baptist who was born in Portsmouth.

In due course Jim Callaghan's name was included in a list which also included George Thomas and Will Nally. The Party had approached Sir William Jowitt but he declined. The son of a Welsh mining MP also expressed some interest, too, but was not nominated. His name was Roy Jenkins. At the selection meeting in Cardiff 23 delegates were present, which seems a small gathering compared with the large meetings that would now be assembled for the selection of a prospective parliamentary candidate. But the political truce and the war took its toll on party organisation and in many parts of the constituency the Labour Party either

116

did not exist or was somewhat rusty, as leading members were on active service throughout the world. Jim Callaghan received twelve votes and George Thomas eleven. Perhaps one of the deciding factors was that Callaghan attended the meeting in his naval officer's uniform and this may have just pulled in that extra vote. As a Welshman, George Thomas was not pleased to lose a Welsh seat but nevertheless went away and was selected for the adjoining constituency, and eventually ended up as Speaker of the House of Commons and later Lord Tonypandy.

Immediately after the selection Jim Callaghan had to dash away to Birkenhead to rejoin his ship, which was on convoy duties in the North Atlantic. He didn't come back until the General Election had commenced. Being on active service it was impossible to nurse the constituency or develop close relationships with particular groups within the area, although his wife Audrey, together with the children, did visit Cardiff for a May Day celebration and delivered a speech that he had written. When the election was announced, Callaghan was aboard the battleship HMS *Queen Elizabeth* in Trincomalee in what used to be known as Ceylon, now Sri Lanka. The intention was that if the Allied forces had invaded Japan, Lieutenant Jim Callaghan would have been a liaison officer with the Japanese authorities. He was summoned by his commanding officer and told to return to England. This was easier said than done since there were no normal scheduled flights back to the UK.

Callaghan made it to Karachi, then remained under canvas for ten days whilst he made friends with an American pilot who gave him a lift back to Cairo. From Egypt he managed to get aboard a York aircraft that was returning to Britain but all he can remember of the flight was that it was bitterly cold and he sat in the baggage locker. By the time he got to Cardiff the election campaign was well under way.

Ian Mikardo, who became MP for Reading, ended up as the candidate by a completely different route. He was active in the Labour Party and was employed locally as a management consultant. The constituency party had commenced the selection procedure and several people were nominated but they all came from outside the area. The local chairman, anxious not to be accused of having no suitable local person, asked Ian Mikardo whether he would accept a nomination. Ian Mikardo's reply was, 'I have no desire whatever to become a Member of Parliament, and that's not assumed diffidence or modesty – I really mean it.'

After Mikardo explained why he did not want to enter Parliament, the Chairman retorted, 'If you accept nomination I don't think you need worry too much about the dangers of becoming an MP. In the first place you might not even get shortlisted; and if you do get shortlisted you're certainly not going to be favourite to be selected against the other nominees who are a very good bunch; and if you do get selected you're not at all likely to win the seat against the pro-Churchill euphoria which will sweep the country in the post-war election.' Convinced by these arguments, Ian Mikardo allowed his name to go forward. He was shortlisted, he was selected and he won the election with a majority of 6,390.

For Jennie Lee (wife of Aneurin Bevan) the position was somewhat more difficult. She had left the Labour Party and stood as an Independent Labour Party candidate in Bristol during the war but in 1944 she reapplied for membership of the Labour Party and this was considered by the National Executive Committee. The Party did not hold out any real objections against Jennie Lee returning to the fold but a statement was considered by the National Executive Committee and this was based on an interview between Jennie Lee and the National Agent of the Labour Party, George Shepherd. It stated:

1   Agreed that the conditions surrounding the departure of the Independent Labour Party from the Labour Party were dead and were no longer a guide to her political views
2. She indicated that her severance from the ILP arose out of the war issue. In her view the military defeat of Hitler was vital
3   She agreed that she had written articles in the American press chiefly the *New Republic*, but that whilst there may have been criticisms of Labour therein, there was no wickedness in it
4   She indicated that Labour's declaration to fight the next election as an independent party had been the chief impulse in the steps she had taken to seek membership. She felt she understood the party case for the General Election, and certainly approved of it. Her view was that in the election, the rival policies of Conservative and

Labour Parties should be sharply defined and kept free from 'splinter' issues

5   She was unconnected with any other political organisation. Her loyalty to the Labour Party would be full and generous. She had no personal aims to achieve. Her activities would be devoted to supporting the broad policy of the Party.

Jennie Lee accepted the thrust of this statement and rejoined the Labour Party in Chelsea. Soon afterwards she received a number of requests from constituencies who were interested in her becoming their candidate. These included Slough, Aberdeen and Cannock but it was in Cannock that she expressed the keenest interest because it was a mining area and she was the daughter of a miner. She recalled,

> when the date for the selection conference approached, I decided it was a waste of time for me to go forward. Hector Hughes, a quaint little lawyer, later a Member of Parliament for Aberdeen had persuaded the local miners' agent to have him adopted as the official miners' candidate. He was the only nominee invited to address the miners' local committee. Frank Beswick [later Lord Beswick], then a young Air Force officer, flew over from the Far East and was sponsored by the Cooperative Party. The General and Municipal Workers Union considered they had the most right to the seat as the previous Member of Parliament had been one of their members. All three promised to meet the election expenses and to make handsome contributions to constituency funds between elections. I could make no offer of financial support of any kind.

Jennie Lee's supporters in the constituency had other thoughts. They suggested she would lose on the first ballot and the three right-wing nominees would split the right-wing vote and only one would remain in the ballot for the second round. In fact, she won on the first ballot. 'I had not been a member of the Labour Party from 1932 to 1944, but what did it matter,' she said. The miners' delegation paid not the slightest heed to the instructions that had been given to them to vote for Hector Hughes.

Sir Stafford Cripps, who as we have seen had been expelled from the Labour Party before the war, was in two minds as to whether he should rejoin or stand as a Common Wealth Party candidate. He was already representing Bristol South-East and had held several senior ministerial posts in the Churchill Coalition Government. The position was somewhat confused because when Cripps was expelled, his active supporters in the constituency, led by their Secretary, Herbert Rogers, resigned in sympathy so in effect there was no Bristol South-East Labour Party to select an alternative candidate. Herbert Rogers kept the membership together and fully supported Sir Stafford Cripps, and indicated to Labour Party headquarters they would only return to the fold when Cripps was allowed back in. When the matter was discussed at a meeting of Labour's National Executive Committee, Attlee reported on a conversation he had had with Cripps. Attlee said that Cripps 'intimated that he intended to maintain his independence in politics until the war had been won but that he could not say at present in what direction his political future would lie'. The committee gave authority for Bristol South-East to go ahead and select a candidate.

A meeting was arranged at Dartington Hall in Devon at which Michael Young (later Lord Young of Dartington) was present when the subject of Cripps rejoining the Labour Party was raised. Michael Young was able to demonstrate that there was a distinct change in the mood of the electorate and this he based on some door-to-door canvassing in St Pancras. He also argued that despite their recent electoral success, the Common Wealth Party was poorly organised, had no clear policies and had a limited future. He was proved right on all counts. Sir Stafford Cripps made a formal application to rejoin the Labour Party, which was considered at the Labour Party National Executive Committee's meeting in February 1945 and duly accepted. Mr Dick Windle, the Assistant National Agent of the Labour Party, spent a good deal of time in Bristol persuading the former active members to return to the fold, whereupon Cripps was officially selected and fought the seat.

Sir Stafford Cripps was a man with high moral virtues and, because he was now no longer an Independent MP, he wrote to Churchill offering to resign his ministerial post. Churchill replied, 'My dear Stafford, I have always considered you a socialist and as belonging to the socialist representation in the Government. Your decision raises no question affecting the balance of the Government, except of course that you will henceforth count as a socialist instead of something even worse.'

In east London Major Elwyn Jones had a different experience. He was a judge advocate in the Army stationed in Germany and was later to become a member of the prosecuting team in the Nuremberg war trials. Elwyn Jones was already on List B of available candidates and had been active in the Labour Party before the war. As a young barrister he played a leading role in the Vienna courts defending Socialists who had been arrested by the government at the time of the Hitler push into Austria. Also helping students who were similarly arrested was a young economics lecturer at Vienna University by the name of Hugh Gaitskell and author Naomi Mitchison who was married to Gilbert Mitchison who later became the Labour MP for Kettering.

With his name on List B, Elwyn Jones began to receive a number of enquiries from constituency parties who were looking for a candidate. He was approached by Twickenham Labour Party and invited to the selection conference but the Army would not allow him to attend since he was serving overseas. This anomaly was later put right by Ernest Bevin as Minister of Labour. It was too late for Elwyn Jones and Twickenham, which was his own local party. Other parties made approaches including Stockton-on-Tees, Peterborough, Macclesfield, Wolverhampton, Newark and Dover. Notwithstanding his Welsh background, only one seat in Wales made an approach: Caernarvon.

Despite his war service, Elwyn Jones found time to put his thoughts into writing and he was responsible for three pamphlets:

Hitler's Drive to the East
The Battles for Peace
The Attack from Within

All these were a modest success and contributed to the wider debate taking place within the Labour Party and the general public about topical issues, and then out of the blue he received nominations from two wards in Plaistow in the West Ham constituency and the selection conference was fixed for 18 April 1945, just three weeks before the end of the war in

Germany and three months before the date of the General Election. West Ham had a long connection with the Labour Party. Keir Hardie had represented the area and Will Thorne, a strong trade unionist, held the seat from 1906 until 1945 when he retired at the age of 88. The local Party thought it was time to find a new (and younger) MP.

Elwyn Jones recalls the selection conference which, like so many Labour Party activities, was held in a school.

> It was a small old-fashioned, dimly lit infants school with asphalt yard and outside toilets. There were four candidates besides me: a young Cooperative Party nominee, an elderly trade union official, Alderman Daisy Parsons who was a suffragette and the first woman Mayor of West Ham, Herbert Willig a local school caretaker and President of the local trades council. Willig had notable claims on the constituency. He was self-educated, served on innumerable local committees and was a fine speaker. He would have been a good MP.
>
> Seventy delegates attended the selection meeting. There were Railwaymen, Dockers, Lightermen, Steverdores, Bargemen, Seamen, Building workers, Tate and Lyle Treacle Blenders, members of the Co-op; altogether a cross-section of the working population of Plaistow. Each of us spoke in turn in the absence of the others. After I had addressed the meeting I was closely but encouragingly questioned by the serious and critical audience. On the first count I had a fair lead over other candidates and at the final count I won by a good margin. During the General Election I had the generous support of all candidates particularly Bert Willig. Will Thorne, somewhat frail by then, sat on the platform at the launching of my election campaign.

Elwyn Jones won the selection, won the election and went on to a glittering career in Parliament culminating in becoming Lord Chancellor in the House of Lords.

Denis Healey never even attended his selection meeting. Whilst serving in the Army in Italy (he was Beachmaster at Anzio), he received a letter from Ivor Thomas the right-wing Labour MP who eventually joined the Tories and changed his name to Ivor Bulmer-Thomas. He wrote, 'From conversation with your parents and knowing your views, I wondered if you would be interested in being put on the list of potential Labour candidates.' Denis Healey (who was twice mentioned in dispatches) said he agreed without great excitement. 'It seemed a very academic prospect at the time. Later I was offered a choice between two safe Conservative seats to fight. I picked Pudsey and Otley because it was nearer home.'

The selection meeting was held in February 1945 but at the time Denis Healey was planning an abortive landing in Yugoslavia so was unable to attend. Based in Pesaro, he wrote to the Pudsey and Otley Labour Party a letter which was read to the meeting by a friend of his father's:

> I am only one of the hundreds of young men, now in the forces who long for the opportunity to realise their political ideals by actively fighting an election for the Labour Party. These men in their turn represent millions of soldiers, sailors and airmen who want socialism and who have been fighting magnificently to save a world in which socialism is possible.
>
> Many of them have come to realise that socialism is a matter of life and death for them. But too many others feel that politics is just another civilian racket in which they are the suckers . . . We have now almost won the war, at the highest price ever paid for victory. If you could see the shattered misery that once was Italy, the bleeding countryside and the wrecked villages, if you could see Casino, with a bomb created river washing green slime through a shapeless rubble that a year ago was homes, you would realise more than ever that the defeat of Hitler and Mussolini is not enough by itself to justify the destruction not just of twenty years of Fascism, but too often twenty centuries of Europe. Only a more glorious future can make up for this annihilation of the past.

Despite his absence and at the age of 27, Denis Healey won the selection but lost the General Election contest. He later became International Secretary of the Labour Party on a salary scale of £600–£750 and beat off a challenge from 168 other applicants. Eventually he became MP for Leeds East in 1952.

In Scotland the Tories did not have quite the same procedures for adopting a candidate. Iain Macleod, who later became Chancellor of the

Exchequer in the Heath Government, dipped his toe in the election pool by a strange but simple process. Nigel Fisher (MP) in his biography of Iain Macleod writes,

> In the early summer of 1945 Iain was on leave from the Army at Scaliscro in Scotland, the home of his father Dr Macleod. The General Election was announced while he was there but there was no Conservative organisation and no Conservative candidate. Dr Macleod was himself a Liberal but he was also an admirer and supporter of Winston Churchill and he thought the Government should be represented in the election in the Outer Hebrides. So he called an inaugural meeting of the non-existent Conservative Association to nominate a candidate.

But there was nothing democratic about the selection process in the 1945 Election in the Western Isles – because there was no competition. The only people who attended the meeting were Dr Macleod and Iain, so they elected Dr Macleod as Chairman and Iain as the candidate. Conservative Central Office were informed, though not consulted, and Dr Macleod sent a telegram to Mr Churchill announcing Iain's selection. The Prime Minister's endorsement and good wishes arrived by return of post. It was a remarkable start in politics for a young man who within seven years was to become a Minister of Cabinet rank and the youngest Privy Councillor in Britain.

The result was a foregone conclusion though Iain Macleod obtained the largest Tory vote ever recorded in a three-cornered contest in the constituency, but he still came bottom of the poll. Macleod used to say that only his cousins voted for him, but 'I've got a lot of cousins in the Western Isles.' He received 2,756 votes in a poll of 13,000. The Labour candidate, Malcolm Macmillan, was elected with a majority of 1,600 over the Liberal who came second.

In some areas where the political organisation was almost defunct the candidate was selected by merely a group of well-wishers who agreed among themselves who would be the popular choice and then attempted to create an organisation and undertake the necessary fund-raising. Today the selection of candidates is organised on well-defined rules, though from time to time someone slips through the system and defies the national offices of the main political parties who like to keep a strict control.

In 1945 the selection procedure was very much a hit-and-miss operation but no one has actually criticised the result and some would argue that democracy works in strange ways and that eventually the general public's clear choice emerges. Because of the war some people who hoped to be candidates missed out. Tony Crosland, who later became Foreign Secretary in the Callaghan government, was such a person. Crosland parachuted into Southern France in June 1944 just after D-Day and was later stationed in Italy. Eleven constituency Labour Parties wrote inviting him to become their candidate. Such was the communication system in wartime Europe that all the letters arrived after the closing date for nomination or that his response could not be made in time. Though disappointed, Tony Crosland spent the election period in Italy and entered the House of Commons in 1950.

Major Donald Bruce was Parliamentary Private Secretary to Aneurin Bevan throughout the 1945 parliament. He fought Portsmouth North in 1945 and later wrote,

> I did not look at the majority otherwise I would have been deterred because it was a naval seat formerly occupied by Admiral Sir Roger Keyes. I was one of those who during the war thought and had good reason to feel by the reaction of my own troops, that a sea change was going to happen. I was in Reims at the time and I came back to Portsmouth and in spite of being in my Army uniform (complete with Sam Browne belt), I was adopted.

George Thomas, who was to make 'Order, Order' delivered with a lilting Welsh accent a famous parliamentary catchphrase, started his political career in Tonypandy, a town whose name he was to bear later in life. Holding slightly pacifist views, Thomas was rejected by a medical board for entry into the services but he joined the Glamorgan police force as a war reserve policeman and shared these duties with his work as a teacher. George was Chairman of his local Labour Party and represented his teaching colleagues on the National Executive Committee of the National Union of Teachers.

In 1944 he was approached by the Women's Organiser of the Welsh Labour Party and asked if he would submit his name for List B of prospective parliamentary candidates. Shortly afterwards he was endorsed as a potential candidate and later received an invitation to attend the two-member Blackburn constituency who were in the process of looking for two candidates. Although he travelled to Blackburn, he had doubts about nursing the constituency since he felt Cardiff and Blackburn were too far apart so he withdrew from the selection process. One of his opponents in Blackburn turned out to be Barbara Castle, who was later elected one of the two MPs for the area and had a long association with the town.

Liverpool was always the scene of immense political activities. The Independent Labour Party, the Communist Party, the Irish, the Church were all protagonists in the task of winning the hearts and minds of the local population. Right in the centre of this turmoil was an industrious couple known as Jack and Bessie Braddock.

When Chamberlain announced that Britain was at war with Germany, Bessie Braddock became a full-time ambulance driver for the next five years and drove her vehicle throughout the blitz on Liverpool docks. Bessie had developed a reputation for challenging authority if it stood in the way of her service to the people of Liverpool. She had a colourful record on the city council but behind the scenes was a dedicated worker for those in need. Eleanor Rathbone, the distinguished Independent MP who represented a university seat and was a champion for family allowances, once said that Bessie Braddock 'will be worth her weight in gold whatever party she supports'. And later, when Eleanor Rathbone entered Parliament she said, 'This is where Bessie should be.' Another description of Mrs Braddock was that she was 'so much of a socialist and so little of a socialite – real working class'.

Bessie became the prospective parliamentary candidate for the Liverpool Exchange constituency in 1936 but because of the war was never able to challenge her opponent, Sir John Shute, who was an ardent Catholic. Bessie won the seat with a majority of 659 but not before she had waged a strong and virile campaign in her usual style. She refused to shake hands with the (Tory) Lord Mayor when she handed in her nomination papers saying, 'I am not shaking hands with any Conservatives during the election.' Her style bore no comparison. 'I am not interested in any other vote but that given by the working class and if returned I have no intention of representing any business interests of the division but only those appertaining to the working people.' She refused to give an assurance to the many Catholics in the Exchange constituency that she would look after their interests unless they were also the best interests of the working people of Liverpool. After her election success, Bessie Braddock denied any personal contribution. 'I didn't win the seat – it was the Labour Party which did it for me,' she said.

Shortly before the 1945 General Election the Boundary Commission decided the Coventry seat should be divided to form two constituencies. Back in 1937 the local Labour Party had selected Richard Crossman, the brilliant academic who later played a prominent role in Harold Wilson's governments and eventually died of cancer.

Because of his activities as Head of Propaganda Warfare, Richard Crossman was not able to nurse the Coventry constituency though he encouraged his wife to take a keen interest, particularly during the time of the extensive bombing of the city. When the Boundary Commission came out with their proposals to create two seats, the question of who should fight the West seat and who should fight the East seat was a subject of much local discussion. The Coventry Labour Party had already decided that the East constituency was the better of the two and, without any selection process at all, Richard Crossman was declared the candidate.

In the West constituency the local full-time Labour Party Agent, George Hodgkinson, expressed some interest in becoming the candidate but the Labour Party had a strange rule which disqualified him from standing on the grounds that he was a paid servant of the Party. The matter was considered by the National Executive Committee but Harold Laski declared the nomination of George Hodgkinson was invalid. The Constituency Labour Party sent a telegram to the NEC urging a change of rules but this would require the endorsement of the Annual Conference so no action was taken.

Jack Jones, the former General Secretary of the Transport and General Workers Union, was at that time the Midlands Regional Organiser for the union and was Chairman of the Coventry Labour Party. He recalls,

The front runner with a lot of local support was Alderman Syd Stringer, a long-time socialist of the old school and Leader of the Labour group. Looking at the assembled delegates I thought, well the majority are middle-aged ladies, the core of the Party and they are bound to vote for Syd. I was to have a shock.

First of the candidates to speak was a civil engineer from Nottingham wearing military uniform. He gave a strong and competent left-wing speech. Syd Stringer followed with a plodding, pedestrian speech dealing with local questions, but it was easy to follow and he got a good reception.

There were other speakers, but none reached the eloquence of Maurice Edelman. Maurice was in the uniform of the Army Press Corps. Young, handsome, he delivered a socialist message which caught the mood of everyone present. It was brilliantly done. The ladies fell for him, as I could see while he was delivering his oration. In the voting he won hands down.

Maurice Edelman went on to win the seat with a 15,013 majority, almost as large as Richard Crossman who romped home with an 18,000 majority.

With the electoral truce well and truly in operation by the major political parties, the process of selection when a by-election occurred during the war was still undertaken. Bernard Taylor, who fought his first parliamentary election in 1945, was already the Labour MP for Mansfield for which he was returned in 1941 unopposed. He nevertheless had to go through the normal selection process even though it was in the depths of the war.

A number of trade union and local parties approached Bernard Taylor. He recalls,

I confess the decision was not easy to make for two reasons: I was now settled in a job as a checkweigh man and was interested in the work of the Union. Naturally I was torn between two loyalties, the industrial and the political. My name went forward to the selection conference with five others. These included Francis Williams, ex-editor of the *Daily Herald*, Evan Durban an author and academic professor, Percy Baistow of the National Union of Railwaymen, Alderman Beck from Mansfield and Albert Wilcox of the Derbyshire Miners Union.

Francis Williams was unable to attend the selection conference but later in life he was appointed one of the first life peers by Hugh Gaitskell. There were two ballots and Bernard Taylor emerged successful and became the candidate. The election was not contested and he was returned unopposed. In effect, the MP was elected by the management committee of the Mansfield Labour Party. In 1945 Bernard Taylor faced a real election. Any misgivings anyone had about the selection process were set aside when he was returned with a 28,000 majority.

It is not often that a sitting MP for a safe seat decides to throw it all in and find another seat but that happened to Herbert Morrison, Home Secretary in the Churchill Government and leader of the Labour Party in London.

Herbert Morrison was MP for Hackney South and was at one time Mayor of the Borough. He was elected in 1924 and played a leading role in various Labour Governments. As Minister for Transport he created the London Passenger Transport Board, which brought together all the different modes of transport in the capital into one unified undertaking. The management structure which he evolved became the model for later public ownership schemes in coal, the railways, air transport and other public bodies. He recalls,

Throughout the war I had visited my constituency as often as I could. The people of Hackney had had a rough time of it; many families had been bombed out and rehoused elsewhere; some had been evacuated and too many regrettably had been killed. My decision to move from a constituency where I could be assured of a comfortable victory was made after considerable thought. I was sounded about transferring to East Lewisham for the post-war election.

As an ex-Minister I could not, nor did I wish to, confine my election speeches merely to local affairs. It was well known that I was editor in chief of 'Let Us Face the Future' [Labour's election manifesto] and my duty to my colleagues was to help the national campaign even when speaking to my constituents. I was worried whether the people of South Hackney would appreciate the point. They were always a good audience but after their wartime experiences they would have been only human if some heckler had cut me short in the middle of a speech on important national affairs with a friendly but impatient interruption, 'that's fine Herbert but what about the roofing felt on the bomb hole in my roof?'

Another factor was my preoccupation with a long-standing inferiority complex among my colleagues about Labour's chances in what they called the respectable suburban areas. I felt that this attitude was at least twenty-five years behind the times and I was ready to put my theory to the test in my own political life, even though at real risk.

East Lewisham was a mixed inner suburb. In its day many of its residential areas had been affluent and a sprinkling of these big houses remained. There was a big section of the solid middle class and as large a population of working-class people. By tradition it was Conservative. At the 1935 election Sir Ashton Pownall, the Conservative Member, had got in with a comfortable majority of 6,500 and this had been the pattern for virtually the entire history of the seat. It was in fact just the sort of constituency I felt assured that Labour could win if it tried hard enough and ran the right sort of public-spirited campaign.

Herbert Morrison went on to contest the seat whilst at the same time making speeches throughout the country. This did not appear to affect the result because he was returned with a majority of 15,219, which compares with the 6,449 majority his Tory opponent received at the 1935 General Election.

The Morrison theory of contesting winnable suburban seats seems to have been proved though it might be stretching a point since Herbert Morrison had generally been a popular Home Secretary, giving his name to the domestic Morrison Air Raid Shelter, but on the other hand he had been criticised for releasing the imprisoned Sir Oswald Mosley, the pre-war Fascist leader some say too soon. Nevertheless he did rather better than if he had stayed in Hackney South. The new Labour candidate, Herbert Butler, had a majority of 5,531.

During the election campaign Winston Churchill toured the East Lewisham constituency as part of a tour throughout South London. In a typical provocative speech at Lewisham Clock Tower before a huge crowd he said that Morrison was cowardly and un-British 'for having blamed him

[Churchill] for the flying bomb tragedy at Lewisham market place when no warning had been given. Of all the colleagues I have lost, Morrison is the one I am least sorry to see the last of. I hope that Lewisham will throw the intruder out. He only came here because he ran away from a Communist.' Churchill's plea fell on deaf ears as the Lewisham East result proved.

Harold Wilson had been a senior civil servant during the war, advising the Cabinet and various Ministries and working closely with Sir William Beveridge in the production of his major report on social security. His father, Herbert Wilson, held strong left-wing views and these were no doubt strengthened in the 1930s when as an industrial chemist he was made unemployed.

In 1943, at the age of 27, Harold Wilson decided that his future career was in politics. He was active in the Fabian Society, a member of the Liskeard Labour Party and his work took him to various depressed parts of the country, particularly in the North. John Parker MP, who was General Secretary of the Fabian Society, encouraged Harold to be nominated for List B of available candidates. Parker had been energetic in persuading several young people to come forward as possible candidates including Jim Callaghan and Tony Benn, though the latter declined since he wanted to resume his university studies after leaving the Royal Air Force. In addition he was a member of Labour's National Executive Committee, and in a strong position to ensure that his hopes were achieved.

At the time Harold Wilson was nominated he was working at the Ministry of Fuel and Power, where Hugh Gaitskell was also employed. He was nominated by a former miner, Tom Smith MP, who was a junior Minister at the Ministry. Harold Wilson gained an intimate knowledge of the mining industry and about this time he delivered a paper at a Fabian Society meeting advocating bringing the mining industry into public ownership. In early 1944, Harold Wilson's name was on List B of available candidates and he received several requests from constituency Labour Parties. His first selection conference was in Peterborough where in the final ballot he was the runner up. At the General Election the Labour candidate, Mr S. Tiffany, a director of the Leeds Cooperative Society, was elected with a slim majority of 571 votes. The late Ben Pimlott in his biography of Harold Wilson stated that Harold's 'second attempt was in the

Lancashire constituency of Ormskirk'. There is another version.

The key people in the selection process for a parliamentary candidate are the regional organisers who determine the selection timetable, vet the nominations, are present on behalf of the National Executive Committee at the selection meeting and ensure the rules are clearly adopted. Reg Wallis was Regional Organiser for the North-West and had a strong influence with constituency parties, often suggesting names and encouraging ideal candidates to come forward. He is reported to have said that Harold Wilson was nominated and selected as prospective parliamentary Labour candidate for Knutsford against the Tory Lieutenant-Colonel Bromley-Davenport. However, as soon as the selection procedure was over there was a complaint that the rules had been infringed. This was examined and the result was declared null and void, which meant the selection procedure had to start all over again. Meanwhile Harold Wilson had moved on to Ormskirk, which is a large constituency embracing mining areas and stretching down to the outskirts of Liverpool.

Wilson's knowledge of the mining industry came in useful with the delegates from the local branch of the National Union of Miners. He was not the strongest candidate. A local alderman, Clifford Kenyon, was on the shortlist and he knew the area intimately not only because of his local government links but because he was a local farmer. Also on the shortlist were two trade union nominees, one from the National Union of Railwaymen and one from the General and Municipal Workers Union. In the final ballot Harold Wilson came first. Later Clifford Kenyon was selected for nearby Chorley, which he went on to win.

Ormskirk was not a safe Labour seat since it had a chequered political history. In 1929 Labour won the seat with a small majority and two years later the MP, Mr S. Rosbotham, became a Ramsay MacDonald supporter, winning Ormskirk for National Labour in both the 1931 and 1935 elections. In 1939 there was a by-election and the National Labour candidate was Commander Stephen King-Hall, a colourful character who was returned unopposed. Stephen King-Hall was a frequent contributor to the BBC radio programme, *The Brains Trust*, and was noted for his somewhat nostalgic views on life in the Navy. He usually commenced his contributions with 'when I was in Patagonia . . .' At the 1945 General

Election the unknown factor was whether the Tories would put up a candidate against both Harold Wilson and Stephen King-Hall. In fact they did. Stephen King-Hall had become a critic of the Churchill government and this did not endear him to the local Tories. They fielded a candidate but on polling day Harold Wilson achieved 30,126 votes, the Tory candidate had 23,104 and Stephen King-Hall, the sitting MP, came third with 11,848 votes.

Securing the nomination and sponsorship of a trade union in a constituency selection process is not a straightforward issue. Each union has its own rules and some seem to change them according to the constituency. But the benefit to a constituency party of a trade union nominee can be extremely helpful, not only in financial terms. Within the trade union movement there is immense loyalty towards the union and any young aspiring trade union officer is encouraged to devote his or her life to the work of the union. If along this path they decide they would like to enter politics then their days on the trade union ladder of promotion become somewhat difficult. The news gets around the union that they are more interested in Parliament than the success of the union and this is often held against them. So if trade union activists decide on a political career with the backing of the union they have to be sure they are taking the right steps.

George Brown had been active not only in the Labour Party but as an officer of the Transport and General Workers Union, and his views and tactics meant he often crossed swords with the General Secretary of the union, Ernest Bevin. The first public indication of this difference came to light at the 1939 Labour Conference when George Brown was a delegate from the St Albans Labour Party. The Conference Chairman was George Dallas, a full-time official of the Transport and General Workers Union and by coincidence a member of the St Albans Labour Party.

The contentious issue was the expulsion of Sir Stafford Cripps, Aneurin Bevan and George Strauss from the Labour Party. George Brown made a useful contribution from the rostrum and this brought him to the attention of key people within the wider Labour movement. During the war Brown was approached to become the joint candidate with John Strachey for the two-member seat in Dundee but rejected this suggestion.

In Belper the sitting MP decided he would not contest the 1945 General

Election and Professor Harold Laski and Hugh Dalton, both members of Labour's National Executive Committee, suggested to George Brown that he might like to let his name go forward. The sitting MP, George Dallas, was sponsored and the local Labour Party was keen to continue these arrangements. But George had to secure the consent of his own union and once again he came into conflict with Ernest Bevin. Bevin was not in favour of George becoming an MP and opposed the idea that he should be sponsored for Belper by the TGWU. As a Cabinet Minister, Bevin did not have day-to-day control of the union, though his influence was always present.

But George Brown did not gain a reputation for being a combatant politician merely by gently accepting an edict. He demanded to meet the National Committee of the union. Appearing before them, he put up a strong case that he should be allowed to contest Belper and the union should sponsor him. At the end of the meeting they agreed, so he was nominated by the TGWU for Belper. He won the selection conference and went on to win the seat with a majority of 8,881 votes. And thus commenced the tumultuous and sometimes exciting political career of George Brown. It was all to end in tears many years later when he abandoned Labour for the Social Democratic Party, left his wife and died a lonely man.

The role of women in politics has never been an easy path. Despite winning the vote and the activities of the suffragette movement, there was always a reluctance first to select a woman as a candidate and second to elect a woman as a Member of Parliament. Invariably they have to be larger-than-life characters with a charisma that cuts through the cant and prejudice against women. Barbara Castle had a vigorous approach to politics, had flowing red hair and was a brilliant orator. She had been an active member of the St Pancras Labour Party and was elected to the St Pancras Borough Council in 1938, and served on the Metropolitan Water Board. During the war she was in the Civil Defence, was a civil servant and developed her skills as a journalist. She was also active in London politics and had many close friends on the Left. Politics in wartime London was a breeding ground for strong arguments about post-war Britain and about the social problems confronting the nation.

Barbara was a delegate to the Labour Party Annual Conference in 1943 and made her mark in a debate on the Beveridge Report on social security. In 1944 when local Labour parties commenced the process of selecting parliamentary candidates, the north-west regional Women's Organiser of the Labour Party was keen to see more women adopted and gave full support to Barbara Castle in her approaches to Blackburn. This was a two-member constituency where the electors had two votes to return two members. Barbara Castle recalls the selection meeting held in July 1944.

> As I stood pale and shaky before them I decided that cunning was my only hope. 'I want you to forget two things, the first is that I am just out of hospital and the second is that I am a woman. Just judge me as socialist.' It did the trick but only just. Inevitably they cast their first vote for a male trade unionist, John Edwards, the intelligent and articulate General Secretary of the Post Office Engineering Union but they decided to use their second vote for the fiery redhead whose fighting speech had attracted them. I had made it.

In fact, Barbara Castle was not the first women Labour candidate in Blackburn. In 1929 Labour fielded Mrs M. Hamilton, a journalist who secured 37,000 votes – 2,000 more than Barbara Castle – and came not only top of the poll but beat her male running mate by more than 2,000 votes. They were both swept away in the disastrous 1931 General Election. At the 1945 General Election Barbara Castle came second to Lieutenant-Colonel John Edwards but only by 37 votes in an electorate of more than 80,000, which could prove that the electors of Blackburn were well trained in giving both their votes to Labour or that Barbara's forceful character demolished any sexual prejudice. It does, however, answer the critics who say that women electors will not vote for a woman candidate. For Barbara Castle this was the commencement of a distinguished parliamentary career which took her into the Cabinet, running major departments of state, a seat in the European Parliament and a title which enabled her to continue her campaigns in the House of Lords. She died in 2002.

The year 1945 was still a time when women were expected to stay at home and look after the children, hence the number of women candidates was extremely low. It used to be argued that women secured the vote in

1918 not by the activities of the suffragettes but by women undertaking traditional men's work during the First World War and thereby demonstrating their skills and prowess. If this was true then in 1945 we should have had more women candidates in the field. But tradition is entrenched in British culture and selection committees were still reluctant to adopt a female. Those who broke through this barrier, like Barbara Castle, demonstrated time and time again that British Parliaments suffered by having too few women MPs.

The Tories only managed to secure one woman MP at the 1945 General Election. Viscountess Davidson fought Hemel Hempstead and achieved a majority of more than 5,000. She first fought and won the seat at a by-election in 1937 when her husband, who was the sitting MP, was raised to the peerage. The Liberal Party could only claim one seat – Lady Megan Lloyd-George who won Anglesey with a majority of 1,081.

In all there were 87 women candidates nominated for all parties and 23 were successful, of which the Labour Party claimed 21 seats. This compares with their target fifty years later when they hoped that women would fill at least half the number of Labour MP's seats.

The Ulster Unionists were able to secure ten seats at the election but strict comparisons with mainland election results can be confusing. At the 1945 General Election the Labour Party fielded candidates in all Belfast constituencies and won one seat in Belfast West but in the more rural areas of Northern Ireland the political picture was different, although the Irish Nationalists were able to win two seats at Fermanagh and Tyrone.

The Communist Party fielded 21 candidates at the election and on polling day they were able to secure two seats. Throughout the war they had been seeking an official affiliation with the Labour Party but this was totally rejected both by the National Executive Committee and the Annual Conference. Failing affiliation, they hoped for some kind of electoral arrangement but this was rejected too. The two successful candidates were Phil Piratin in Stepney Mile End and Willy Gallagher in Fife West. Gallagher was the only Communist MP in the 1935–45 Parliament. He beat the Labour candidate, Lieutenant William Hamilton, by 2,000 votes but Hamilton won the seat at the 1950 General Election and was a keen anti-monarchist. Piratin's seat was next door to Stepney Limehouse, which was won by Attlee. Piratin won a seat on Stepney Council in 1937, becoming the first Communist on the council, and used this as a stepping stone to Parliament. By the 1950 General Election almost all constituency boundaries were redrawn and Piratin's short time in Parliament was over.

Among the other Communist candidates was Harry Pollitt, who was General Secretary of the Communist Party of Great Britain. He fought the Rhondda East seat against Labour and Welsh Nationalist candidates and lost by 972 votes. Pollitt was the driving force behind the Communist Party's desire to affiliate to the Labour Party A skilled boilermaker by trade, he was converted to Communism following the Russian Revolution in 1917. His mother gave him a copy of Marx's *Das Kaapital* for his twenty-first birthday. In his election address he claimed he had been arrested four times. Many years after the 1945 General Election, one of Harry Pollitt's supporters suggested the arrangements for the counting of the votes in Rhondda East were less than perfect and that a bundle of ballot papers for Mr Pollitt were inadvertently placed on the Labour candidate's pile.

Another of the leading Communist Party candidates was Mr R. Palme Dutt, a political theoretician who edited their monthly journal. Educated at Balliol College Oxford, he served a period in gaol for refusing to be conscripted. He fought Birmingham Sparkbrook but only secured 1,853 votes and lost his deposit. In some other areas, particularly in Scotland, the Communist Party recorded reasonable polls and in Hornsey they were able to secure more than 10,000 votes. But this was their peak and throughout the post-war period their support went into decline.

The 1945 General Election also had that curious category known as university seats. Dating back to 1603, the practice first started with Oxford and Cambridge Universities having the power to elect one of their graduates to become a Member of Parliament and this was later extended to embrace other universities and combined universities. The Labour Party attempted to abolish this privilege in 1931 but did not succeed, so in 1945 we had 25 largely Independent candidates contesting these twelve seats. Contesting might be too fine a word to describe these elections since they were all conducted in a polite manner. There were no public meetings, no heckling, no canvassing and electors voted by post in a simple form of proportional representation. Whereas in other elections the returning officer would be in charge, in the university elections they were run by the vice-chancellor.

The university candidates were often distinguished academics and among them was Sir John Anderson, who played a key role in Churchill's Coalition Government, and Sir John Boyd Orr, a distinguished scientist and medical authority. Whilst they stood as Independents they all had political opinions and when elected declared their hand by voting for or against the government and sometimes abstaining. Under the 1949 Representation of the Peoples Act, university seats were abolished.

At the 1945 General Election there was considerable freedom at local level to select the candidate that best fitted the area, but from time to time there was mild criticism about the narrow range of candidates who came forward, though this was not always true. The Tories were accused of selecting candidates who had a wealthy background and Labour was criticised for selecting too many full-time trade union officers. The general complaint was that there were too many barristers, but of course their natural ability to speak in court may have been an asset when they were addressing selection meetings. The accepted criticism today is that prospective parliamentary candidates are drawn from too narrow a field – almost professional parliamentary careerists – people who have left university, worked for a short period in a political lobbying organisation, in public relations or as an assistant in an MP's office. In 1945 the range of candidates was immense.

In Paddington North, Labour fielded an army general who had been Governor of Gibraltar, the chief officer of the Allied Control Commission in Italy and the senior army liaison officer with the Russian Army. And he won the seat with a 6,000 majority, ejecting Brendan Bracken, a close confidant of Churchill. The Liberal Party candidate in Middlesbrough was a 34-year-old air vice-marshal, probably the youngest serving officer holding one of the highest posts in the Air Force. He lost the election. In Wembley North the Tory candidate was Lieutenant-Commander Peter Scott, who saw service in the Navy and was responsible for creating the Wildlife Trust and other environmental projects. He failed to win the seat.

By complete contrast, in Manchester Clayton the Labour candidate was a hairdresser and in Moss Side their candidate was a consulting ophthalmic optician. Whilst the Tory Party fielded a large number of candidates who were farmers or came from the landed gentry, they rarely had a working-class candidate. With a wide range of candidates to choose from, the outcome of the election was that Parliament was more representative of the nation and covered a wider cross-section of society than ever before. People were allowing their names to go forward for election more on the basis of a service to the nation and because of their desire to see that Parliament was a way of changing society. It is not as if an elected MP were well paid. The salary of an MP at this time was £600 per annum compared with a London bus driver who might earn £5 a week. MPs virtually had no office; they paid their own postage (except letters to Ministers); there was no free telephone service and unless they had alternative sources of income they had to pay for the services of a secretary. In addition there was no pension.

But 1945 was different. It was no ordinary General Election. It was like a bubbling cauldron. Five years of war had destroyed not only thousands of homes and tens of thousands of service personnel and civilians, it had wrecked the traditional ways of running a modern society. It had killed off the concept that unemployment was an accepted way of life and eroded the class basis where some people employed servants and 'skivvies', and others lived in slums and poverty. The very nature of this revolutionary period was that it attracted people who wanted to do something about changing society and many eventually found themselves as parliamentary candidates.

In the immediate days after the war, when candidates were being selected a service background was often useful. In part this was because candidates with a service background had seen the war at first hand and this must have strengthened their views and opinions. Many had no practical experience of fighting an election but if you have taken an active role in defeating the enemy in all theatres of war then your views and opinions became that much more effective and forceful, and your desire for dramatic changes in the way society was managed and organised were more relevant.

The impact of the war on local political organisations and structure cannot be overemphasised. Where there was a sitting MP some kind of organisation existed though it was not unknown for MPs to make only periodic visits to the constituency. The modern concept of an MP running a weekly or fortnightly surgery where local constituents could bring their problems was extremely rare so there was no need to maintain a strong organisation. If the MP did not live in the constituency he or she would descend on the area only for high days and holidays which, because of the war, were often abandoned. The constituency parties who wanted to win the seat were often faced with a situation where the key players were otherwise involved either in the services or in some kind of war work which took them away from the area. The electoral truce meant in effect the end of political activities since there was no point in meeting. Despite this, total membership of the Labour Party rose from 2.6 million in 1939 to 3 million in 1945. The Communist Party claimed their membership in 1938 was 15,000 and by 1942 it had risen to 56,000.

The key person at Labour Party headquarters in reviving the Party from its non-active period was the newly appointed General Secretary, Morgan Phillips. He was a former Labour Party Agent in East Fulham and later the Regional Organiser in East Anglia. He came to Transport House (Labour Party headquarters) as the Propaganda Officer and spent every weekend visiting constituency Labour parties reviving their spirits and encouraging them to prepare for the General Election. He also played a key role in the development of Party policies both in 1945 and in the post-war years. Although he was a former Welsh miner he failed to win the nomination for a mining constituency when he sought membership of the House of Commons after the 1951 General Election.

In December 1943 the Labour Party NEC turned its collective mind towards the next General Election when they asked the Party officers to prepare a report regarding the necessary development costs of:

1   New propaganda staff
2   Loudspeaker vans
3   Conferences and schools
4   Training of party agents
5   Organisation of women in the Party
6   Survey of marginal seats

The whole area of press and publicity was another in which they called for detailed costs including:

1   Production of party journal
2   Local Labour press services
3   Film propaganda
4   Party publications – pamphlets, leaflets
5   Sales organisation
6   Newspaper advertisements
7   Broadcasting
8   Staff costs

The Labour National Committee put in train the production of policy reports and the development of new services to affiliated organisations. It was at this meeting that the Labour Party embarked on a recruitment drive for potential parliamentary candidates, reviewing the procedures for selection and the political education of selected candidates.

Clearly the tempo for preparing for the General Election was on the increase and in the weekend of 26–27 February 1944 (three months before D-Day), the National Executive Committee had a special meeting at St Ermin's Hotel in Westminster to discuss:

1   the present political situation including the continuance or ending the Coalition Government after the war with Germany was over
2   the problems of the next General Election

St Ermin's was the nearest hotel to Parliament and Whitehall, and seemed popular with members of the Labour Party. The building was largely used as offices during the war and at one stage it was considered as a possible headquarters for the Labour Party after the war, though the TUC who shared accommodation at Transport House had their own plans for a separate headquarters. The idea was not pursued.

The St Ermin's meeting laid out the strategy for the Labour Party in the crucial period towards the end of the war. It agreed:

1   that the Coalition should continue to be supported until the conclusion of the war in Europe
2   that there should be no question of a Coalition 'coupon' election as

141

far as the Labour Party was concerned

3   that the question of any future Coalition Government, its nature and terms should be left over for further discussion

4   that the modification of the Electoral Truce should be discussed by Labour Cabinet Ministers with their immediate Cabinet colleagues and by respective Party national agents

5   the question of local elections to be considered after the Speaker's conference

6   the question of supporting the principle of the Alternative Vote to be remitted to the Election Subcommittee

The reference to the Alternative Vote appears to be the result of a study of voting systems which showed that the existing systems were 'glaring examples of unfairness'. The advocates for change included Jim Griffiths and John Parker – two MPs who had large Labour majorities. They were opposed by Clement Attlee, Arthur Greenwood, Pethic Lawrence and Lord Ammon. The campaign to change the voting system never achieved widespread support within the Labour movement, though the Liberal Party were advocates of change.

The results of the St Ermin's meeting, together with the range of important reports called for at the December 1943 meeting, clearly put the Labour Party in the lead among all political parties in preparing for the next General Election. The decision of the National Executive Committee set the tone for galvanising the wider Labour movement into developing the necessary election-winning machinery and was subconsciously in tune with the thoughts of the electorate as demonstrated by the results of various by-elections.

Towards the end of 1943 the Labour Party began to think about the General Election in more practical terms. It called a meeting of affiliated trade unions to discuss the internal financial situation and the need to increase subscriptions to 6d per month. It agreed to purchase eleven propaganda vehicles – one for each region – with an estimated total cost of £2,200 plus staff costs. At the time there were 67 trade unions affiliated to the Labour Party and the combined direct and affiliated membership was 2,156,156, whilst the Trades Union Congress claimed they had 5,385,212 members.

In 1944, with peace now in focus, the hearts of some activists began to stir and they looked forward to the next election, though the feeling was not universal. In the larger urban areas the Labour Party took steps to rouse the constituency parties from their slumber but in rural areas, where transport was a problem, the process was much slower. Trying to assemble a meeting when there were virtually no local buses, no petrol and where telephone ownership was confined to the local doctor, vicar and squire was an organisational feat. But the latent enthusiasm for political change could be harnessed and this manifested itself when off-duty servicemen and women stationed in the area volunteered to create some kind of structure that would select a candidate and engage in raising funds for the campaign. It was this somewhat casual process that made the 1945 General Election different from any previous election and any since. Although it was inevitable that rules were broken, local well-wishers and party activists ran campaigns that were motivated by sheer political enthusiasm rather than strict organisational guidelines.

Francis Beckett, in his book, *The Enemy Within* claims 'about a dozen of the 393 Labour MPs [elected at the 1945 election] were either secret Communist Party members or were close to the Communist Party, sharing its beliefs and enjoying the company of its leaders.' This view is endorsed by Douglas Hyde, former news editor of the *Daily Worker*, who claimed, 'By the end of the night we knew we had at least eight or nine "cryptos" in the House.' Douglas Hyde resigned from the Communist Party in 1948 and wrote a book which exposed the operation of the Party.

But democracy moves in strange ways. No one appears to have criticised the way candidates were selected in 1945 and eventually the general public's choice emerged. We have to remember there was great respect for Parliament, the political parties and national institutions, and anyone standing for election was regarded as a citizen performing his or her national duties. Facing the hustings is a daunting challenge even for experienced candidates but in 1945 the majority had never fought a parliamentary election and most lacked public-speaking skills or the capacity to put across a convincing case. The head offices of the various parties produced 'speaker's notes', which were a great help but they could only go so far and were never helpful when it came to local issues.

The National Executive Committee of the Labour Party was hoping that candidates would be selected in all constituencies and this claim was endorsed by Reg Wallis, the Labour Party North-West Organiser. In fact, Labour did not have candidates in every constituency. Of the 600 candidates fielded by Labour, 130 were serving in the services apart from those who were employed in Civil Defence and government departments.

In Northern Ireland the major parties have always kept away from the hustings though there have been various attempts to replicate the party organisation in the province. After the war, the Labour Party employed John Hill as a full-time organiser in Ulster to create local parties but even his skills had no long-term effect. The Tories have often flirted with the idea of putting up candidates when their relations with the Official Unionists were at a low ebb but they have not been successful. As a result of a possible legal threat, the Labour Party now accepts into membership residents of Northern Ireland.

Excluding Northern Ireland, there were a number of constituencies which the main parties did not contest and this is possibly due to the lack of an efficient organisation at a local level. With Common Wealth Party candidates popping up throughout the country, one or two did not have a Labour Party opponent. The City of London has always been a difficult seat for Labour. A constituency dominated by the business vote (which was still in operation in 1945) meant that support was limited to a few hundred electors tucked away in streets dominated by office blocks or in caretaker's accommodation at the top of a building.

For the Liberal Party, Lord Samuel claimed that several hundred constituencies would be fought by what he called 'free Liberals'. Although this was a hope, in the final analysis they fielded 306 candidates. The Liberal Party position was confused by their relationship with the National Liberal Party. This situation went back to the National Government created by Ramsay MacDonald in 1931, which split the Labour Party and had a devastating effect on the Labour vote at the 1931 General Election. The Liberal Party was split too. Some of their MPs supported MacDonald and later Baldwin, and became National Liberals or Liberal Nationals, whilst others remained loyal to the mainstream Liberal Party. The National Liberals kept together until the 1945 Election was over when they finally dissolved and their members joined other parties. But their existence as a separate organisation competing for votes with the Liberal Party was bound to have a damaging effect and created confusion for the average elector.

The Liberal Party had other problems too. The decline of the Liberal vote since the great days of Lloyd-George meant that not only were they losing public support, their organisation was limited to specific parts of the country (known later as the Celtic fringe) and their finances suffered because they did not have the support of big business or the trade union movement and had to rely on individual donors. Nevertheless, considering it had been ten years since the last General Election they had a reasonable spread of candidates throughout the country.

The Common Wealth Party, which had done well during the electoral truce, ended the election campaign by only winning Chelmsford. Wing Commander Millington won the seat in April 1945 at a by-election when he secured a 28 per cent swing against the Coalition Government. Three months later he faced the electors again and won the seat with a 2,080 majority. Shortly afterwards he joined the Labour Party when the Common Wealth Party decided to dissolve itself. One of the founders of the Common Wealth Party, Sir Richard Acland, scored only 2,686 votes in his contest at Putney.

Another of the Common Wealth's candidates was Tom Sargant who had the doubtful privilege of being returned bottom of the poll in Petersfield where there was no Labour candidate.

The Tories had difficulties in fighting all seats. If it was a hopeless seat and a candidate was prepared to finance his or her own election campaign then the chances of being selected were that much better. If the local Tory Association had little in the way of funds and the chances of winning were somewhat remote, no contest was forthcoming. Out of a possible 640 seats the Tories contested 624 seats and this included National candidates and the particular position in Northern Ireland.

The Tories had a narrow base from which to select their candidates. In pre-war elections the aristocracy, which never numbered more than 25,000 people, managed to provide an average of 200 seats in Parliament. In the 1935 Parliament Tory MPs held more than 800 company directorships.

Because of the limit on the number of candidates they could field and the severe shortage of funds, the Communist Party sought to forge an alliance with the Labour Party. They argued that they would be reducing the number of their candidates as a contribution towards limiting a split in the progressive vote, which they claimed would lead to the return of Tory candidates. This plea by the Communist Party was ignored by the Labour Party, as was an overture by the Independent Labour Party who wanted to work closely with Labour.

A midsummer election in July posed several problems for those areas where one industry dominated the town and where it was the tradition to close the factory and allow all staff to have their holidays at the same time, known locally as 'wakes weeks'. Emergency legislation was passed by Parliament to defer their elections until 12 July except for Nelson and Colne who voted on 19 July. The towns involved were Carlisle, Bolton, Farnsworth, Nelson, Turton, Westhoughton, Barrow, Ulverston, Crewe, Greenock, Falkirk, Renfrew, Midlothian, Berwick and Stirling. It was pointless for candidates to campaign in these areas since most of the shops were closed and the inhabitants had decamped to the seaside. This did not stop the enterprising Labour candidate for Bolton, who took his campaign to Blackpool, Southport and Morecambe. The decision to defer polling day in these constituencies had no effect on the wider General Election because the count did not take place until 26 July.

With so many new candidates in the field and a lack of knowledge about election law by temporary election agents drafted in to the campaign, the Parties embarked on a crash programme of education. Classes in election procedures for both full- and part-time workers were held throughout the country and the Labour Party organised one-day conferences on election policies for new candidates. Election law clearly spelt out the limit a candidate could spend on the campaign. For urban seats a candidate could spend 5d (old money) per elector. Rural areas were allowed to spend 6d (old money) per elector. Because of the shortage of paper, candidates were limited to one ton of paper each plus an extra 5 cwt for every 10,000 electors over 40,000. If you were an Independent candidate you could claim an extra 25 per cent. The party national headquarters were also allocated a ration of paper.

Petrol, too, was restricted though this was never a problem for the Labour Party since so few of their supporters had cars. James Callaghan recalls that he had one car and one three-wheel tricycle to move goods and people around his Cardiff constituency. Each candidate in a rural seat could use 750 gallons and 500 gallons if you campaigned in an urban area. It is difficult to understand how these restrictions were monitored, though in the case of petrol it was a matter of being allocated coupons which had to be exchanged at the petrol station.

The electoral registration officers had their problems too. They were responsible for compiling the election register and were faced with evacuation, bomb damage and thousands of potential electors in the services who could vote by post. The qualifying date for inclusion in the election register was 7 May 1945, which was the eve of VE-Day when the nation was more interested in celebrating the defeat of Hitler rather than the more prosaic process of a General Election. The qualifying date for the business vote was 28 February 1945.

In the days before computers, election registers were compiled from forms left at homes and followed up by canvassers but severe staff shortages in the council offices made this impossible. During the war everyone was issued with an identity card which included your home address. If you moved you were supposed to notify the town hall of your old and new addresses and this information helped the electoral registration officer to compile the election register.

There is no accurate evidence that the public stuck rigidly to the rules and with bombing, direction of labour, evacuation and the general movement of people, the election register was far from perfect. Due to an oversight even Winston Churchill was not on the election register! Almost certainly there were tens of thousands of people who were excluded from the register since the period between the end of the war in Europe (8 May) and polling day (5 July) saw many returning to their urban homes from evacuation in rural areas. Similarly, a start had been made in demobilising people from the services and those employed in war factories.

Bombed-out areas were particularly bad in creating an accurate register of electors since many houses were unoccupied and thousands of electors had moved away. Two examples come to mind. The combined Tory and Labour vote in Clem Attlee's Limehouse constituency in 1935 was 21,000. After six years of bombing and evacuation, the number of people in this

147

dockland constituency who voted in 1945 was just under 10,000 – a considerable drop. In Shoreditch the combined vote in 1935 was 29,000 whereas it was down to 15,000 in 1945.Bethnal Green had a population of 90,000 in 1939 – by 1941 it was down to 47,000.

The movement of population throughout the war presented electoral registration officers with distinct problems. Within a few months of the commencement of hostilities it was estimated that more than 2 million people had moved home. By 1942 20 million people had notified the national registration officer of their change of address. The normal practice was for election registers to be printed by hand-set printing methods with the printers retaining the type until changes were made for the next issue. But the demand for scrap metal to build aircraft and other tools of war meant that many printers disposed of their election register type for war salvage and electoral registration officers had to compile their new register operating without the advantage of previous printed records. One town clerk pleaded with the Home Office that 'he had only one experienced man, a boy of sixteen and two girls' to prepare the register.

Other ideas about compiling the election register were discussed in Whitehall including printing by stencils on office duplicators and using the air-raid precaution officers and wardens to compile the names and addresses in their district. Suggestions were also made to use post office counters and police stations where electors could come and register their names. Another idea was to use the food ration book distribution system. All these suggestions might have been acceptable in towns and cities but were impracticable in the Western Isles or remote rural areas. It was estimated that it would take 3,500 man-hours to make a full canvass in urban areas and 5,000 in the countryside. In the end, most electoral registration officers used the identity card as the basis for compiling their election register.

The drive to have the widest possible election franchise came from the Cabinet, who set up a powerful subcommittee headed by the Chancellor of the Exchequer to 'consider the practicability of extending the postal voting to members of the Forces and seamen overseas and war workers abroad over as wide a geographical area as possible'. When this was announced in Parliament Tom Driberg, who was then an Independent MP, sought an assurance that 'servicemen who have no fixed domicile in this country and do not know exactly where they will live after the war' should be taken into account.

In the general discussion about the franchise George Shepherd, the National Agent of the Labour Party, wrote to Herbert Morrison, the Home Secretary, stating, 'I do not believe that the voting age should be reduced as in the 1914–18 war. There will however be an outcry in favour of it. I can quite see, however, that on this occasion reduction in the voting age would have to apply not merely to men and women serving in the armed services but to those who have been "conscripted" for other forms of National Service.' Whether George Shepherd was expressing the view of the National Executive Committee of the Labour Party was not made clear but it seemed that you could be conscripted into the services at the age of eighteen and fight for your country but that you would have to wait until you were 21 before you could vote. The position was changed after the war when the voting age was reduced to eighteen.

In 1945 there was no general postal voting for the sick and those away on holiday but service people were allowed to appoint a proxy, which led the *Daily Mirror* to urge its readers at home to 'Vote for him' who was away in the services throughout the world.

Because of the uncertainties about their future prospects in the post-war field, several candidates had second thoughts about contesting a General Election. At its meeting on 26 April 1944 the Labour Party NEC endorsed the selection of ten new candidates and at the same time it was reported that eleven had withdrawn. In one case the selected Labour candidate for Banff, Mr G. Mair, had been killed in action.

Three months later John Belcher withdrew from Faversham, Louis Fenn from Widnes, William Warby from Wimbledon and Mr H. Pennington from Pudsey and Otley. Other prospective candidates also withdrew from Altrincham, Carlisle, Portsmouth North, Peterborough, Isle of Thanet and Manchester Hulme. In some cases it was not a simple decision to withdraw but of candidates finding what they thought were better seats. The Labour candidate for Henley on Thames, Wogan Philipps, withdrew for other reasons. He married the Countess of Huntingdon who was a member of the Communist Party so he joined too but whether it was part of the marriage bargain is not known. The immediate effect, however, on leaving the Labour Party and joining the Communist Party meant that his father, the second Baron Milford, disinherited him.

In Maldon, Essex, the sitting Independent MP was Tom Driberg but the Labour Party had already selected Captain Morris Jarvis. The difficulty that arose was that following his selection, Captain Jarvis was sent overseas and was captured by the Japanese and became a prisoner of war. Communist members of the Amalgamated Engineering Union used their union's affiliation to the Labour Party to urge that Captain Jarvis's candidature should be withdrawn in favour of Tom Driberg. The Labour Party was in some difficulty as they could not promote Captain Jarvis at the election since he would not be able to sign the nomination form and other legal documents. They had no alternative but to withdraw his candidature, which left the door wide open for Tom Driberg MP to become the official Labour candidate for the constituency.

Although the Labour Party had its suspicions about some candidates who might be sympathetic towards the Communist Party there is only one case where the candidate had links with the other end of the political spectrum. In 1945 the Labour Party was asked to include in the list of available candidates, the name of Charles Wegg-Prosser. Mr Wegg-Prosser came to live in Paddington in 1937 and was active with Sir Oswald Mosley and the British Union of Fascists even to the extent of being a BUF candidate at local elections. When Mosley developed his extreme Fascist policies, Mr Wegg-Prosser left the BUP and joined the Labour Party. Hinley Atkinson, the London Labour Party Regional Organiser, came to his defence and argued that Mr Wegg-Prosser had been an active member of the Labour Party for six years. After some discussion it was agreed that his name should go forward as a possible candidate and later he was adopted for Paddington South, a seat which he fought and lost on several occasions. Though he never made it to Parliament he played an active role as a member of Paddington Borough Council and was a vociferous opponent of the slum landlord who gave his name to Rachmanism. Mr Wegg-Prosser died in 1996.

Some fifteen candidates decided to fight the election as National candidates. They had the backing of their local Tory association but they somehow felt the National banner was above politics. For Harold Nicolson this presented a problem. He had been elected an MP for Leicester West in 1935 as National Labour – an indication of his support for Ramsay MacDonald, the 1931 Labour Prime Minister who reneged on the Labour Party. When it came to 1945 he refused to call himself Conservative 'but equally he would form no part of an alliance ranged against Churchill', whom he held in high esteem. As regards the 'National Labour Party', this had almost ceased to exist since Malcolm MacDonald (son of Ramsay) decided not to return from Canada and contest his own seat. Harold Nicolson came up with the original slogan, 'Support Churchill and vote for Harold Nicolson, the National Candidate'. The electors of Leicester West saw through this ruse and decided to reject their erstwhile MP in favour of Barnet Janner, the Labour candidate. But to give Nicolson some credit, after his defeat he joined the Labour Party and fought without success a by-election in Croydon, then spent many happy years cultivating his garden with his wife Vita Sackville West at Sissinghurst and hoping that some day he would be elevated to the peerage, something which always alluded him.

Another candidate who fought under the National banner was Leslie Hore-Belisha at Devonport in Plymouth. Hore-Belisha gave his name to the street crossing signals and fought in previous elections under different banners. He was up against Michael Foot, the skilful propagandist who easily exposed him for his true Tory beliefs. The result was the demise of Hore-Belisha and the election of someone who was to become a distinguished politician for more than 60 years.

General Elections always attract their fair share of Independent candidates, and in 1945 there were 76 and they included many academics for the university seats. The author and wartime broadcaster, J. B. Priestly, fought the Cambridge University seat but was only the runner-up. Eleanor Rathbone, who was largely responsible for the introduction of family allowances, was returned again for the Combined English Universities seat as an Independent.

Except on rare occasions, Independents are seldom elected since the electors clearly prefer someone with a party label. There are times, however, when independence is seen as an essential qualification. Mr D. N. Pritt was the Independent Labour candidate for Hammersmith North, He was a distinguished lawyer, a King's Counsel and had been expelled from the Labour Party in 1940 because of his opposition to policies relating to Russia and Finland. Some have described Mr Pritt as an able lawyer but a naïve politician. He once said that 'many people thought it did not matter who was in Parliament because all politicians were a pack of rascals. But people's lives and indeed deaths depended on who was in Parliament.' The electors of Hammersmith North were of the opinion that Pritt was a good MP who looked after his constituents and he was re-elected to Parliament. Shortly after his victory he applied to rejoin the Labour Party. The matter was considered by Hammersmith North Labour Party, the London Labour Party and the National Executive Committee but they all rejected his application. Mr Pritt continued his activities in Parliament and spent much time being fêted by Iron Curtain governments who showered him with awards and medals.

Another Independent was Vernon Bartlett who fought and won Bridgewater in Somerset. He was first elected to Parliament in 1938 at a crucial by-election when he defeated the Tory candidate during the Munich crisis. Bartlettt was a journalist and had travelled extensively throughouut Europe and from 1922 to 1932 was the London Director of the League of Nations. Attempts were made to persuade him to join the Labour Party and in 1945 he was interviewed by Harold Laski, Arthur Greenwood, Hugh Dalton and Herbert Morrison.

The selected Labour candidate for Bridgewater offered to withdraw his nomination if Vernon Bartlett joined the Labour Party but despite these overtures he decided to continue as an Independent though he did support the Labour Party on many issues. He won the seat in 1945 with a majority of 2,312, defeating both the Labour and Tory candidates.

David Kendall, who won a by-election in 1942 as an Independent at Grantham with a 367 majority, was returned again in 1945 with a majority of 15,513, putting the Labour candidate at the bottom of the poll. Mr Kendall was a works manager at a car manufacturing company and had a reputation of being a good employer. He formed the Grantham Production Company, which produced the 'people's car' but it never became a mass sales product. He lost the seat in 1950.

General Elections also attract their fair share of candidates who profess

'Here you are! Don't lose it again!'
Philip Zec's *Daily Mirror* VE Day cartoon

This cartoon by Zec was first used by the *Daily Mirror* on the front page of their issue for VE-Day and again on 5 July 1945 – polling day. Zec also produced eight posters for the Labour Party election campaign.
(reproduced by kind permission of the *Daily Mirror*)

Despite the rain, Winston Churchill out campaigning with his wife much to the amusement of the crowd.

One of the Labour Party posters used in the campaign which is deliberately linked to the service vote.

The end of the 1945 Labour Party Conference in Blackpool when the platform party leads the delegates in singing the 'Red Flag', the 'Internationale' and 'Auld Lang Syne'.

Sir Stafford Cripps (right) with General Mason Macfarlane, the Labour Candidate who defeated the Tory Minister Brendan Bracken at Paddington North with a 6,545 majority.

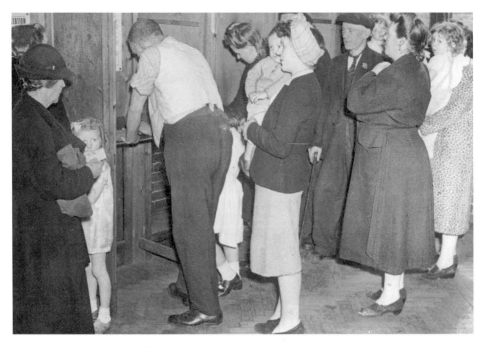

Polling day at Webber Street, Southwark

Ernest Bevin, the Minister of Labour (right) in conversation with Arthur
Greenwood who was Leader of the Opposition during the Coalition Government.

INDUSTRY MUST SERVE THE PEOPLE
—NOT ENSLAVE THEM!

FOR PUBLIC OWNERSHIP—NOT PRIVATE MONOPOLY
vote LABOUR

A Labour Party election poster arguing the case for public ownership.

Some of the successful Labour Candidates arriving for the first meeting of the Parliamentary Labour Party. (Centre) Herbert Morrison who won Lewisham East but previously represented South Hackney and Barbara Castle who won one of the two seats at Blackburn with a majority of 8,000 over her nearest Tory opponent.

Clement Attlee receives warm applause from supporters at Labour Party headquarters when it became clear that Labour had won the election.

Election workers in Ernest Bevin's Wandsworth Central constituency – note the Army corporal lending a hand.

Two winners from Scotland (left) George Mathers who was first elected for Linlithgow in 1935 and Mrs Jean Mann the new MP for Coatbridge who was previously organising secretary of the Town & Country Planning Association.

Not quite smiles all round – (left to right) Mr and Mrs Bevin, Mr and Mrs Attlee and Mr and Mrs Morrison.

The victory rally at the Central Hall, Westminster on 26 July 1945 when Attlee announced the King had charged him to form a Government.

strong beliefs for their party and then begin to change their allegiance – described by some as being on the road to Damascus. In Eastern Dorset the Labour Party selected before the war Charles Fletcher-Cooke, a former President of the Cambridge Union, as their candidate. During the war Mr Fletcher-Cooke joined the Navy and served in Naval Intelligence, ending up with the rank of lieutenant-commander. He fought the election in 1945 and lost by 1,468 votes. Shortly after losing Fletcher-Cooke decided he no longer supported the Labour Party, promptly joined the Tories and served in Parliament as Tory MP for Darwen for many years and was eventually knighted. There must be something about Eastern Dorset for in 1950 the same thing happened again when Evelyn King, a former Labour MP, contested Poole, lost the election and joined the Tories, becoming a Tory MP for South Dorset. Another who changed sides was Flight-Lieutenant Aiden Crawley who fought and won Buckingham as a Labour candidate and, after losing the seat in 1951 by 54 votes, joined the Tories and became a Tory MP for Derbyshire West.

The case of Albert Edwards was somewhat different. He was elected a Labour MP for Middlesbrough East in 1935 and served the constituency until 1950. He started out in life working as a labourer in a Middlesbrough foundry and later became a director of a pig-iron firm and many other companies. He was opposed to Labour's plan to bring the iron and steel industry into public ownership and was eventually expelled from the Labour Party. He joined the Tory Party and was their standard-bearer in Newcastle upon Tyne East at the 1951 General Election but he was not successful.

Another Labour MP who changed sides was Ivor Thomas, the Labour MP for Keighley from 1942 to 1948. He left Labour in 1948 and continued in Parliament as a Tory until the 1950 General Election. It was Mr Thomas who encouraged Denis Healey to become a Labour candidate. Ivor Thomas not only changed his party but changed his name too, becoming Mr Ivor Bulmer-Thomas and contesting Newport (Mon) for the Tories in 1950.

In some families, politics must play an important part in their way of life. The West Country Foot family no doubt had many arguments and discussions around the kitchen table. Isaac Foot (father) contested Tavistock for the Liberals; Major John Foot (son) fought Bodmin for the

Liberals; Dingle Foot (son) fought Dundee for the Liberals and Michael Foot (son) was the Labour candidate at Devonport. Only Michael Foot was successful.

Two members of the Noel-Baker family contested the 1945 General Election, both for Labour and both were successful. Philip Noel-Baker (father) fought Derby and Francis Noel-Baker (son) won Brentford and Chiswick. The Jeger family also fielded two Labour candidates and both won. Captain George Jeger made the surprising gain at Winchester and Dr Santo Jeger, a founder of the Socialist Medical Association, won St Pancras South-East.

Some families seem to have a long association with Parliament. The Hurd family is an example. Sir Percy Hurd was a Tory MP for Devizes from 1924 to 1945 and his son Anthony Hurd became the MP for Newbury in 1945 where he had a Tory majority of more than 8,000. Later Douglas Hurd became the Tory MP for Witney and was Home Secretary and Foreign Secretary in Margaret Thatcher's governments.

The Guinness family were strong in Southend. Henry Channon won the constituency first in 1935 when he succeeded his mother-in-law, Lady Iveagh, as MP. Later he was succeeded by his son, Paul Channon, who became Minister of Transport under Margaret Thatcher. Almost a pocket borough seat.

Among the other personalities contesting the 1945 General Election was Randolph Churchill, the son of Winston Churchill. He was returned unopposed in Preston at a by-election in 1940 but when he faced the electors for the first time he lost out to Labour. He persisted in his attempt to get back to Parliament in 1950 at Plymouth Devonport against Michael Foot but despite the support of his father, he was not returned by the electors of Plymouth.

By polling day on 5 July there were 1,682 candidates in position. These were made up as follows:

Tories	624
Liberal	306
Labour	604
Communist	21
Common Wealth	23
Others	104

Included in these figures were a variety of National Candidates: National Liberal, Nationals, Welsh Nationals, Scottish Nationals and Irish Nationals. The Speaker, Colonel D Clifton Brown also sought re-election as a Tory though by 1950 he dropped his party connection. The Independent Labour Party fought separately to the Labour Party.

In January 1945 the Boundary Commission undertook a short survey where they thought the constituencies were too large with more than 100,000 electors. This resulted in an increase in the number of seats by 25, bringing the total up to 640. The new seats were:

Barking	Heston and Isleworth
Barnet	Hornchurch
Bexley	Ilford South
Birmingham Acocks Green	Orpington
Blackpool North	Southall
Bucklow	Sutton and Cheam
Carshalton	Sutton Coldfield
Coventry East	Thurrock
Dagenham	Wembley South
Ealing West	Wembley North
Eton and Slough	Woodford
Harrow East	Worthing
Hendon South	

In January 1945, Megan Lloyd-George, who was then a Liberal MP, proposed to Parliament that plural voting should be abolished. She argued that everyone should only have one vote. A situation could arise when electors could have a vote where they resided, another as a business elector and, if they had been to a university, have a vote there too. Her proposal was defeated by 121 votes to 53. Parliament eventually abolished both the business vote and the university vote in 1949.

For those in the services there was the opportunity to vote either by post or by appointing a proxy. Almost 3 million were eligible to vote and just under 2 million appointed a proxy. A separate election register was compiled for service voters and legislation was passed by Parliament in early 1945 which enabled ballot papers to be flown to service personnel in bases overseas. Most of the Western world was covered but it was found impossible to send ballot papers to servicemen and servicewomen in Australia and New Zealand. The returning officer for the election had the task of sending off ballot papers and election addresses to all absent voters and the RAF flew more than 6 tons of paper via Blackbushe, Down Ampney, Prestwick and Lyneham airports. The inclusion of a candidate's election address with the ballot paper was a major departure and has never been repeated again at subsequent elections. Without an election address, a serviceman or woman would be unable to know whom to vote for since the ballot paper contained only a minimum of information. One airman serving in Burma managed to write home and sought information from the family, and Major Denis Healey said he knew who the Labour candidate was because he was a friend of the family. But these were exceptions.

The military authorities took these responsibilities very seriously. Instructions were issued which emphasised that secrecy in voting was a fundamental principle and that arrangements should 'not be considered a routine administration task but the intimate concern for Commanders at all levels'. The instructions stated that no censor 'will interfere on political matters and no officer may attempt to influence any personnel to vote or not to vote'. Each unit was asked to create a postal voting officer and personnel were not to be marched to polling stations. Indeed, everyone was given a full day to read the election addresses and make up his or her mind which way to vote.

The act of voting by the fighting services was considered by the authorities to be compatible with military operations 'whenever local conditions are such that troops are able to send and receive personal mail.' Inevitably there were isolated problems. More than 1,000 troops in India complained that despite making an application for a postal vote only seventeen had received the necessary papers. They all signed a petition which they sent to Tom Driberg who was then an Independent MP. But sending complaints via the post during the war would take some time and before action was taken the election was over.

The question of how to enable prisoners of war to vote was also considered by the Ministry of Home Security and various service units. The lawyers said that a prisoner of war would have to complete an application form to vote by post or even to appoint a proxy. The immediate problem that arose was how to get the necessary forms to prisoners who were incarcerated in Europe and the Far East. Any idea of getting the Japanese government to cooperate was ruled out but possibilities with Germany were explored. The conclusion of this exercise, after consultation with the International Red Cross, was that only a limited amount of mail was allowed through the system and there would be a large number of complaints if official mail took precedence over personal mail from families and loved ones. It was argued that German authorities were very suspicious of official communications to prisoners of war. Another suggestion was that the prisoner's next of kin should automatically be made a proxy but objections were made that the appointment of a proxy was the personal responsibility of an elector and some might not want their next of kin to use their vote.

But the electoral scene moves on. As Allied troops swept through France, Germany and the Low Countries, prisoners of war were released and flown home, and Parliament agreed that ex-prisoners could register for a vote 'any time after the qualifying date and up to 4 days before nomination day'. This enabled ex-prisoners to use their vote but it did not help those who were in Japanese prisons for whom nothing could be arranged because the war was still being fought.

Concern about the General Election procedures and facilities was expressed on both sides of the House of Commons Chamber and resulted in a cross-party deputation of ten MPs meeting not only the Home Secretary but also the First Lord of the Admiralty, the Secretary of State for War and the Air Minister.

Major Quintin Hogg who led the delegation said that existing procedures for service personnel to register a service vote were defective.

157

He argued that it would 'create a dangerous feeling of political dissatisfaction, just at the time when such sentiments would be most harmful'. Herbert Morrison, the Home Secretary, assured the meeting there was no 'lack of goodwill to enable that all persons eligible should be entered on the service register'. Later that month (31 July 1944) service chiefs issued a press statement reminding all those in the fighting services of the opportunity to register their vote in their home town and made available the necessary application forms.

Looking back after 60 years, it is clear that civil servants did everything possible to enable the maximum number of people to register for the election. But we are talking about a period long before office computers, before fax machines, before there was an extensive telecommunications system and when there was dislocation in industry caused by the war effort. A determination to win the war was the priority and creating accurate election registers was not top of the agenda.

With a dual choice of voting, returning officers had the task of separating proxy votes from postal votes to ensure that a service elector did not vote twice. Postal votes were examined on the day before the count and proxy votes, which were on coloured paper, were extracted from the ballot boxes and checked against those that arrived by post. For scrutineers and counting agents this was the first opportunity they had for estimating the likely result but all were sworn to secrecy so nothing appeared in the press on the real counting day – 26 July.

Although the service vote was vitally important, the bulk of candidates had great difficulty in making contact with those in uniform. In modern elections the ballot paper informs the elector of the name of the political party, the name and address of the candidate plus a logo. In 1945 it was different. The name and address of the candidates together with their occupation were the only details the humble voter could elicit, though if you managed to get to a polling station you might gather some information as to the names of the people who had nominated the candidate. With servicemen and women scattered all over the globe, candidates had no details where the particular electors were serving so there was little or no personal contact. Although returning officers were allowed to include a candidate's message with the ballot paper, this assumes that all constituency parties were efficient in availing themselves of the opportunity. One Labour Party agent said he relied entirely on the goodwill of families to forward on to their sons and daughters any political literature. In the case of proxy voters the task was easier because the absent voter would nominate someone to be their proxy and they could turn up at the polling station and cast a vote for the candidate the absent elector had chosen.

The 1945 General Election was therefore unique. Many of the candidates were novices; the election organisation somewhat creaky; electors were all over the world and the election register left a lot to be desired in terms of accuracy. It was fought against a background of six years of war: some 100,000 homes destroyed; thousands of people had been killed both at home and overseas; industry had been geared up for war and needed to change; Europe was reduced almost to rubble; Britain's finances were in a perilous state and the population existed on limited food rationing. But the war in Europe was over and spirits were high. The nation had the daunting task of deciding whether they wanted a change in direction or whether they would give Churchill a vote of confidence.

With all the candidates in position on nomination day – 25 June – and an electorate of 33,240,391 waiting to cast their vote, we must now return to the hustings to see how the campaign was waged on the doorstep, on the radio and in the towns and villages of Britain.

CHAPTER SEVEN

The Campaign

In choosing 5 July as polling day, Churchill took an unusual step by consulting the Chief of the Imperial General Staff, Field Marshal Lord Alanbroke. At a celebratory lunch held in Downing Street on 7 May with all the Chiefs of Staff present, the Field Marshal recalls,

> Winston discussed the pros and cons of elections in June. We stressed the 'cons' from the military point of view, stating that it could lead only to dispersal of effort which would be better concentrated onto the war.

But with the break-up of the Coalition Government there was a scramble to find sufficient numbers of candidates by the major parties and though the Tories and Labour had a good national spread throughout the country, the Liberal Party organisation was weak and they only contested 306 seats out of a possible 640.

Between the period when the Labour Party left the Coalition Government and the General Election, the country was governed by a Caretaker Government which consisted mainly of Tory MPs as Ministers, together with a few people from outside to give the impression that it was a National Government.

The Caretaker Government met for eleven days in session and this was the opportunity for both the Labour Party and the Tories to parade their policies and differences. In April 1945 the Labour Party had published its manifesto under the general title of 'Let Us Face the Future' and the Tories responded with their 'four years' plan'. Whilst the Labour Party held a conference to finalise their policies and programmes, the Tories and the Liberal Party left the compilation of the manifestos to their leaders.

The clear difference of opinion between Labour and the Tories was crystallised in their different approaches to tackling the enormous human, social, financial and administrative problems that confronted the nation at the end of the war.

For Labour it was simple. The nation must organise the nation's resources for the benefit of the nation. Priorities must be created and the economy managed. For the Tories it was away with wartime controls and let private enterprise create and meet the public's demands. Sir Stafford Cripps put it succinctly when he said, 'During the war it was through Government enterprise and initiative that we had been able to secure victory. History has been brought about by the spirit of enterprise shown by the people of Britain under Government control and planning.'

With the Tories promoting Churchill as the saviour of the nation, Ernest Bevin insisted, 'The war was not a one man show or a one man Government.' He argued, 'One would imagine that if there was any sense of responsibility among politicians, they would have been anxious to face the electors, not with the old tricks but with solemn facts upon which judgement could be given. Only by careful thought and judgement can a repetition of the fraud perpetrated after the first world war be avoided.' He went on to say, 'The Tories had been in office for 20 years and they had brought the nation to the verge of disaster by the complete failure to prepare for defence and then claim credit for winning the war.'

The first major impact in the campaign came with Churchill's party political broadcast on 4 June 1945 when he suggested that returning a Labour Government would mean the introduction of the Gestapo. He stated that Socialists were opposed to a free Parliament and that everyone's savings would be at risk if the public voted Labour: 'I declare to you from the bottom of my heart that no socialist system can be established without a political police.' Continuing his vitriolic attack on the Labour Party he said that Labour would be

> monkeying with the credit of Great Britain and would see that no man or woman in the country who has by their thrift or toil accumulated a nest egg will not run the risk of seeing it shrivel before their eyes.

In a typical Churchillian flourish he added:

> Leave the socialist dreamers to their Utopias or their nightmares. Let us be
> content to do the heavy job that is right on top of us. And let us make sure that
> the cottage home to which the warrior will return is blessed with modest but
> solid prosperity, well-fenced and guarded against misfortune and that Britons
> remain free to plan their lives for themselves and for those they love.

The broadcast was a complete disaster and was an affront to all intelligent
electors. To associate the Labour Party with all the evils of Hitler's Gestapo
system was ludicrous, particularly since the Labour Party had played a key
role in defeating Germany and thousands of Labour supporters were in the
services fighting a bitter war. Churchill's reputation never really recovered
from this gaffe. D. N. Pritt, the Independent Labour candidate at
Hammersmith North, suggested that Churchill's speech was worth 50 seats
to Labour. Churchill's wife Clementine was also appalled at his Gestapo
reference and told him so before the broadcast.

The response to Churchill's howler was widespread and from his own
Party too. The Chief Whip of the Tory Party, James Stuart, is reported to
have telephoned Chequers stating, 'If that is the way he wants to conduct the
campaign he must decide. He is the Leader of the Party but it is not my idea
of how to win an election.' Churchill had the difficult task of converting
himself from being the leader of the nation into becoming leader of the Tory
Party – something he did not relish. In many respects he felt he was somehow
supreme – above party politics.

Sir John Colville, Churchill's private secretary, was present at Chequers
when he delivered this amazing party political broadcast. Some 20 years later
he tried to explain away the incident in his book *Footprints of Time*. He
argued,

> Part of Churchill's strength stemmed from his simplicity. He had always had
> a gift for eliminating the complex and concentrating on the essential. If a
> particular theme seemed to him to contain an essential truth he would seize
> on it, play with it like a cat with a mouse, expatiate on it at the dinner table
> and provided it stood up to all his own tests, finally offer it to the public. He

had recently been reading two books – *The Life of the Bee* and *The Life of the Ant*. The latter in particular with its description of the orderly, unthinking regimentation of life in an ant hill, seemed to Churchill a realistic picture of what society would eventually become under Socialist control. This was the background to the so-called Gestapo speech. Contrary to the general belief, neither Beaverbrook or Bracken had a hand in preparing it.

For the first time he was speaking to the country within a given time limit, for the BBC could not allow the Prime Minister one second longer for a Party Political Broadcast. This new and unwelcome restriction on his oratory put Churchill off balance, so that he spoke hurriedly, without the pauses and unscripted interpolations which had always been a feature of his oratory.

In defending Churchill's use of the Gestapo phrase, Sir John Colville wrote that Churchill was drawing his conclusions from Russia, 'the only country in which the experiment of Marxist Socialism had then been made'. Some would describe this as a lame excuse.

Attlee's response was modesty itself. In a calm, responsible manner he set out the record, corrected Churchill's misinformation about the creation of Labour Party policy and went on to attack the Tories for their blind faith in private enterprise. In arguing his case for public control, Attlee recalled the various measures that had been taken during the war for the benefit of the nation's war effort and suggested that a similar method was necessary to tackle the problems of peace. He said that it had been impossible to leave the management of the coal industry in private hands and that a Labour Government would be selective about nationalising various aspects of British industry.

Clem Attlee also took the opportunity in his first party political broadcast to emphasise the broad membership of the Labour Party and the need to tackle the post-war problems for the benefit of the nation and not for any sectional interest. He was thus able to enlist the support of all electors who wanted to see a national approach, and recognised the real public-spirited attitude towards post-war Britain. Whether this was a deliberate attempt on the part of Attlee is not certain but it bears out the results of a Gallup poll the previous November when the public were asked 'what form of Government would you like to see lead Britain in the period following the war'. The answer: 35 per cent wanted an all-party government; 26 per cent wanted a Labour Government and 12 per cent wanted a Tory Government.

But whilst Attlee and Churchill toured the country making dozens of speeches, no one could have predicted the behaviour of the maverick Harold Laski, who was then Chairman of the Labour Party and felt that he should play a major role in determining its issues and policies. Laski's first intervention arose just before the election when Churchill invited Attlee to be an observer at the Potsdam Conference in Germany where the war leaders thrashed out various issues emerging from the war. All the British leaders attending the conference flew back to London in separate planes. Laski's approach was to warn everyone that Attlee could not be party to any decision made at Potsdam – 'Labour should not accept responsibility for agreements which on the British side will have been conducted by Churchill,' he wrote in an article in the *Daily Herald*. Laski's intervention was not popular and clearly upset many Labour leaders. It is not often recalled that he actually wrote to Churchill suggesting there should be a continuation of the Coalition Government after the war under Churchill, something which the Labour Party Conference was clearly against. Fortunately for Labour, Laski's proposal was not acted upon.

But Churchill was able to use this episode to illustrate that Labour was controlled by a political caucus which had no relationship with an elected Parliament. This did not stop Laski from making speeches and always the adroit Lord Beaverbrook's reporters were not far away. In one speech made at Newark referred to by a Tory correspondent in the *Nottingham Guardian*, Laski was alleged to have argued that a Labour Government would use force to bring about a Socialist state and this was reproduced in the *Daily Express* and Beaverbrook's other newspaper, the *Evening Standard*. As in so many interesting election meetings, the facts were somewhat different since Laski was replying to a question about the French revolution and a speech on Revolution he had made in 1941. Laski sued the *Daily Express* and the *Nottingham Guardian* in a classic court case held before Lord Goddard, the Lord Chief Justice of England in 1946. He lost his case. Some argue that Harold Laski never really recovered from this defeat and that his enthusiasm for public political activity began to decline. He died in 1949.

All these goings–on provided the national press with an immense amount of interesting material, which inevitably distracted the electorate from the main issues of the campaign. Laski was portrayed as some kind of unelected political figure who carefully controlled the activities of Attlee and the other Labour leaders. Nothing could be further from the truth but it did provide the opportunity for the press to describe the Parliamentary Labour Party as being controlled by outside influences such as the trade union movement and the National Executive Committee. At one point Churchill suggested the return of a Labour Government would mean that state secrets would have to be passed to the National Executive Committee.

These issues resulted in an exchange of correspondence between Attlee and Churchill when Attlee was able to explain the role of the Labour Party Conference and the National Executive Committee in relation to a Labour Government. Nevertheless the subject was picked up by Tory candidates all over the country and used to attack the Labour Party rather than debate issues facing the nation. Harold Macmillan, who was defending his seat in Stockton, voiced the view of many Tory candidates when he asked, 'Who is this Gauleiter Laski to tell British statesmen what they are to do?' Harold Laski continued to make speeches during the election and afterwards, and his position as Chairman of the Labour Party always gave the impression that he was speaking with the authority of a Labour Government. Attlee decided he would have to reprimand Laski and wrote to him after the election stating, 'Foreign affairs are in the capable hands of Ernest Bevin. His task is quite sufficiently difficult without the embarrassment of irresponsible statements of the kind which you are making . . . a period of silence on your part would be welcome.'

Laski and Churchill had a curious relationship. Laski described Churchill as a 'gallant and romantic relic of eighteenth century imperialism'. And yet in 1944 Laski proposed 'that a fund should be raised in token of the nation's gratitude to the Prime Minister'. Churchill declined and in his reply wrote, 'If however when I am dead people think of commemorating my services, I should like to think that a park was made for the children of Londoners on the south bank of the Thames where they suffered so grimly from the Hun.' This idea has never been pursued.

Throughout the election, both on the public platform and in correspondence to Attlee, Churchill continued to hammer away at the relationship of the Parliamentary Labour Party and other constituent parts of the wider Labour movement. His essential theme was that Labour Ministers would not be free to act in the public interest but would first have to seek approval for their actions from the Labour Party National Executive Committee.

Attlee's reply emphasised that 'neither by decision of the annual party conference nor by any provision in the party constitution is the Parliamentary Labour Party answerable to or under the direction of the National Executive Committee. There are consultations between them, but never has the National Executive Committee given instruction to the Parliamentary Labour Party.' With a particular reference to Harold Laski, Attlee said, 'The Chairman has not the power to give me instructions nor do his remarks to a press correspondent constitute the official authoritative and reiterated instructions of the Executive Committee of the Labour Party.'

Although the Laski interventions provided material for all the newspapers, it is doubtful whether they had any real effect on the outcome of the election. Nevertheless, Beaverbrook was in his element and one critic suggested that there may even have been a streak of anti-Semitism in the way Laski's activities were portrayed. This was illustrated by a sarcastic remark of the Tory peer, Lord Croft, who referred to him as 'that fine old English Labour man'. But Laski was a strong opponent of Attlee and was keen to see him removed from office. This opposition continued right up until Attlee was invited by King George to form a government. Laski, as Chairman of the Labour Party, argued that after the General Election all Labour Members of Parliament should assemble and elect a leader who would then go forward to receive the King's commission to form a government. He wrote to Attlee along these lines.

This was a narrow interpretation of the Labour Party constitution, though it was used many years later when, following an election for the Greater London Council, the leader of the Labour group, Andrew Mackintosh, was deposed on the following day and the new group met and elected Ken Livingstone as its leader.

In his reply to Laski, Attlee was his usual man of few words: 'Thank you, the contents have been noted.' And with that he got on with the job of leading the Labour Party.

Attlee conducted an exhausting campaign, speaking at up to eight meetings a day, largely in the Midlands, Lancashire, Yorkshire and the eastern counties. He was driven around by his wife in a small Standard car, in contrast to Churchill's entourage in a fleet of vehicles operating from his private train parked at a nearby station. Whilst in London, Churchill used Claridge's Hotel as his campaign headquarters.

When Attlee arrived in Birmingham he was told by Jim Cattermole, the Labour Party city organiser, that he had been allocated one hour to speak to the electors of Birmingham. Attlee replied, 'Any good politician needs only twenty minutes to get his case across' and spoke for twenty minutes before moving on to another town.

Churchill made an extensive whistle-stop tour of the country with large-scale meetings during the evening at a theatre, stadium or arena. His journey commenced on 25 June, visiting the Midlands, Lancashire, Yorkshire and Scotland. He covered, in four days, 1,000 miles making 40 speeches. Wherever he went the crowds turned out in their thousands in an almost idolatrous way. It must not be forgotten that he had been a household name throughout the war. He endeared himself to the public by his regular broadcasts and there was a genuine interest in seeing the man. Churchill was a master orator. He knew how to move a crowd but it did not follow that everyone listening to his pearls of wisdom agreed with him or would vote for his party. Naturally, he indicated his role in winning the war and in his last political broadcast stressed that 'a vote for his political opponents was a vote for his dismissal from power'. The simple point he was making was to frighten the electors about his concept of the threat of Socialism.

Rereading some of Churchill's speeches during the election one comes to the conclusion that he was sorry the Coalition Government had collapsed and his real hope was that some kind of Coalition Government with himself at the helm would exist after the war. He was moved and touched by the enormous crowds that came to see him and his speeches were coloured with sentimental references to the kindness he had received. He mentioned the children 'who in vast numbers with bright eyes and vigorous voices assembled by the roadside' or the 'magnificent part our women had played in this total war'. He concluded his final broadcast with a traditional flourish:

I have an invincible confidence in the genius of Britain. I believe in the instinctive wisdom of our well-tried democracy. I am sure they will speak now in ringing tones and that their decision will vindicate the hopes of our friends in every land and will enable us to march in the vanguard of the United Nations in majestic enjoyment of our fame and power.

Churchill was not a born orator. He learned and practised his skills until he was perfect by standing in front of a mirror. He overcame his natural lisp to make a dramatic presentation worthy of a Shakespearean actor. His speeches sounded good and they raised morale at a time when the nation's spirits were very low, and it was this same technique that he used in his nationwide campaign as the Prime Minister seeking re-election. His speeches and delivery had a ready response compared with a pedestrian performance from an unskilled orator. But other features became transparent during the campaign.

Clem Attlee, Ernest Bevin and Herbert Morrison came across as people who had made a major contribution towards winning the war. They were good administrators, they understood the problems facing the nation and their solutions appealed to their listeners. The arguments the Labour Party deployed were in retrospect quite simple. As a nation we had combined to face the challenge of Hitler and by determination, common sense and utilising the country's resources we had won the war. Labour argued that these same skills and abilities should now be directed at winning the peace, where the problems were no less great but of a different kind. By the judicious use of controls, argued the Labour Party, the national benefit was put before the claims of individuals. With the nation facing dire shortages in food, housing, natural resources and almost every commodity, the Labour Party said there should be fair shares for all. This appears to have found a ready response from the electorate.

Churchill's essential theme was to urge the electors to return a National Government with a good majority and though he never explicitly mentioned a new Coalition Government it was clearly his desire. It is doubtful whether the Labour Party would have agreed to join such an arrangement in peacetime since the wartime Coalition Government was largely held together by the support of Labour's national leaders without the wholehearted support of backbenchers and local constituency parties.

It must, however, be said in Churchill's favour that he had some sympathy for the underdog, though the miners in Tonypandy in 1910 may have held different views when he authorised the Army to become involved in an industrial dispute. Churchill accepted the Beveridge plan for social security and an elementary amount of the Welfare State proposals but that was the limit of his thoughts. The less the state undertook the better he liked it. He thought that state control was the beginning of totalitarianism – it would destroy the British character. But his beliefs were out of touch with the general public, who wanted a more radical approach to life.

Churchill returned to the theme of a Coalition Government in his final party political broadcast. He said, 'Under the ordinary workings of the British constitution the Coalition Government which had rescued our nation from ruin and carried it to victory . . . should have presented itself to the nation as a united body and asked for a renewal of their confidence. Although this would have been the true interest and the wish of the nation, it was brushed aside by the overwhelming strong opinion of the Socialist Party.'

Emmanuel Shinwell, the Labour candidate at Seaham and a colourful and outspoken Labour critic of Churchill, said, 'The Labour Party will decline Churchill's offer to be associated with the Tory Party after the election. We are not going to walk into a conservative parlour in order to make a tasty dish for the Tory Party. We are going to win the General Election ourselves.' As regards Shinwell himself, he was returned at Seaham in Durham with the second-largest majority of any Labour candidate: 32,257.

Whilst Churchill made his oratorical flourishes, the real issues of the election were being debated at a local level. Barbara Castle recalls speaking at an eve-of-poll meeting in her Blackburn constituency when 3,000 people occupied every seat in the St George's Hall.

There was an unbelievable buoyancy in the atmosphere, as though people who had had all the textile depression years, the men and women who had suffered in the forces and the women who had been working double shifts, making munitions and the rest of it, suddenly thought, 'my heavens, we can win the peace for people like us.' That faith carried one along through all one's physical fatigue and I have never experienced before or since anything like the atmosphere of that meeting.

169

Although miles apart both in physical and political terms, a similar effect was experienced by Roy Jenkins, who was the unsuccessful Labour candidate in Birmingham Solihull. He recalled that his was an active campaign.

> We had long light evenings, but it was a campaign mostly of very well-attended meetings. Typical meetings would be in the main hall of the school, therefore there would be seats for about a hundred and fifty to two hundred people and normally there would be another hundred people standing around the edges. I hardly recollect a single badly attended meeting. Occasionally after a meeting, we'd go out and have a thing outside a pub and people would gather round. I remember seas of faces looking up in the twilight, a mixture of exhaustion, hope, some kind of doubt. A sea of tired faces looking up in hope, that's the best phrase I can make of it.

Throughout the campaign, Tory candidates were arguing for the end of wartime controls and this issue epitomised the difference between the two major parties. The Tories wanted a return to complete freedom and to allow private enterprise to decide the market. The Labour Party, on the other hand, saw that by the judicious use of controls the national benefit was put before the claims of individuals. With the nation facing dire shortages in food, housing, natural resources and almost every commodity, the Labour Party argued there should be fair shares for all.

An indication of the mind of the electorate on a public enterprise issue was explained in a Gallup Poll on state ownership of railways published in the *News Chronicle*. In response to a question as to whether the state should own and control Britain's railways, 54 per cent were in favour, 28 per cent were against and 28 per cent had not made up their minds. Yet the implications of this survey were never really understood by political analysts, politicians and the press. The swing to Labour was clearly demonstrated but not accepted.

In Clem Attlee, despite his diffidence and shyness, there was a determination to achieve and his general theme was 'to win the peace as we won the war'. If elections are won on personality grounds then Churchill would have been an outright winner but the message hammered home by Attlee and the hundreds of Labour candidates about using the nation's resources for the benefit of the nation clearly had a greater effect on the electorate than issues of personality. Ernest Bevin in one of his speeches said, 'This is a people's war and it must lead to a people's peace.' Alan Bullock in his biography of Bevin said he was not devoted to any political theory or any economic system – he just wanted to do what was right for the ordinary men and women of Britain.

Morgan Phillips, the General Secretary of the Labour Party who played a key role in determining Labour's strategy for the General Election, visited Southampton and made a speech crystallising Labour's overall approach. He said

> that men and women were turning their minds more and more to the problems of what kind of world was to follow the end of hostilities. We must convert their fear into something constructive in which people would all act as a team seeking to serve the wider public interest and to secure a fair deal for all.

Halfway through the election campaign the demobilisation scheme by which servicemen and women were released commenced and by the end of June 1945, 44,500 people who had served in the forces were back in 'civvy street'.

Throughout the campaign local candidates put their own gloss on specific issues. Mr Noel-Baker, the Labour candidate at Derby who at one time worked for the League of Nations, naturally discussed foreign affairs in many of his speeches. His constant theme was:

> The Tories pledged themselves to the League of Nations in election times but in practice helped the Japanese over Manchuria. They made the Hoare-Laval agreement within a month of being elected and allowed Hitler to re-arm without a protest. I see no sign that the majority of the Tory Party had abandoned these doctrines or beliefs.

The theme of returning Churchill the war leader as Churchill the peace leader was taken up by most Tory candidates. Lord Woolton declared in Diss, Norfolk that Churchill 'is the greatest leader and patriot this country has ever had'. Henry Willink, the Tory Minister of Health, echoed this thought when speaking in North Cornwall. He said, 'Mr Churchill's dynamic leadership and Mr Eden's experience and idealism are assets which the country would be mad to throw away.'

Major Quintin Hogg echoed this view when he stated, 'Are we to be represented in the councils of the world by the two greatest statesmen of international repute, Churchill and Eden, or by two other men, the names of whom we do not even know?'

The role of the service vote appeared to be a problem for Churchill. In his final broadcast he had a special message for people in the forces. He said, 'Beware that you are not deceived about the workings of our political system at this election. There is no truth in the stories now being put about that you can vote for my political opponents without at the same time voting for my dismissal from power.' There was a somewhat naïve belief among Churchill's advisers that electors did not know what they were doing when they put an 'X' on a ballot paper. They were under the impression that many people thought they could have Churchill returned as Prime Minister at the head of a Labour Government.

The role of the Liberal Party in the election was somewhat confused with the role of the National Liberals. The National Liberals were supporters of Churchill and some held office in his administration. The Liberal Party were sometimes described as 'Sinclair' Liberals after their leader and they argued for traditional Liberal policies, which were echoed in post-war years by Joe Grimond, David Steel and Paddy Ashdown. Sir Archibald Sinclair held office as Secretary of State for Air in the Coalition Government under Churchill but the Liberal Party would not take any seat in a Chamberlain administration. When the Coalition Government broke up in 1945, the Liberal Party were prepared to continue with Churchill but came out when Labour declared its hand.

The National Liberals were in effect a breakaway party from the traditional Liberal Party. When they stood as General Election candidates they were usually not opposed by a Tory candidate so they had the field to themselves against Labour and Liberal candidates. National Liberal members were part of the Caretaker Government which Churchill formed after the Coalition Government collapsed. There were accusations of a pact between the Liberal and Labour Parties but there is no evidence to prove this allegation. Nevertheless, Lord Roseberry in a speech at Wrexham during the election suggested, 'The Sinclair Liberals had a pact with the Labour Party. They were opposing ten of the principal members of Mr Churchill's present Government although not Mr Churchill himself because they tried in some slimy way to make people think they were on his side. On the other hand no fewer than 26 of the principal Socialist ex-Ministers were not being opposed by Sinclair Liberals.' If that was not a pact he did not know what was, he declared. The Liberal Party fielded 306 candidates whereas the National Liberals only contested 49 constituencies.

In reality the Liberal Party fought the election under immense difficulties. Their organisation was in complete tatters as a result of the war and was the minority political party in most parts of the country. In many constituencies they never had a semblance of an organisation, which meant they were unable to find a candidate, let alone conduct a campaign. This was one of the primary reasons why the Liberal Party would have preferred an autumn election so that they could have had more time in which to organise themselves. They did, however, have an articulate women's membership who among other policies called for new sweeping powers on housing.

The National Liberals were treated by the electorate as Tories and they received a similar fate. Their candidates were defeated all over the country and shortly after the war the remnants met and decided to wind up the Party, and members went their own political way.

Although the Labour Party had an ambitious and radical programme of public ownership, the creation of the Welfare State and council housing, these issues never became headline news with violent attacks by their opponents. Of course, they were debated and mentioned by speakers but it would appear the public had made up their minds and those who intended to vote Labour were not going to be influenced by any newspaper story or speech by a visiting politician. They would listen politely because for many it was their first experience of attending a political meeting. Of the electorate, 21 per cent were voting for the first time and an analysis after the election showed that 61 per cent of new voters supported the Labour Party.

In the absence of party political broadcasts on television, the general public attended political meetings in large numbers. The *Acton Gazette*, circulating in West London, said 'that more than 1,000 people attended a Labour election rally. They came to enjoy themselves, to laugh, cheer and clap. Every reference to working–class unity was warmly applauded.' In another report they claimed, 'The Tory candidate was listened to in complete silence.'

The Churchill meetings reflected more the traditional type of open-air political jamboree when hecklers came into their own. This was particularly noticeable in London, where cockneys demonstrated their extensive knowledge of the English language. When Churchill visited Walthamstow in north-east London he faced an audience of 20,000 and though he had a large number of supporters present who gave vent to their feelings, there was a big hostile audience. But Churchill was adept at dealing with hecklers. It gave colour to the meetings and often he was able to turn the heckle round and make a serious political point. At some meetings the opposition consisted of merely booing the speaker. The *Times* correspondent described the scene at Walthamstow when Churchill was clearly playing with his audience:

> When more booing started Mr Churchill said, 'I am sorry that one hurts. I cannot help it. I did not mean it to hurt but I repeat – improvement of human hearts and human heads before we can achieve the glorious Utopia that the Socialist woolgatherers place before us. Now where is the boo Party? I shall call them henceforward in my speech the booing Party [boos].
>
> Mr Churchill: 'Everyone have a good boo.' He turned from the hostile side of the stadium whilst looking at the other side and said, 'Any help from this side?' and cheering broke out. 'Where I think the booing Party are making such a mistake is dragging all this stuff across the practical tasks we have to fulfil. They are spoiling the tasks that have to be done in order to carry out their nightmares. They have no chance of carrying them out. They are going to be defeated at this election in a most decisive manner [Cheers]. Their exhibition here shows very clearly the sort of ideas they have of free speech'. [Cheers]

Churchill very much enjoyed the rough and tumble of election meetings but compared with today's television audience he only reached a fraction of the nation in his triumphant tours. The campaign was left very much for local candidates to pursue their own individual efforts since in the final result electors vote for local candidates and not national leaders. But it was the enthusiasm of Labour candidates for a new beginning, for the creation of a new society and a determination to tackle the immense problems that faced the nation, that came across to an electorate ready for change.

However, although there was a giddy enthusiasm that carried candidates forward, some of their ideas had not been thought through. Denis Healey, who was unsuccessful as the Labour candidate at Pudsey and Otley, freely confesses,

> I was incredibly ignorant. I remember during the campaign itself I was asked a question about exports and I said I thought it was criminal to be exporting shoes to people in Australia when there were kids in Barnsley who had no shoes at all.
>
> The extraordinary thing in a way is that for the wartime generation economics scarcely existed. It was all about ideals and building a better world.

Some candidates, whilst giving support to their party, developed their own individual approach. The maverick but effective Tory politician Bob Boothby was a typical example. Boothby was seeking re-election at his East Aberdeen seat which, being a fishing constituency, was fraught with problems. He was also a member of the Tory Reform Group and tended to take a more progressive attitude to political and economic issues than his more staid fellow candidates. In a letter to Beaverbrook he said that in his election campaign he was 'standing uncompromisingly on my own policy – economic expansion, full employment, high wages, control of food imports, no deflation and no gold standard'. Boothby supported the Beveridge plan for social security '100 per cent'. He won the election, though he found 'a political hostility in his audiences that he had not experienced since 1929'. Commenting on his election success, he said it was due 'to the personal goodwill of the people of East Aberdeenshire and nothing to do with the Conservative Party policy'. Boothby's independent approach to politics was further demonstrated after the election, when he voted for public ownership of the Bank of England.

Two leading politicians fought the election from their bedside. Hugh Gaitskell, who was contesting Leeds South, became ill in March 1945 with severe chest pains. After visiting a heart specialist it was agreed he was suffering from a minor coronary thrombosis. Although only 38 years of age he was ordered to have a complete rest and only visited the constituency in the last few days of the election. It does not appear to have had any effect since he was elected with a majority of 10,402. Active members of the Leeds South Labour Party were aware of the position but whether the electors realised they were voting for a sick man is not known.

Anthony Eden, who had played a key role in the Churchill Coalition Government, was seeking re-election at Warwick and Leamington, and spent most of the election in bed suffering from a duodenal ulcer. All his life he had been stricken with one ailment after another and it was ill health that ended his political career. He left the election campaigning to his wife. As a leading member of the Tory Party he was expected to make one of the radio political broadcasts and this he did by making a recording from his country retreat. From all accounts it was the best broadcast he had ever made and one report said it was done 'with a sincerity and sensitivity that, far more than the content, made a deep impression'.

By some strange collusion between the Parties it was agreed that in their campaigns no one would use films or use newsreels for party purposes, or projectors or mobile viewing vans. During the war the Ministry of Information conveyed the war message (propaganda) to towns and factories by successfully using sound films. In some cases they set up their projectors in village halls and schools, and introduced into market squares and other open spaces large removal vans with a built in screen at the back, round which the public stood and viewed. The decision not to use film was no doubt put down to cost but others may have thought it was alien to political campaigning.

Until the advent of television, public meetings and doorstep canvassing were the main areas of activity for parliamentary candidates. Many of these meetings were held in the open air, partly because it was the height of the summer, they were free to organise and a good crowd could often be assembled. Today all candidates are entitled to use any school building for election meetings but in 1945 they had to be paid for and in some cases access was denied to Labour candidates if the school governors decided they would not allow their premises to be used for election purposes.

But public meetings call for a special technique. Great orators like Lloyd-George or Aneurin Bevan could move a crowd almost to tears with their dramatic oratory. In 1945 there were so many new and untried candidates that many of them had to learn their public speaking skills as the campaign went along. Some were adept and learnt quickly but others created amusement as the humorous heckler intervened.

For much of the time, voters depended on national newspapers for their diet of election news. Because of severe shortages of newsprint, the size of newspapers was seriously curtailed and the novelty of tabloid size was restricted to a few of the popular papers. For example, the *Daily Mail*, which had a sale of 1,500,000 a day, was broadsheet in size consisting of four and six pages. Likewise the *Daily Herald*, which sold more than 2 million copies a day, was a broadsheet and carried the same number of pages. With severe shortages in most commodities display advertising was limited too. The age of full-page spreads had not arrived. Nevertheless, the amount of editorial material carried in such few pages was surprising, ranging from the runners and riders at race meetings to extensive coverage of the election and international news.

Where the main newspapers pledged their loyalty was predictable. The *Daily Herald* and the *Mirror* were clear supporters of the Labour Party though the *Mirror* never precisely told its readers to 'vote Labour'. The *Telegraph*, which had a circulation of 648,317 copies a day, plus the *Mail*, the *Sketch* and the *Express*, were four-square behind Churchill and the Tories. *The Times* (165,000) seemed to sit on the fence but was at heart a Tory supporter, whilst the *Manchester Guardian* (now the *Guardian*) and the *News Chronicle* supported the Liberals and were anti-Tory, which in some small way was of benefit to the Labour Party.

Despite paper shortages, the *Daily Express* sold more than 2,700,000 copies a day. In its own unique way it campaigned vigorously for the Tories right up until the ballot boxes closed and argued strongly that Labour had lost the election. It even came out with a headline which suggested – 'Socialists decided they have lost', though how it reached this conclusion was never clearly explained. The Sunday newspapers reflected similar tribal support, though their diet of scandals and depravity was not in any way compromised. The *Daily Mirror* (almost 2 million copies a day) claimed the four most important issues at the election were: housing, full employment, social security and international cooperation. This tabloid newspaper, which had a flair for colourful journalism and vigorous campaigning, clearly was in touch with public opinion. At its height in post-war days the *Mirror* could claim a circulation of 5 million copies a day.

The international press who had correspondents in London were all convinced that Churchill would be re-elected – the *New York Times* suggested that he would have a 100 majority. Reuters, the worldwide news agency, was perhaps more cautious when, as polling day came to an end, it stated that possibly it would be a close race.

Local newspapers also played a useful role, though in some areas the election was considered an unnecessary interruption to their rounds of flower shows and funerals. Like other industries, key members of the editorial team were in the services and the weekly papers were produced with a minimum of staff. The *Mid-Devon Advertiser*, which circulated in the Totnes constituency, managed to get through the election without reporting in any detail what it was about and the issues confronting their readers.

In one aspect of the campaign all parties and candidates spoke with one voice: foreign affairs. They were united in their desire to see the war against Japan brought to a successful conclusion and to witness the creation of the United Nations organisation. The role of the Commonwealth was recognised and the maintenance of good relations with Russia and the United States of America was deemed essential. International economic and political affairs did not play a significant part in the campaign.

The real differences emerged on home policies, with Labour advocating public ownership of key industries, reform of social security, the introduction of a national health service, full employment for returning servicemen and women and a drive to produce homes 'fit for heroes'.

Churchill and the Tories argued for free enterprise as opposed to state control, an examination of industries on their merits, protection of purchasing power, an extension of social security, development of overseas trade and removal of all controls as soon as possible.

The Liberal Party in a 20-point manifesto argued for public ownership of the railways, coal mining and electric power generation, plus the acquisition of land development rights outside built-up areas and a periodic levy on all increases in site values, and total reform of the voting system.

The task of getting the message and the arguments across to the electorate was left primarily to the party political broadcasts and to the individual candidates at the grass roots. But even the most energetic of candidates could only reach a small percentage of their potential electors.

Radio listeners had a choice of two BBC programmes: Forces and Home Service. For Saturday, 21 April 1945, the nearest the Forces listener had to a documentary programme was a 15-minute item, *As the Commentator Saw It*, which went out at 8.15 p.m., and the fact that it was followed by the football results indicates it had more to do with sport than current affairs. Home Service listeners had a choice of a 25-minute programme called *The World Goes By* and a 15-minute programme, *The Week in Westminster*, which would have been a kind of radio Hansard. So for political thought the listener had to be content with party political broadcasts, which went out after the 9 p.m. news. Unlike today's programmes, these were not slick productions with music and dramatic presentation but merely a voice reading a script straight to the microphone.

With only the BBC to cover the nation, each Party was allocated a series of broadcasts which lasted 20 minutes and all the national leaders were fielded by the different Parties. Labour and Tories were allocated ten broadcasts each, the Liberals had four and the Communist Party and the Common Wealth Party had one broadcast each.

Clearly, the broadcasts had a major impact on the election and the BBC claimed that on average 44.9 per cent of the adult population were listening to them. When Churchill spoke the audience rating went up to 49 per cent. He spoke four times whereas in the Labour broadcasts they had ten speakers who all spoke once. In 1945, although electricity was fairly widespread, there were large parts of the country, particularly rural areas, that had to rely on battery radios so although almost half the population listened to Churchill there must have been sizeable sections of the nation that did not listen to him because they did not have the facilities. What was said on radio was often picked up by the national press so that statements over the air were debated in the columns and arguments taken a stage further.

Clem Attlee suggested, 'The influence of radio has operated to make election audiences more thoughtful and more desirous of listening to solid reasoning than in the old days.' There were, of course, no hecklers or even radio presenters to cross-examine the politicians. Neither were there facilities

179

for the public to 'phone in' and make their points. In effect, the politicians had a free time to develop their party points and philosophies.

In Churchill's four broadcasts he adopted a strong attack on the Labour Party about their Socialist beliefs, which he saw as alien to the British way of life. Attlee used a more friendly approach and reminded his listeners that two nations that had made a considerable contribution to winning the war – Australia and New Zealand – both had Labour Governments.

The fundamental differences that separated the two main parties in their broadcasts was Labour's passionate belief in the nation coming together to work for the benefit of the nation and its people, and the Tory belief that the return of a Labour Government would lead to a loss of freedom and a period of discord and party strife 'such as had never been seen in our history'.

In the absence of large-scale opinion polls, it is difficult to measure the effect these broadcasts had on the mood and minds of the electorate. Some people argue that political broadcasts have very little effect in winning support for a party but merely reinforce the prejudices and opinions held by the public. There is, however, now clear evidence that the electorate had made up their minds before the election had commenced and the activities of candidates were almost an entertaining ritual. There was also some evidence that the majority of women supported the Tory Party.

Compared with post-war elections, the 1945 General Election was on the quiet side. Michael Foot described it as a 'mild and good-humoured election'. For most of the electorate, voting was a new procedure, almost a citizen's duty, and for a large proportion of candidates of all political persuasions electioneering was something new too. Today, opposition parties have a vast array of 'shadow' Ministers covering every conceivable subject and present themselves as an alternative team in the hope that the public will support them rather than the existing set of Ministers. Because the Coalition Government was somewhat unique and the opposition (for patriotic reasons) was inevitably muted, in 1945 there were only the big guns: national leaders versus national leaders.

In today's multimillion-pound election campaigns, with glossy TV productions, national poster campaigns and expensive constituency tours for the inevitable photo opportunity, it is difficult to comprehend the kind of monies that were spent and available in the 1945 election. The Labour Party estimate amounted to just under £100,000 and this covered printing costs for leaflets and posters plus making grants to marginal constituencies and to local parties who were short of cash. Inevitably, the estimates had to be revised as the election campaign developed. In the original plan it was deemed that only 50,000 copies of the m anifesto would be printed at a cost of £600 but as the campaign got under way the public wanted to know what Labour intended to do if they were elected. As a result of this demand more than 1,300,000 copies of the manifesto were printed and distributed. As for leaflets, the Labour Party produced more than 12 million on a range of subjects and issues.

Among literature produced was the *Speaker's Handbook*, written by Michael Young. This book was of immense help to new and struggling candidates since it provided all the information and arguments on the main political issues to deploy at public meetings. Another item of printed material was the 'Speaker's Cards', which were a source of valuable information when making a speech. Most candidates had several meetings each evening in various parts of the constituency so there was a need for a large number of supporting speakers to help keep the show going until the candidate arrived. One of the new features of the election was the introduction of a sixteen-page pictorial magazine – looking something like a woman's magazine – but it only had a limited circulation partly due to cost and partly to the shortage of paper.

Such was the enthusiasm for the Labour Party by the professionals that the artwork for posters was freely donated by the designer John Armstrong, who was also responsible for the cover of the manifesto. The *Daily Mirror* cartoonist, Zec, worked day and night to make eight designs for posters, which were used by constituency candidates throughout the country. His most famous drawing, depicting a wounded soldier amid the bomb and battle ruins holding a wreath marked 'Victory and Peace in Europe' with the caption, 'Here you are! Don't lose it again!', was used originally on the front page of the *Daily Mirror* on VE-Day and the *Mirror* with great panache used it again on polling day to great effect. Meanwhile the *Daily Express* was still telling its readers that the 'Tories have won', which was as far from the truth as you could possibly get.

In the West London constituency of Acton, where Joe Sparks was the Labour candidate his campaign costs amounted to £950. Sparks was a local councillor and was nominated by the National Union of Railwaymen who contributed £530 towards his expenses. The remainder of the money came from collections at public meetings, which raised £301. Collecting sheets were passed round factory workshops and door-to-door donations raised £161. Local trade union branches also raised £184.

The successful Labour Party Election Agent in Acton, Don Barwick, claimed that he had so many helpers 'we were dizzy with success'. He also claimed that more than 200 helpers came from the local Communist Party who had withdrawn their own candidate. This was not typical of the national scene because most candidates were not sponsored and had to rely entirely on local resources, but the enthusiasm for the Labour Party was such that in some cases the local parties made a 'profit' out of the election. In only one case did a Labour candidate lose his election deposit and the Deposit Insurance Fund, which the Labour Party operated, completed the election with £5,800 left in the coffers. In Aldershot the Tory candidate, Oliver Lyttelton, who won the seat, spent £787 whereas his Common Wealth Party opponent, Tom Wintringham, spent £647.

The Labour Party at national level had enough money to cover the expense of the General Election since they had been able to build up their resources without any real drain on the election fund since 1935. From time to time they recorded in their balance sheet the generosity of individuals, including 125 shares in the Buenos Airies Town and Docks Tramways Ltd, worth about £25 and 55,000 shares in Victoria House Printing Company, worth every bit of £2,750. For most of the time the Labour Party depended on the affiliation fees of trade unions and Socialist organisations, together with the membership subscriptions of individual members. Several wealthy supporters made large donations to party funds.

When the electors had completed their duty, the ballot boxes were sealed up and locked away for the next three weeks awaiting the arrival of the service postal vote from overseas. In some constituencies they were kept safe in police station cells and in others a permanent guard was mounted on a locked room at the town hall. The total register amounted to 32,240,391 electors, which compared with the 1935 General Election when 29,400,476 could vote. The total number of people voting in 1945 was 25,085,978 and the national turnout was 72.7 per cent. Labour achieved 47.8 per cent of the vote and the Tories 39.8 per cent. The Liberal Party scored 9 per cent.

Those closely involved in the election at a local level were dispatched to some kind of limbo land. They could relax, awaiting the verdict of the nation, whilst much of the country including its leaders got on with the war in Japan, tackling the immense problems of a defeated Germany and coming to terms with a new semi-peace situation. The result of Britain's first post-war election would amaze the candidates, the press, the nation and indeed international public opinion. It was the last General Election when the electors could freely make an individual choice and judgement unencumbered by all the manifestations of modern publicity campaigns that were about to descend and dominate post-war elections. For candidates there was no election 'battle bus' on nationwide tours, no spin doctors, no party political broadcasts on television, no photo opportunities, no lavish advertising, no daily press conferences, no glossy pamphlets – simply, this is what I believe in and this is what I want to do for our country, please give me your vote.

CHAPTER EIGHT

The Result

The first indication of the likely result of the 1945 General Election came from the votes of servicemen and women flown in from all theatres of war and counted in most parts of the country on Wednesday, 25 July – the day before the official count. The ballot papers arrived back in Britain, were sorted into constituencies and dispatched to constituency returning officers. Because service personnel were given a choice of either voting by post or appointing a proxy it was necessary for the returning officer to extract from the ballot boxes all the proxy votes which were printed on coloured paper so as to ensure the service voter had not voted twice.

Nearly 3 million service personnel were eligible to vote and the final number of those voting by proxy was 986,784 and 1,032,688 voted by post. The view has been expressed by several commentators that it was the service vote which decided whether there would be a Labour Government. Whilst there is evidence that many in the services did support Labour with their vote, the actual number of service personnel voting was just over 50 per cent and that figure included votes for all parties. The comparable figure among ordinary electors was 72 per cent. Nevertheless there is anecdotal evidence that a majority of servicemen and women voted Labour, but since this would have been spread over 640 constituencies it does somewhat take the gloss off the argument that were it not for those in the services, the nation would not have returned a Labour Government.

Sergeant George Wallace, the successful Labour candidate at Chislehurst commented, 'I should say about 90 per cent of the forces vote was for me.' At his count when they were dealing with the service vote, they found a rifle bullet wrapped up in a ballot paper. The returning officer awarded him the vote but not bullet! Roy Jenkins, who failed to win Solihull for Labour, stated, 'The forces vote was very strong. That's attributed to a great deal of educational work during the war, but educational work can't do all that much unless a mood is running in a certain direction.'

A former gunner in the Royal Artillery, Jack Goldberg, recalled the position in his regiment which was serving in northern Italy. 'The troops were puzzled by the system of voting which was not clear to the ordinary soldiers. Many men appointed their wives as proxies, but the wives never exercised their votes. In my own regiment the number who voted was almost certainly under a third.'

Under the provisions of the voting system that existed in 1945, only those people who were 21 years of age could vote. The call-up age for the services reached 18 so all people in the services between the ages of 18 and 21 did not have a vote; this would have represented a large number and is a further argument against the theory that a Labour Government was elected merely because of the service vote. In fact, the 1945 service vote was only 7 per cent of the total votes cast.

Because of the technicalities of the election, servicemen abroad were at a disadvantage. Most did not have access to BBC radio nor were national newspapers widely circulated. Some army newspapers emerged, which tried to keep their readers informed, but most troops were isolated from the election campaign. There is some evidence that many in service uniform who were based in the UK worked and assisted local Labour candidates when they were off duty although their vote would have been in another constituency. One newspaper report stated the British troops in Berlin were heard to be chanting 'Attlee . . . Attlee'. The service vote was therefore important to the Labour Party but it was not crucial. It formed part of the general swing towards the Party that existed in all sections of society.

One of the contributory factors in determining the way in which service people voted was the existence of educational schemes introduced to some extent to overcome the boredom of military life. Debates on major post-war policies took place in 'mock parliaments' and educational circles when those in the services began to understand for the first time the economic and social background to important strands of everyday life. The dividing line between education about current affairs and active political campaigning became difficult to measure when Leo Abse, who was later a Labour MP, was arrested in the Middle East for political activities whilst serving in the RAF in 1944. This precipitated a debate in Parliament.

Although there was a strong full-time regular element in the services, the vast majority of servicemen and women were conscripts and they came from all walks of life including people who were natural lecturers and teachers. In the Army there was the Army Bureau of Current Affairs staffed in many cases by people from the Workers Educational Association and similar adult education services who issued pamphlets and discussion documents on topical subjects every week. In addition to filling in the time between active service, these classes and pamphlets acted as morale boosters and informed service personnel what the war was about and how the peace could be won. These classes and seminars prompted service personnel to think for themselves. The political result of this activity is difficult to assess and some critics claim it was a breeding ground for left-wing thought and action. Clearly a well-informed fighting force was desirable in itself, but almost certainly it clarified in many people's minds the problems of the thirties and how Parliament had dealt with the issues. The next step from understanding the problem was to take some action and for most people the only step they could take was to use their vote.

Major Leonard Caplan, who was the Tory candidate in North Hammersmith, wrote,

> What was not readily appreciated until after the election was the effect many people believed the Army Bureau of Current Affairs had upon the soldiers vote because a large number of people who were manning ABCA, and who were responsible for the lectures on public affairs given to soldiers, were, in fact left wing.

Lieutenant Willie Hamilton, who fought West Fife for Labour, recalled his army days:

> I'd been attached to the Education Corps when the Beveridge Report came out. We talked about Beveridge and I think the Army vote went almost solidly in favour of the Labour Party because we advocated the implementation of

186

Beveridge so far as the health service, national insurance and the rest were concerned. The military vote was normally a patriotic vote but they'd had a basin full and they were determined we'd won the war and the only way to win the peace was to get a Labour Government.

The Liberal view was recalled by Lieutenant Basil Wigoder who fought the election at Bournemouth. He wrote,

> Part of my job was to be a lecturer in current affairs in the ABCA which involved trying to talk to the troops in as reasonably impartial way as any Liberal could, and one got a very strong feeling from them that they were pretty disillusioned with the Conservative Party as a whole and particularly with the days of appeasement and events before the war. The swing in that sense didn't surprise me but of course in my youthful naïveté I thought we might get it rather than the Labour Party.

Many in Whitehall and Parliament were fully aware of the influences of these service education schemes and Churchill at one point suggested they should be wound up and the Cabinet should have an official inquiry. But the very success of the schemes put them in a strong position to survive and though there was in 1943 an inquiry, Churchill took no further action on the subject.

The composition of the new Parliamentary Labour Party demonstrated that for the 1945 General Election the Labour Party was able to crash through the middle-class barrier both in the selection of candidates and in the votes they received from the public, though there is some evidence that women in general terms continued to vote for Tory candidates. During the war the Women's Voluntary Service recruited more than a million women into their ranks and most of these came from the upper and middle classes. Some social scientists have argued that as a result of bringing these ladies into contact with the harsher side of wartime life they were democratised, with the result that they drifted away from their normal and traditional conservative and class beliefs. But James Hinton in his book, *Women, Social Leadership and the Second World War*, argues the reverse. He believes that 'among women, the war reinforced not democracy, but the continuities of class'.

Since its creation, the Labour Party has always relied on its natural core vote – the working class – but as we move through the thirties and into the forties it was able to draw on a wider cross-section of society. In 1945 the range of Labour candidates was almost a complete reflection of the nation. Of course, the trade union movement was still in a strong position but in constituencies where there were no union-sponsored candidates, the local party seemed to opt for articulate middle-class candidates. They came from the professions, from the officer ranks of the services, from management and from academia. This general radical move was reflected in many areas when local committees threw off their inhibitions and selected a woman as their candidate. Attlee claimed, 'We are no longer a class party.' This was borne out by the election results when for the first time Labour was able to appeal to 'middle England' and to a certain extent has retained this ever since.

The average age of elected Labour MPs was 43 – the youngest majority party on record. It was a complete cross-section of society and included men and women from the armed services, factory workers, technicians, business executives, lawyers, journalists, architects, teachers and housewives. The group grossly under-represented in the new Parliament were women; nevertheless, Labour returned 21 women MPs compared with one each for the Tories and Liberals. The 1935–45 Parliament included fifteen women members.

The policies on which Labour contested the election were clearly far-reaching, particularly in the areas of public ownership and the creation of the Welfare State. These policies in any other part of the twentieth century would have incurred the wrath of Labour's opponents and the press. But 1945 was very different. Labour's policies were relevant and to many were a consolidation of all that had taken place during the war. To advocate public ownership of the railways, when during the war they were virtually publicly owned, was not a great step. To suggest having a national health service when those in the services had already experienced a national scheme did not stretch one's imagination or excite opposition.

The same could be said for other policies. If you accepted public ownership of transport then arguments for coal and steel did not seem too far away. Gwilym Lloyd-George (a Liberal), who was Minister of Fuel and Power in the Coalition Government, argued that to raise production in the pits the state must take over the ownership of the mines for the duration of the war. No action was taken on a report prepared by Sir John Anderson, which came to the same conclusion, since Churchill was opposed to nationalisation and because he did not want any controversial legislation to pass through Parliament that would take people's minds off the war.

But it was the mood of the nation that determined the result of the election. The role of the Tory Party before the war was still very clear and fresh for most electors. The Tories meant unemployment and war. They meant slums and deprivation, and a class structure in society. The war had somehow put all these issues into a new perspective and there was a great urge to change the way the nation was governed. It was quite simple. The nation had come together to win the war and by harnessing its resources could win the peace.

People were also able to make their own judgement about how they were going to cast their vote without the influence of the press. Paper shortages meant that all newspapers operated under severe restrictions, they were extremely small and to maintain their circulation they needed to cover the normal subjects in a very abbreviated form. With war reports dominating their front pages, editors were unable to build up a climate of opinion that was hostile to Labour since the period between the end of hostilities in Germany and polling day was too short. An interesting comparison about the role of the press can be made with the 1950 and 1951 General Elections. At these, the anti-Labour press was able to build up over several years a clearly hostile approach to the Labour Government, drawing on rationing, shortages of almost every kind plus a reorganised Tory Party, which had overcome its 1945 defeat. If the Labour Party had faced a similar hostile press at the 1945 General Election the result might have been somewhat different.

A further and important factor about the role of the press is that it failed or ignored to take account of the changes that were happening within society. Operating with limited staffs, the newspapers had to concentrate on printing the news with little time to analyse the changes that were taking place. Today many universities and think tanks have whole departments just looking at society and all the numerous changes that have an impact on the way we live, whether it is crime, transport or world affairs. In 1945 this existed only in a very limited way since academics were in the fighting forces operating 'Enigma' or intelligence services. In addition, newspaper editors in 1945, plus many leading politicians, failed to understand the political impact that was reflected in all the by-elections. The swing of the pendulum was under way.

Perhaps the most important reason for the failure of the press to recognise the political and social changes that were taking place was the role and status of Churchill. Here the Tories had the strongest possible candidate. He was invincible, unbeatable and the nation was merely going through the process before his return to Downing Street. To some he was above the normal party strife – he was a national leader who had won the war. Many in Fleet Street believed he was bound to win the election – how could anyone defeat such a successful Prime Minister, someone who had brought us safely through the perils of war and offered us the pearls of victory?

Churchill must have made a deep impression on the electorate too. For those without strong political opinions he must have had a ready appeal – a way of saying thank you for all his efforts on our behalf. He won the war, now let him win the peace. Many recalled his stirring wartime broadcasts, which had a profound effect on morale. If it had been a presidential election similar to those in the United States, Churchill would undoubtedly have been the winner, but in Britain we have parliamentary elections where the crucial vote is in the constituency.

If the Tories had not had Churchill as their candidate, the chances are they could have been routed and the Labour Party returned with an even larger majority. In pre-war days the Tory Party had little time for Churchill. He was a lone voice and in May 1940, when Chamberlain was toppled, it was by no means certain that Churchill would succeed since Lord Halifax was a very strong candidate and had considerable support in the upper reaches of the Party. It did not help that he was a member of the House of Lords and not the House of Commons. One report suggested that at the crucial moment when the Tories were deciding who should follow Chamberlain, Lord Halifax was at the dentist's having his teeth examined. So the Tories went into the 1945 General Election camouflaged by Churchill's achievements and hoping the nation's grateful thanks would be offered up in abundance.

One of the most important aspects of the 1945 General Election was the calibre of Labour leaders. Attlee, Bevin, Dalton, Cripps and Morrison were national figures. They were running great offices of state and were household names. As Deputy Prime Minister, Attlee was in effect running Parliament and responsible for most of the home policies, whilst Churchill concentrated on major international issues and the prosecution of the war with the Chiefs of Staff. Ernest Bevin played a major role in mobilising the nation into a fighting force, whether it was for the services, aircraft production or the manufacture of ammunition. He was responsible, too, for preparing the demobilisation scheme and a whole raft of progressive policies covering conditions at work, which were very much appreciated by trade unions and their members.

Bevin was immensely loyal to Churchill and this was reciprocated. Bevin came into the Coalition Government without any practical experience of Parliament or Whitehall. Having left school at the age of twelve he became an active trade unionist and his organising skills welded together a whole series of small trade unions into the mighty Transport and General Workers Union. He was known as the dockers' KC (King's Counsel) and was a great believer in joint consultation whereby everyone was invited to get round a table to sort out their problems. It was Ernest Bevin who led the public in a round of 'three cheers for Churchill' from the balcony of the Ministry of Health on VE-Day when the Cabinet paraded before the excited crowds celebrating the victorious end to the war in Europe. Earlier that day Bevin performed a more mundane role when he addressed the Institute of Wallpaper Manufacturers in London's Guildhall and spoke about the problems of peace facing the nation.

When he took over the Ministry of Labour in 1940, his first task was to mobilise the nation's manpower resources. He asked Sir William Beveridge to create a Manpower Requirements Committee to find out precisely how many people the armed services required, how many people were needed in industry, what were the nation's skills and where we should site the factories to manufacture the essentials of war.

Bevin was a born organiser and a true radical. Before the war he was arguing for an international currency and for training schemes for black people in the British Empire. He was shrewd and had the support of Churchill, who quickly brought him into the War Cabinet. Bevin had immense impact on the war economy and gained the respect of both sides of industry and the editors in Fleet Street. In May 1945 the *Manchester Guardian* writing about Bevin said, 'He came out of the war second only to Churchill in courage and insight.'

Herbert Morrison was a strong and powerful Minister too. He was leader of the London County Council and the brains behind the creation of the London Passenger Transport Board, which became the organisational format for most nationalised industries. As Home Secretary he was in charge of Civil Defence and the National Fire Service, which played a key role in the blitz, and his impact on the public was close since a large number of domestic activities were controlled by the Home Office.

The Labour Party had household names in Stafford Cripps and Hugh Dalton, and even the Coalition's critics like Aneurin Bevan and Emmanuel Shinwell had a ready response from certain sections of the public. But it was Clement Attlee, the Deputy Prime Minister, who was greatly respected throughout the country. He had served in the First World War, was closely identified with all the problems of deprivation and bad housing that abounded in the East End of London, and had played a major role in the prosecution of the war. He was a completely different character from Churchill but nevertheless was able to press home his ideas throughout Whitehall and, more importantly, in Cabinet and its committees. He was in no way flamboyant but was a great judge of character and competence. He was utterly straightforward and honest, and gained the respect of all his colleagues. He was completely devoted to his wife Vi. Some thought he was too modest and terse, and believed the Labour Party should have a leader with charisma. Harold Laski, the Chairman of the Labour Party believed Attlee should make way for Herbert Morrison who he thought had greater public appeal. But he did not count on the influence of Ernest Bevin who was extremely loyal to Attlee and recognised his virtues. The fact that he detested Morrison was also a contributory factor.

The historian Ben Pimlott argued that Attlee had 'greatness thrust upon him'. If so, Attlee had the character and the ability to respond to the situation, and to use his full faculties to develop sensible, practical policies which were relevant to the time and appropriate to the developing events and problems. But Attlee also had widespread respect throughout the country. John Colville, who was private secretary to Chamberlain, Churchill and Attlee, gave an insider's view when he wrote, 'Attlee may well have been the only British Prime Minister in all history without a touch either of vanity or conceit. Personal ambition played no part and he cared nothing for money or position.'

So the Labour Party went into the election with a strong team at national level and an abundance of talent at local level. The Tory national team bore no comparison with Labour's men and women of experience. There were hundreds of new and distinguished candidates who were carried along partly by their own enthusiasm and partly by the response they received from the general public. The policies on which they fought the election appeared to be relevant and appropriate to a post-war situation, and in tune with what the electorate was seeking. Writing in 1959, Denis Healey suggested that in 1945 there was no gap between the active worker in the Labour Party and the average voter.

For the Tories, Churchill was their greatest asset. They could bask in his glory but behind this idolatry was their recent past and this was never far away throughout the campaign. Their pre-war record on unemployment was still fresh in the minds of many, particularly those in the forces who did not want to return to a situation that was evident after the First World War with widespread unemployment, poverty and deprivation.

Among the Tories' national figures was Anthony Eden, who had performed on the international stage for many years but who spent most of the election in bed nursing a duodenal ulcer. He was smart and debonair but never quite in touch with the man on the Clapham omnibus. Mr R. A. Butler was another well-known figure, particularly since he had played a key role in the 1944 Education Act. But the Coalition Government included people who came from outside the political arena and played little or no role in the 1945 General Election. Similarly, the Tories had several leading parliamentary figures who came from the House of Lords and were therefore not seeking re-election and among the rest of their team none was a household name except perhaps Lord Woolton, one-time Minister of Food and later in charge of Reconstruction.

Of the two frontbench teams, Labour fielded the strongest element. They had men and women of ministerial experience and the public could make a judgement on whether they had been good Ministers by their activities during the war. If they had little or no parliamentary experience, this might have been a disadvantage for Labour since the electorate might have had reservations about voting for a party which had good intentions but no experience of running the offices of state, particularly in the difficult post-war situation. The Labour Party and its candidates also presented themselves as moderate and reasonable people. They were not Communists à la Russian style who were about to banish the royal family or set fire to Buckingham Palace. Even 'disgusted' of Tunbridge Wells could have a pleasant sleep at night.

After what has been described as a quiet election campaign, candidates and their election helpers turned up at town halls and Assembly Rooms throughout the country at 9 a.m. on Thursday, 26 July to see who had won the election. The ballot papers had been carefully locked away since 5 July, awaiting the service votes that had been flown in from around the world.

The first result to come in was from Salford and this augured well for the Labour Party. It was 10 a.m. and this was Labour's first gain when Mr E. A. Hardy, the Area Secretary of the Hospitals and Welfare Services Union, defeated the Tory candidate with a majority of 4,791. As the day went on, Labour was to gain the two other Salford seats. Throughout the day one Tory stronghold after another fell to Labour's onslaught. By 9.45 p.m. the last Labour gain for the day was recorded at Hornchurch when Captain Geoffrey Bing, a barrister who was injured whilst serving with the British Liberation Army in North Africa, came home with a majority of 11,756 over his Tory opponent.

The Tory defeat was widespread. Brendan Bracken, a close confidant of Churchill and a member of the Cabinet, was defeated at Paddington. Twelve other Cabinet-ranking Ministers were rejected by their electors and nineteen other Ministers had the doubtful pleasure of seeing the Labour candidate win their seats. All the service Ministers were defeated. It made no difference whether you played a leading role in Parliament or were a household name, the same universal swing to Labour could not be halted.

Names such as Harold Macmillan were defeated at Stockton, Hore-Belisha at Plymouth, Sir James Grigg, who had been Secretary of State for War, went too in Cardiff, as did Duncan Sandys in Norwood. Lord Dunglass, who eventually became Prime Minister as Lord Home, was rejected by the electors of Lanark and Peter Thorneycroft, who was a Junior Minister at the Ministry of Transport and later became a Minister in a Macmillan's administration, went out at Stafford. Leo Amery, the Secretary of State for India, lost his seat at Sparkbrook in Birmingham and at Crewe it was all change as the Caretaker Government's Home Secretary, Sir D. Somervell, lost his seat too.

In former safe Tory seats the Labour Party won through and where the Tory did win the majority was drastically reduced. In two constituencies, Bromley (Sir E. T. Campbell) and Monmouth (Mr L. R. Pym) the Tory candidates died after polling day and before the count; both were elected, which in effect meant there would be by-elections. Alfred Dodds, who was elected as Labour MP for Smethwick, was killed in a road accident within 24 hours of the announcement of his success. An analysis of the election results showed that 79 seats won by Labour had never had a Labour MP before and eighteen had always voted Tory for the past hundred years. The bulk of the election results were declared on Thursday, 26 July.

For the Liberal Party the 1945 General Election was a disaster. The peak of their public support was in the days of Lloyd-George and his radical governments in the early part of the century. They held eighteen seats when the 1945 Election was called and ended up on polling day with twelve seats, though this disguises the fact that they won three seats – at Buckrose in Yorkshire and in North Dorset, both from the Tories, and Carmarthen from Labour.

The Liberals were at a great disadvantage compared with the other two major Parties. The existence of the Liberal Nationals confused the situation in the minds of the electorate and they were only able to contest 306 seats. Nevertheless, they managed to win the support of more than 2 million electors, whereas the Liberal Nationals achieved 750,000 votes. If the Liberals had contested more seats and if the Liberal Nationals had sunk their differences and fought under one banner, they might have won a few more. In fact, they lost Berwick-on-Tweed, where the candidate was Sir William Beveridge, the distinguished social scientist and author of the Beveridge Report, and Caithness and Sutherland where their leader, Sir Archibald Sinclair, came bottom of the poll. Among other casualties were Sir Percy Harris at Bethnal Green and Lady Violet Bonham-Carter who came bottom of the poll at Wells. The name of Lloyd-George did, however, hold some sway with electors. Lady Megan Lloyd-George succeeded in holding Anglesey in a straight contest with a Labour candidate and her brother Major Gwilym Lloyd-George, who had been a Minister in the Coalition

Government, held his seat at Pembroke with the slender majority of 168 votes.

The 1945 Liberal Party was very different from their modern–day counterparts, the Liberal Democrats. They drew their support from an elderly section of the electorate who were not quite prepared to cast their votes for Labour candidates and, indeed, were suspicious of the trade union movement. Their leaders were not household names like Paddy Ashdown, David Steel or Jo Grimond and they were seen very much as the third party. Despite this they were able to see off the Liberal Nationals who started the election with 26 members and ended up holding thirteen seats. The Party later met and dissolved themselves with members going their own political way.

The demise of the Liberal Party was all part of the general swing towards Labour, which became abundantly clear as the results poured in from all over the country. Nicholas Henderson, who was Private Secretary to Anthony Eden, described the scene at Downing Street when he called to take John Colville, Churchill's Private Secretary, out to lunch on the day of the count.

> Just before 1 o'clock I went round to collect him from the annexe of No. 10. 'Come look at the map room,' he said. For five years the map room had formed the backcloth to Churchill's command of the British war effort, by land, sea and air. There night and day members of the three services had stuck coloured pins and flags into the battlefronts of the world. For the election the room had been transformed; instead of war maps and orders of battle there were charts of constituencies and the latest state of poll. The change in the bearing of the Prime Minister himself was no less striking. Here was a war he had lost; no oratory or inspiration could make any difference now. He was glum. Round the room sat Mrs Churchill, Mary Churchill and Lord Beaverbrook, their lengthening faces cupped in their hands. Mary Churchill said as she saw us, 'The news is very bad.' Churchill said, 'It's very hot in here. Why isn't there more air? Open the windows and let's have some more air.' Inexorably a WAAF officer continued to pin up Labour gains.
>
> John and I withdrew to our lunch, the Churchills to theirs.

He records at this point how Mrs Churchill tried to comfort him by saying,

'It may well be a blessing in disguise,' to which Churchill replied, 'At the moment it seems quite effectively disguised.'

Colville, with hindsight, wrote about this period in his book, *Footprints in Time*:

> It must be doubtful whether Churchill's speeches that summer, whatever their content and however delivered, would have made any difference at all to the result. The country wanted a change of Government. The voters had been taught to believe that the nation's unreadiness for war in 1939 had been exclusively the fault of the pre-war National Government.

Churchill spent most of polling day in Downing Street and did not attend the counting of the votes in his own constituency but instead sent Mrs Churchill to represent him at Woodford, where he secured a 17,200 majority against a solitary Independent candidate who nevertheless managed to obtain more than 10,000 votes.

And then, at 5.30 p.m., when the result of the election was unmistakably clear, Churchill invited all the service Chiefs of Staff to Downing Street to say his farewells. Field Marshal Lord Alanbrooke recalls, 'It was a very sad and very moving little meeting at which I found myself unable to say much for fear of breaking down. He was standing the blow wonderfully well.' Reflecting later, he wrote,

> During the last years Winston had been a very sick man, with repeated attacks of pneumonia, and very frequent attacks of temperature. This physical condition together with his mental fatigue account for many of the difficulties in dealing with him. I shall always look back on the years I worked with him as some of the most difficult and trying ones in my life. For all that I thank God that I was given the opportunity of working alongside of such a man, and having my eyes opened to the fact that occasionally such supermen exist on this earth.

Of the 87 women who stood as candidates, 24 were elected. The Labour Party gained 21 of these seats and both the Tory Party and the Liberal Party won one seat each, and an Independent won a seat for the Combined English Universities.

The Sutton seat at Plymouth was made famous in 1919 by Lady Astor becoming the first elected woman to take a seat in the House of Commons. In 1945 the electors maintained their support for a woman MP, but this time it was a Labour woman, Lucy Middleton, the wife of the former General Secretary of the Labour Party.

The result of the election clearly indicated that electors gave their support to either of the two main political parties. The Tories lost 181 seats, the Liberal Nationals lost thirteen, the Liberals eleven. Independents lost six seats and the Common Wealth Party, which had made great strides during the electoral truce, lost two seats. Despite the major gains made by the Labour Party, in fact it lost three seats (Mile End to the Communists, Carmarthen to the Liberals and Eddisbury to the Liberal Nationals). Three candidates were returned unopposed.

The result was a great surprise, not least to the successful candidates. Kenneth Younger, who won Grimsby for Labour, wrote in his diary,

> We ended up with 28,484, a majority of 9,643. That was of course much bigger than any of us had hoped. I was delighted but knew that I personally could claim only minor credit for it. For old Labour supporters who had been on the losing side so often (scarcely even daring to believe in victory), it was tremendously exhilarating.

A similar view was expressed by Lieutenant James Callaghan at Cardiff South. He recalled,

> I was carried literally shoulder high from the City Hall almost before the speeches had been concluded. My supporters were so enthusiastic. There were men and women with tears in their eyes. It was so unexpected. I don't think we had really imagined a victory of that sort. It was the consummation of so many hopes and aspirations over such a long period and here we seemed to be on the point of achieving it all.

Similar scenes were enacted throughout the country. From Accrington to

York, Labour took seats that not even the wildest dreamer could imagine. In Birmingham, Labour swept the floor by winning ten seats from the Tories and traditional-sounding Tory towns like Winchester, Taunton, Stroud and Buckingham went Labour's way. All the major conurbations had strong Labour representation and in many provincial cities such as Stoke-on-Trent, Nottingham, Newcastle on Tyne and Wolverhampton, Labour captured all the seats.

The highest Labour majority was in Wentworth, where Wilfred Paling achieved a majority of 35,410 votes, and in Bournemouth Sir Leonard Lyle had the largest Tory majority of 20,312. There were some small majorities too. Group Captain Ward, standing for the Tories in Worcester, squeaked home with a majority of four and in the Rusholme seat of Manchester Mr H. L. Hutchinson became a Labour MP with just a ten vote majority.

All the Labour leaders romped home. Sir Stafford Cripps saw his majority rise from 6,000 to 17,000 and Herbert Morrison, who deliberately chose a difficult seat in Lewisham which he had not contested before, had a clear 15,000 majority. The election also saw the return of most of the 1950 generation of Labour leaders – Harold Wilson in Ormskirk, Jim Callaghan at Cardiff South, George Brown at Belper, Barbara Castle at Blackburn, Dick Crossman at Coventry East, Hugh Gaitskell at Leeds South, Jennie Lee at Cannock, Alf Robens at Wansbeck, Sir Hartley Shawcross at St Helens, George Thomas at Cardiff Central and John Strachey at Dundee.

Lost deposits were also a feature of this election. Compared with the previous election, when 84 candidates lost their deposits, this time the number was up to 149. More than a fifth of Liberal Party candidates went home without receiving back their deposit and the national coffers benefited to the tune of £22,000, since lost deposits were sent direct to the Treasury and not retained locally.

Absent on the day of the count were TV and radio analysis programmes where experts measure the swing in votes on 'swingometers' and pontificate about the political implications of the result. In 1945 the electors rejoiced or commiserated at a local level and relied on BBC news programmes to inform them about results in other parts of the country. (Lord) Jack Ashley recalls that the workers at Bolton's, a factory where he worked in Widnes, chalked up the results as they came in and were jubilant at the outcome.

It was the surprise of the result, coupled with the enthusiasm of the public, that dominated the day. The City of London took a different view. They were shocked with the result and reacted in the normal way that city investors do: stock exchange prices fell sharply and government stocks went down about 5 per cent.

The Workers Educational Association could justly claim they were strongly represented in the return of 393 Labour MPs. When the 1945 Labour Government was formed their members included the Prime Minister, the Chancellor of the Exchequer and twelve other Government Ministers. Furthermore, 56 of their tutors, executives and students were MPs.

The Labour Party fielded 120 candidates who were in the services and a large number of these were elected to Parliament. In that sense the new Parliament represented the views of the fighting services and this became evident when the new MPs could speak about service problems based on their own practical experience.

As is usual after every successful election, individuals advance their own claim about their responsible role. Hugh Dalton, who clearly played a leading role as a member of Labour's National Executive Committee, said, 'I think I can take a good deal of personal credit. In the last year or two, I have taken pains to ensure that our electoral machine was in put in good order.'

In the evening when the election results were declared, the Labour Party organised a victory rally at Central Hall, Westminster, when victorious candidates and their supporters congregated to welcome their leaders. Even at this stage there were people within the Labour Party who were trying to replace Clem Attlee with Herbert Morrison as Leader. They were encouraged in their activities by Morrison himself who had grandiose ideas that given a vote in the Parliamentary Labour Party he could win. But they had not counted on the loyalty and forthrightness of Ernest Bevin, who was outraged and argued that the public had voted Labour with Attlee as its leader.

At 7.30 p.m. Attlee was summoned to Buckingham Palace and asked by the King to form a government, and that settled the issue. He was driven to the palace by his wife Vi in the family car and then on to Central Hall where the audience, including the remaining members of the Attlee family, were ecstatic. Also in the audience was a young Tony Benn who lived just round the corner at Millbank. He recalls,

> I was up in the gallery looking down and I saw Clem come on to the platform and he said, 'I have just returned from the Palace where the King has asked me to form a Government.' The whole place erupted. But what was so exciting about it was that everybody was so surging in confidence. Here we were so utterly bankrupt, saved by the skin of our teeth by the Red Army who carried the brunt of the Nazi attack and then by the Americans who came over and provided the main forces at D-Day, and yet my generation thought they could beat Hitler, beat Mussolini, end the means test, end rearmament, build the welfare state, have the health service. And we did.

All the Labour leaders spoke at the rally. Harold Laski proclaimed, 'We have won a great victory for socialism and we send a message of hope to every democracy in the world.' Clement Attlee said,

> The country has put its confidence in Labour. It will not put that confidence in vain. Let us look at the tasks and not underestimate them. We intend to conquer and overcome all difficulties.
>
> We want the fullest cooperation with all nations. We want a security that will banish war forever. We want a widespread prosperity among all peoples and nations of the world.

Ernest Bevin put the election result into context when he stated, 'When I saw the election results, I had a feeling the British people had put an end to the very conception of personal government. It is a great thing to have lived to see the day when the British electorate cast their votes for policies and not personalities.'

Professor Alan Bullock's view was that 'the war had stirred up a conservative nation into one of its rare bouts of radicalism. For the first time the Labour Party was the beneficiary of this radical mood which in the past (1886 and 1906) had carried reforming Liberal Governments into power.'

The Liberal Party said they had 'suffered a reverse as overwhelming as it was unexpected . . . Electors were mainly concerned to defeat the Tory Party.

They were naturally and justifiably resentful of the Tory record before the war and deeply suspicious of their lukewarm attitude towards projects of reconstruction. This was undoubtedly the principal reason why they elected a Labour Government and the Liberal Party appeared to offer a less effective alternative.'

Jo Grimond, who later became leader of the Liberal Party, fought and lost the Orkney and Shetland constituency by 329 votes. He never thought he would win and did not even bother to go to the count.

His view of the General Election was that

> though Churchill was popular, the Tories were still held to blame for 'appeasement'. Some hold that servicemen and women had been quietly making up their minds to set off on a new course. It has been suggested that Churchill's 'Gestapo speech' lost many votes. It has also been suggested that while the Tories had let their organisation rust while they attended to winning the war, the Labour organisation had been kept well oiled. None of these reasons was obvious to me at the time.

After every major change in society come the alternative possibilities. If Churchill had retired at the end of the war and devoted the remainder of his life to painting and writing, the Tories would have had to find another leader for the election. The only real name they could have come up with was Anthony Eden and, whilst the public respected his efforts on the international stage, he never had the appeal of Churchill and would not have attracted the kind of votes that Churchill with his war record was able to achieve. In that case the Labour Party would have had an even larger majority in Parliament.

Secondly, if the service vote had been higher, this might have had a significant effect on the result. The service vote was just over 50 per cent whereas the vote by the general public was 72 per cent. All the indications are that a majority of servicemen and servicewomen supported Labour candidates and again this might have led to an even larger Labour majority. But these are suppositions and the reality was that the Labour Party, armed with a strong Socialist programme, was returned with a comfortable majority and was able to dominate the political scene at home in the full knowledge that it had the mass of the public behind it in the difficult days ahead.

One of the most significant outcomes of the 1945 election was that the new Parliament represented more accurately the state of the nation. Because of the ten-year gap between elections, the age level was lower since there was a missing generation. The 1945 Parliament represented a greater cross-section of society and out of this emerged a frontbench team that was strong and formidable.

The unmistakable result of the election meant there was only one thing that Winston Churchill could do. He drove to Buckingham Palace complete with cigar and gave the V sign to a small group of people outside the gate. He tendered his resignation to the King and so ended his term of office as Prime Minister, which had commenced on 10 May 1940. According to his diaries, the King thought the nation had been 'very ungrateful' to Churchill. In a final message to the country Churchill said, 'I have laid down the charge which was placed upon me in darker times. I regret that I have not been permitted to finish the work against Japan. Immense responsibilities abroad and at home fall upon the new Government, and we must all hope that they will be successful in bearing them.'

Clement Attlee in his first press statement after the election said,

> Labour went into this election on a carefully thought out programme based on very definite principles. We are facing a new era and I believe that voting at this election has shown that the people of Britain are facing the new era with the same courage as they faced the long years of war. I am confident that British democracy can make a tremendous contribution to the building up of world peace and prosperity on a firm foundation. I believe we are on the eve of a great advance of the human race. That will mean not only the work that must be done here in reconstruction, but above all cooperation with other nations and particularly with our great allies the United States of America and the Union of Soviet Republics.

Good wishes for the new Labour Government flowed in from around the world. The Australian Labour Prime Minister, Mr Chifley, said there was great jubilation in the Australian Parliament and Signor Nenni, the Italian

Socialist leader, expressed similar views and went further by stating, 'This defeat does not lessen the greatness of Winston Churchill or the task that he has hitherto performed. But there comes a time when great men have completed their function and their continuance in power would be dangerous. The British people have recognised that moment.'

The new Government was not short of advice from the press. *The Times*, whilst recognising that the Tories 'undergo an eclipse and the Liberal Party is virtually extinguished' said the result was 'not a "doctor's mandate" or a "blank cheque". It is a vote decisive in its effect, for specific courses of action. Their mandate now is national not sectional. It has been furnished for a national programme, not for narrow doctrines or extreme experiments.' But *The Times* and other newspapers failed to convey the natural and genuine exuberance and enthusiasm for the new government. Jim Callaghan recalls that following his victory in Cardiff he went by train to Paddington and hailed a taxi to take him to the first meeting of the new Parliamentary Labour Party at Beaver Hall in the City of London. The taxi driver 'refused to accept the fare. Like millions of others he was full of excitement at the political upset that had taken place and at the prospect of the first ever Labour Government with a substantial majority.'

The silent and slow revolution, which had begun to take shape immediately after the 1935 General Election and gathered pace in the inter-war years, took on a new urgency during the war. Society's values had changed, people had changed, their views about the way the country should be governed had changed; alongside these changing attitudes had developed a new comradeship among the fighting services and the emergence of a community spirit at home. And all these significant changes were bound to be reflected in the democratic process which took place on Thursday, 5 July 1945. A new light dawned to overcome the dark past. For the first time in British history the Labour Party was returned with a substantial working majority, which meant it could carry out its entire manifesto promises. By the time of the next election in 1950, the 38th United Kingdom Parliament had achieved all its manifesto goals.

Whilst the 1945 Labour vote of 11,995,152 gave it a majority of seats over the Tories of 180, by 1951, with an 82 per cent turnout, the Labour vote had increased still further to 13,948,605 but elected only 295 Labour MPs.

Although the Tory vote in 1951 was less – 13,717,538 – it produced 321 MPs, giving the Tories a majority of 26. Such are the vagaries of election statistics under our democratic process.

And the 'little man' – Clement Attlee – who was imbued with a passionate desire for social justice and a radical reforming Socialist zeal, remained at No. 10 Downing Street for six years and 92 days. He led a Government that created a new society and was the most radical of the twentieth century.

Postscript

The results of the 1945 General Election were announced on Thursday, 26 July and the following day Clement Attlee issued the names of his Cabinet, which included most of the Labour leaders who had played a significant role in the wartime Coalition Government. The major surprise was to find Hugh Dalton as Chancellor of the Exchequer and Ernest Bevin as Foreign Secretary. Most observers thought the roles would have been reversed. But later reports suggested that Attlee believed that there would be friction if Bevin and Morrison were both in charge of 'home' Government Departments.

Before completing his new government, Attlee and Bevin flew off to Potsdam to finish their talks with Marshal Stalin and President Truman, the new United States President, about post-war Germany and the future of Europe. On his return, Attlee completed his other appointments and the stage was set for the new Parliament to meet.

On Wednesday, 1 August members of the new House of Commons assembled in the Chamber with the Mace under the table rather than in its usual position. Their purpose was to elect a Speaker of the House. As Winston Churchill entered the Chamber, the Tories sang 'For he's a Jolly Good Fellow'. Immediately George Griffiths, a checkweigh man and Salvation Army chorister representing Hemsworth with a 26,000 majority, stood up and sang the 'Red Flag' and this was taken up by government supporters and echoed around the House of Commons. On his election as Speaker of the House, Colonel Douglas Clifton Brown commented, 'I wondered whether I was going to be elected Speaker or director of a musical show.' The Mace was then placed in its official position and for the following two days members took their Oath of Allegiance and made preparations for the State Opening of Parliament.

Because the original House of Commons Chamber had been bombed, MPs used the House of Lords Chamber and the Lords used a robing chamber in the Palace of Westminster, but this had to change when it was agreed there should be an official State Opening with all pomp and ceremony. The next time MPs met, on Wednesday, 15 August, they assembled in St Stephen's Hall – the last time the House had met in this hall was 15 August 111 years before. After the ceremonies and the King's speech, Attlee rose at 4.05 p.m. to make an historic announcement – the war with Japan was over. The House adjourned to proceed to St Margaret's Church for a Service of Thanksgiving. The atomic bomb had been dropped on Hiroshima and Nagasaki and a new chapter in civilisation was about to begin.

1945 General Election Result

Party	Votes	Candidates	Elected	% Vote
Labour	11,995,152	604	393	47.8
Tory	9,988,306	624	213	39.8
Liberal	2,248,226	306	12	9.0
C/Wealth	110,634	23	1	0.4
Comm	102,780	21	2	0.4
Others	640,880	104	19	2.0
Total	25,085,978	1,682	640	100.0

(C/Wealth = Common Wealth; Comm = Communist)

ELECTORATE
33,240,391

TURNOUT
72.7%

GROWTH IN LABOUR VOTE

Year	Vote	Members Elected
1922	4,241,383	142
1923	4,438,508	191
1924	5,489,077	151
1929	8,389,512	288
1931	6,649,630	52
1935	8,325,491	154
1945	11,995,152	393
1950	13,266,592	315
1951	13,948,605	295
1955	12,404,970	277
1959	12,215,538	258
1964	12,205,814	317
1966	13,064,951	363

(Source: David Butler and Jennie Freeman, *British Political Facts 1900–1968*)

The Labour Manifesto

LET US FACE THE FUTURE

Victory in War Must Be Followed by a Prosperous Peace
Victory is assured for us and our allies in the European War. The war in the East goes the same way. The British Labour Party is firmly resolved that Japanese barbarism shall be defeated just as decisively as Nazi aggression and tyranny. The people will have won both struggles. The gallant men and women in the Fighting Services, in the Merchant Navy, Home Guard and Civil Defence, in the factories and in the bombed areas – they deserve and must be assured a happier future than faced so many of them after the last war. Labour regards their welfare as a sacred trust.

So far as Britain's contribution is concerned, this war will have been won by its people, not by any one man or set of men, though strong and greatly valued leadership has been given to the high resolve of the people in the present struggle. And in this leadership the Labour Ministers have taken their full share of burdens and responsibilities. The record of the Labour Ministers has been one of hard tasks well done since that fateful day in May 1940, when the initiative of Labour in Parliament brought about the fall of the Chamberlain Government and the formation of the new War Government which has led the country to victory.

The people made tremendous efforts to win the last war also. But when they had won it they lacked a lively interest in the social and economic problems of peace, and accepted the election promises of the leaders of the anti-Labour parties at their face value. So the 'hard faced men who had done well out of the war' were able to get the kind of peace that suited themselves. The people lost the peace. And when we say 'peace' we mean not only the Treaty, but the social and economic policy which followed the fighting.

In the years that followed, the 'hard faced men' and their political friends kept control of the Government. They controlled the banks, the mines, the big industries, largely the press and the cinema. They controlled the means by which the people got their living. They controlled the ways by which most of the people learned about the world outside. This happened in all the big industrialised countries.

Great economic blizzards swept the world in those years. The great inter-war slumps were not acts of God or of blind forces. They were the sure and certain result of the concentration of too much economic power in the hands of too few men. These men had only learned how to act in the interest of their own bureaucratically-run private monopolies which may be likened to totalitarian oligarchies within our democratic State. They had and they felt no responsibility to the nation.

Similar forces are at work today. The interests have not been able to make the same profits out of the war as they did out of the last. The determined propaganda of the Labour Party, helped by other progressive forces, had its effect in 'taking the profit out of war'. The 100 per cent Excess Profits Tax, the controls over industry and transport, the fair rationing of food and control of prices – without which the Labour Party would not have remained in the Government – these all helped to win the war. With these measures the country has come nearer to making 'fair shares' the national rule than ever before in its history.

But the war in the East is not yet over. There are grand pickings still to be had. A short boom period after the war, when savings, gratuities and post-war credits are there to be spent, can make a profiteer's paradise. But Big Business knows that this will happen only if the people vote into power the party which promises to get rid of the controls and so let the profiteers and racketeers have that freedom for which they are pleading eloquently on every Tory platform and in every Tory newspaper.

They accuse the Labour Party of wishing to impose controls for the sake of control. That is not true and they know it. What is true is that the anti-controllers and anti-planners desire to sweep away public controls, simply in order to give the profiteering interests and the privileged rich an entirely free hand to plunder the rest of the nation as shamelessly as they did in the nineteen-twenties.

Does freedom for the profiteers mean freedom for the ordinary man and woman, whether they be wage earners or small business or professional men or housewives? Just think back over the depression of the 20 years between the wars, when there were precious few public controls of any kind and the Big Interests had things all their own way. Never was so much injury done to so many by so few. Freedom is not an abstract thing. To be real it must be won, it must be worked for.

The Labour Party stands for order as against the chaos which would follow the end of all public control. We stand for order, the positive constructive progress as against the chaos of economic do-as-they-please anarchy.

The Labour Party makes no baseless promises. The future will not be easy. But this time the peace must be won. The Labour Party offers the nation a plan which will win the Peace for the People.

What the Election Will Be About
Britain's coming Election will be the greatest test in our history of the judgement and common-sense of our people.

The nation wants food, work and homes. It wants more than that – it wants good food in plenty, useful work for all, and comfortable, labour-saving homes that take full advantage of the resources of modern science and productive industry. It wants a high and rising standard of living, security for all against a rainy day, an educational system that will give every boy and girl a chance to develop the best that is in them.

These are the aims. In themselves they are no more than words. All parties may declare that in principle they agree with them. But the test of a political programme is whether it is sufficiently in earnest about the objectives to adopts the means needed to realise them. It is very easy to set out a list of aims. What matters is whether it is backed up by a genuine workmanlike plan conceived without regard to sectional vested interests and carried through in a spirit of resolute concentration.

Point by point these national aims need analysis. Point by point it will be found that if they are to be turned into realities the nation and its post-war

Governments will be called upon to put the nation above any sectional interests, above any cheap slogan about so-called free enterprise. The problems and pressures of the post-war world threaten our security and progress as surely as – though less dramatically than – the Germans threatened them in 1940. We need the spirit of Dunkirk and of the Blitz sustained over a period of years.

The Labour Party's programme is a practical expression of that spirit applied to the tasks of peace. It calls for hard work, energy and sound sense.

We must prevent another war, and that means we must have such an international organisation as will give all nations real security against future aggression. But Britain can only play her full part in such an international plan if our spirit as shown in our handling of home affairs is firm, wise and determined. This statement of policy, therefore, begins at home.

And in stating it we give clear notice that we will not tolerate obstruction of the people's will by the House of Lords.

The Labour Party stands for freedom – for freedom of worship, freedom of speech, freedom of the Press. The Labour Party will see to it that we keep and enlarge these freedoms and that we enjoy again the personal liberties we have, of our free will, sacrificed to win the war. The freedom of the Trade Unions, denied by the Trade Disputes and Trade Unions Act, 1927, must also be restored. But there are certain so-called freedoms that Labour will not tolerate: freedom to exploit other people; freedom to pay poor wages and to push up prices for selfish profit; freedom to deprive the people of the means of living full, happy, healthy lives.

The nation needs a tremendous overhaul, a great programme of modernisation and re-equipment of its homes, its factories and machinery, its schools, its social services.

All parties say so – the Labour Party means it. For the Labour Party is prepared to achieve it by drastic policies of re-planning and by keeping a firm constructive hand on our whole productive machinery; the Labour Party will put the community first and the sectional interests of private business after. Labour will plan from the ground up – giving an appropriate place to constructive enterprise and private endeavour in the national plan, but dealing decisively with those interests which would use high-sounding talk

212

about economic freedom to cloak their determination to put themselves and their wishes above those of the whole nation.

Jobs for All

All parties pay lip service to the idea of jobs for all. All parties are ready to promise to achieve that end by keeping up the national purchasing power and controlling changes in the national expenditure through Government action. Where agreement ceases is in the degree of control of private industry that is necessary to achieve the desired end.

In hard fact, the success of a full employment programme will certainly turn upon the firmness and success with which the Government fits into that programme the investment and development policies of private as well as public industry. Our opponents would be ready to use State action to do the best they can to bolster up private industry whenever it plunges the nation into heavy unemployment. But if the slumps in uncontrolled private industry are too severe to be balanced by public action – as they will certainly prove to be – our opponents are not ready to draw the conclusion that the sphere of public action must be extended.

They say, 'Full employment. Yes! If we can get it without interfering too much with private industry.' We say, 'Full employment in any case, and if we need to keep a firm public hand on industry in order to get jobs for all, very well. No more dole queues, in order to let the Czars of Big Business remain kings in their own castles. The price of so-called "economic freedom" for the few is too high if it is bought at the cost of idleness and misery for millions.'

What Will the Labour Party Do?

First, the whole of the national resources, in land, material and labour must be fully employed. Production must be raised to the highest level and related to purchasing power. Over-production is not the cause of depression and unemployment; it is under-consumption that is responsible. It is doubtful whether we have ever, except in war, used the whole of our productive capacity. This must be corrected because, upon our ability to produce and organise a fair and generous distribution of the product, the standards of living of our people depends.

Secondly, a high and constant purchasing power can be maintained through good wages, social services and insurance and taxation which bears less heavily on the lower-income groups. But everybody knows that money and savings lose their value if prices rise, so rents and prices of the necessities of life will be controlled.

Thirdly, planned investment in essential industries and on houses, schools, hospitals and civic centres will occupy a large field of capital expenditure. A National Investment Board will determine social priorities and promote better timing in private investment. In suitable cases we would transfer the use of efficient Government factories from war production to meet the needs of peace. The location of new factories will be suitably controlled and where necessary the Government will itself build factories. There must be no depressed areas in the New Britain.

Fourthly, the Bank of England with its financial powers must be brought under public ownership, and the operation of other banks harmonised with industrial needs.

By these and other means full employment can be achieved. But a policy of Jobs for All must be associated with a policy of general economic expansion and efficiency as set out in the next section of this Declaration. Indeed it is not enough to ensure that there are jobs for all. If the standard of life is to be high – as it should be –The standard of production must be high. This means that industry must be thoroughly efficient if the needs of the nation are to be met.

Industry in the Service of the Nation

By the test of war some industries have shown themselves capable of rising to new heights of efficiency and expansion. Others, including some of the older industries fundamental to our economic structure, have wholly or partly failed.

Today we live alongside economic giants – countries where science and technology take leaping strides year by year. Britain must match those strides – and we must take no chances about it. Britain needs an industry organised to enable it to yield the best that human knowledge and skill can provide. Only so can our people reap the full benefits of this age of discovery and Britain keep her place as a Great Power.

The Labour Party intends to link the skill of the British craftsmen and designers to the skill of British scientists in the service of our fellow men. The genius of British scientists and technicians who have produced radio-location, jet propulsion, penicillin and the Mulberry Harbours in wartime, must be given full rein in peacetime too.

Each industry must have applied to it the test of national service. If it serves the nation, well and good; if it is inefficient and falls down on its job, the nation must see that things are put right.

These propositions seem indisputable, but for years before the war anti-Labour Governments set them aside, so that British industry over a large field fell into a state of depression, muddle and decay. Millions of working- and middle-class people went through the horrors of unemployment and insecurity. It is not enough to sympathise with these victims: we must develop an acute feeling of national shame – and act.

The Labour Party is a Socialist Party, and proud of it. Its ultimate purpose at home is the establishment of the Socialist Commonwealth of Great Britain – free, democratic, efficient, progressive, public-spirited, its material resources organised in the service of the British people.

But Socialism cannot come overnight, as the product of a weekend revolution. The members of the Labour Party, like the British people, are practical-minded men and women.

There are basic industries ripe and over ripe for public ownership and management in the direct service of the nation. There are many smaller businesses rendering good service which can be left to go on with their useful work.

There are big industries not yet ripe for public ownership which must nevertheless be required by constructive supervision to further the nation's needs and not prejudice national interests by restrictive anti-social monopoly or cartel agreements – caring for their own capital structures and profits at the cost of a lower standard of living for all.

In the light of these considerations, the Labour Party submits to the nation the following industrial programme:

Public ownership of the fuel and power industries. For a quarter of a century the coal industry, producing Britain's most precious national raw material, has been floundering chaotically under the ownership of many hundreds of

215

independent companies. Amalgamation under public ownership will bring great economies in operation and make it possible to modernise production methods and to raise safety standards in every colliery in the country. Public ownership of gas and electricity undertakings will lower charges, prevent competitive waste and open the way for co-ordinated research and development, and lead to the reforming of uneconomical areas of distribution. Other industries will benefit.

Public ownership of inland transport – co-ordination of transport services by rail, road, air and canal cannot be achieved without unification. And unification without public ownership means a steady struggle with sectional interests of the enthronement of a private monopoly, which would be a menace to the rest of industry.

Public ownership of iron and steel – private monopoly has maintained high prices and kept inefficient high-cost plants in existence. Only if public ownership replaces private monopoly can the industry become efficient.

These socialised industries, taken over on a basis of fair compensation, to be conducted efficiently in the interests of consumers, coupled with proper status and conditions for the workers employed in them.

Public supervision of monopolies and cartels with the aim of advancing industrial efficiency in the service of the nation. Anti-social restrictive practices will be prohibited.

A firm and clear cut programme for the export trade – we would give State help in any necessary form to get our export trade on its feet and enable it to pay for the food and raw materials without which Britain must decay and die. But State help on conditions – conditions that industry is efficient and go-ahead. Laggards and obstructionists must be led or directed into better ways. Here we dare not fail.

The shaping of suitable economic and price controls to secure that first things shall come first in the transition from war to peace and that every citizen (including the demobilised Service men and women) shall get fair play. There must be priorities in the use of raw materials, food prices must be held, homes for the people must come before mansions, necessities for all before luxuries for the few. We do not want a short term boom followed by collapse as after the last war; we do not want a wild rise in prices and inflation, followed by a smash and widespread unemployment. It is either sound economic controls – or smash.

The better organisation of Government departments and the Civil Service for work in relation to these ends. The economic purpose of government must be to spur industry forward and not to choke it with red tape.

Agriculture and the People's Food

Agriculture is not only a job for the farmers, it is also a way of feeding the people. So we need a prosperous and efficient agricultural industry ensuring a fair return for the farmer and farm worker without excessive prices to the consumer. Our agriculture should be planned to give us the food we can best produce at home, and large enough to give us as much of those foods as possible.

In wartime the County War Executive Committees have organised production in that way. They have been the means of increasing efficiency and have given much practical assistance, particularly to the small farmer. The Labour Party intends that, with suitable modifications and safeguards, their work shall continue in peacetime.

Our good farm lands are part of the wealth of the nation and that wealth should not be wasted. The land must be farmed, not starved. If a landlord cannot or will not provide proper facilities for his tenant farmer, the State should take over his land at a fair valuation. The people need food at prices they can afford to pay, This means that our food supplies will have to be planned. Never again should they be left at the mercy of the city financier or speculator. Instead there must be stable markets, to a great gain of both producer and consumer.

The Ministry of Food has done fine work for the housewife in war. The Labour Party intends to keep going as much of the work of the Ministry of Food as will be useful in peace conditions, including the bulk purchase of food from abroad and a well organised system of distribution at home, with no vested interests imposing unnecessary costs.

A Labour Government will keep the new food services, such as the factory

217

canteens and British Restaurants, free and cheap milk for mothers and children, fruit juices and food supplements, and will improve and extend these services.

Houses and the Building Programme

Everybody says we must have more houses. Only the Labour Party is ready to take the necessary steps – a full programme of land planning and drastic action to ensure an efficient building industry that will neither burden the community with a crippling financial load nor impose bad conditions and heavy unemployment on its workpeople. There must be no restrictive price rings to keep up prices and bleed the taxpayer, owner occupier and the tenant alike. Modern methods, modern materials will have to be the order of the day.

There must be a due balance between the housing programme, the building of schools and the urgent requirements of factory modernisation and construction which will enable industry to produce efficiently.

Housing will be one of the greatest and of the earliest tests of a Government's real determination to put the nation first. Labour's pledge is firm and direct and it will proceed with a housing programme with the maximum practical speed until every family in this island has a good standard of accommodation. That may well mean centralised purchasing and pooling of building material and components by the State, together with price control. If that is necessary to get the houses as it was necessary to get the guns and planes, Labour is ready.

And housing ought to be dealt with in relation to good town planning – pleasant surroundings, attractive lay-out, efficient utility services, including the necessary transport facilities.

There should be a Ministry of Housing and Planning combining the housing powers of the Ministry of Health with the planning powers of the Ministry of Town and Country Planning; and there must be a firm and united Government policy to enable the Ministry of Works to function as an efficient instrument in the service of all departments with building needs and of the nation as a whole.

The Land

In the interests of agriculture, housing and town planning alike, we declare for a radical solution for the crippling problems of land acquisition and use in the service of the national plan.

Labour believes in land nationalisation and will work towards it, but as a first step the State and the local authorities must have wider and speedier powers to acquire land for public purposes wherever the public interest so requires. In this regard and for the purposes of controlling land use under town and country planning, we will provide for fair compensation; but we will also provide for a revenue for public funds from 'betterment'.

Education and Recreation

An important step forward has been the passing of the recent Education Act. Labour will put that Act not merely into legal force but into practical effect, including the raising of the school leaving age to 16 at the earliest possible moment, 'further' or adult education, and free secondary education for all.

And above all, let us remember that the great purpose of education is to give us individual citizens capable of thinking for themselves.

National and local authorities should co-operate to enable people to enjoy their leisure to the full, to have opportunities for healthy recreation. By the provision of concert halls, modern libraries, theatres and suitable civic centres, we desire to assure to our people full access to the great heritage of culture in this nation.

Health of the Nation and Its Children

By good food and good homes, much avoidable ill-health can be prevented. In addition the best health services should be available for all. Money must no longer be the passport to the best treatment.

In the new National Health Service there should be health centres where the people may get the best that modern science can offer, more and better hospitals, and proper conditions for our doctors and nurses. More research is required into the causes of disease and the ways to prevent and cure it.

Labour will work specially for the care of Britain's mothers and their children – children's allowances and school medical and feeding services, better maternity and child welfare services. A healthy family life must be fully ensured and parenthood must not be penalised if the population of Britain is to be prevented from dwindling.

219

Social Insurance Against the Rainy Day

The Labour Party has played a leading part in the long campaign for proper social security for all – social provision against rainy days, coupled with economic policies calculated to reduce rainy days to a minimum. Labour led the fight against the mean and shabby treatment which was the lot of millions while Conservative Governments were in power over long years. A Labour Government will press on rapidly with legislation extending social insurance over the necessary wide field to all.

But great national programmes of education, health and social services are costly things. Only an efficient and prosperous nation can afford them in full measure. If, unhappily, bad times were to come, and our opponents were in power, then running true to form, they would be likely to cut these social provisions on the plea that the nation could not meet the cost. That was the line they adopted on at least three occasions between the wars.

There is no good reason why Britain should not afford such programmes, but she will need full employment and the highest possible industrial efficiency in order to do so.

A World of Progress and Peace

No domestic policy, however wisely framed and courageously applied, can succeed in a world still threatened by war. Economic strife and political and military insecurity are enemies of peace. We cannot cut ourselves off from the rest of the world – and we ought not to try.

Now that victory has been won, at so great a cost of life and material destruction, we must make sure that Germany and Japan are deprived of all power to make war again. We must consolidate in peace the great wartime association of the British Commonwealth with the USA and the USSR. Let it not be forgotten that in the years leading up to the war the Tories were so scared of Russia that they missed the chance to establish a partnership which might well have prevented the war.

We must join with France and China and all the others who have contributed to the common victory in forming an International Organisation capable of keeping the peace in years to come. All must work together in true comradeship to achieve continuous social and economic progress.

If peace is to be protected we must plan and act. Peace must not be

220

regarded as a thing of passive inactivity: it must be a thing of life and action and work.

An internationally protected peace should make possible a known expenditure on armaments as our contribution to the protection of peace; an expenditure that should diminish as the world becomes accustomed to the prohibition of war through an effective collective security.

The economic well-being of each nation largely depends on world-wide prosperity. The essentials of prosperity for the world as for individual nations are high production and progressive efficiency, coupled with steady improvement in the standards of life, an increase on effective demand, and fair shares for all who by their effort contribute to the wealth of their community. We should build a new United Nations, allies in a new war on hunger, ignorance and want.

The British, while putting their own house in order, must play the part of brave and constructive leaders in international affairs. The British Labour Movement comes to the tasks of international organisation with one great asset: it has a common bond with the working peoples of all countries, who have achieved a new dignity and influence through their long struggles against Nazi tyranny.

And on all this worthwhile work – whether political, military or economic – the Labour Party will seek to promote mutual understanding and cordial cooperation between the Dominions of the British Commonwealth, the advancement of India to responsible self-government and the planned progress of our Colonial Dependencies.

Labour's Call to All Progressives

Quite a number of political parties will be taking part in the coming Election. But by and large Britain is a country of two parties.

And the effective choice of the people in this Election will be between the Conservative Party, standing for the protection of the 'rights' of private economic interest, and the Labour Party, allied with the great Trade Union and co-operative Movements, standing for the wise organisation and use of the economic assets of the national for the public good. Those are the two main parties; and here is the fundamental issue which has to be settled.

The election will produce a Labour Government, a Conservative

Government or no clear majority for either party: this last might well mean parliamentary instability and confusion, or another election.

In these circumstances we appeal to all men and women of progressive outlook, and who believe in constructive change, to support the Labour Party. We respect the views of those progressive Liberals and others who would wish to support one or other of the smaller parties of their choice. But by doing so they may help the Conservatives, or they may contribute to a situation in which there is no parliamentary majority for any major issue of policy.

In the interest of the nation and of the world, we earnestly urge all progressives to see to it – as they certainly can – that the next Government is not a Conservative Government but a Labour Government which will act on the principles of policy set out in the present Declaration.

The Tory Manifesto

MR CHURCHILL'S DECLARATION OF POLICY TO THE ELECTORS

I had hoped to preserve the Coalition Government, comprising all Parties in the State, until the end of the Japanese war, but owing to the unwillingness of the Socialist and Sinclair Liberal Parties to agree to my proposal, a General Election became inevitable, and I have formed a new National Government, consisting of the best men of all Parties who were willing to serve and some who are members of no Party at all.

It is a strong Government, containing many of those who helped me to carry the burden of State through the darkest days and on whose counsel and executive ability I have learned to rely.

We seek the good of the whole nation, not that of one section or one faction. We believe in the living unity of the British people, which transcends class or party differences. It was this living unity which enabled us to stand like a rock against Germany when she overran Europe. Upon our power to retain unity, the future of this country and of the whole world largely depends.

Britain is still at war, and must not turn aside from the vast further efforts still needed to bring Japan to the same end as Germany. Even when all foreign enemies are utterly defeated, that will not be the end of our task. It will be the beginning of our further opportunity – the opportunity which we snatched out of the jaws of disaster in 1940 – to save the world from tyranny and then to play our part in its wise, helpful guidance.

Having poured out all we have to beat the Germans, holding nothing back, we must now take stock of our resources and plan how the energies of the British people can best be freed for the work that lies ahead.

This is the time for freeing energies, not stifling them. Britain's greatness has been built on character and daring, not on docility to a State machine. At all costs we must preserve that spirit of independence and the 'Right to live by no man's leave underneath the law'.

Britain and the World

The settlement of Europe and the prosecution of the war against Japan depend on decisions of the utmost gravity, which can only be taken by resolute and experienced men. Our alliance with Soviet Russia and our intimate friendship with the USA can be maintained only if we show that our candour is matched by our strength.

We have, during the years of our history, gained the confidence of the smaller nations, because although our power has been formidable, we have tried to use it with restraint and for high purpose, and have always respected the rights and interests of others. There is no small country which does not welcome our strength. This was plainly shown in the recent events in Greece. The irresponsible attitude towards the interest of the Greek people adopted by many sections of Left Wing opinion is, by its example, a warning not to put the conduct of foreign affairs into untried hands.

The main hope of the world is now founded upon the setting up of a World Organisation strong enough to prevent future wars of aggression whether by the weak or the strong. The United Nations have lately been assembled at San Francisco with the object of devising the necessary machinery. We have taken our full part with other Nations and have acted by natural inclination in full agreement with the United States.

There are still many difficulties to overcome. It would be wrong to pretend that so far full success has been gained. Despair would be a crime. We must persevere by any road that opens towards the uplands on which will certainly be built the calm temples of peace. Our prevailing hope is that the foundations will be laid on the indissoluble agreement of Great Britain, the United States and Soviet Russia.

The British Empire and Commonwealth

We shall base the whole of our international policy on a recognition that in world affairs the Mother Country must act in the closest possible concert with all other parts of the British Commonwealth and Empire. We shall never forget their love and steadfastness when we stood alone against the German Terror. We, too, have done our best for them.

The prowess of the Indian Army must not be overlooked in the framing of plans for granting India a fuller opportunity to achieve Dominion Status. We should remember those friends who stood by us in our hour of peril, and should be ever mindful of our obligations towards minorities and the Indian States.

The arrangements made in war for constant mutual consultation with the Dominions and India on all matters of joint interest must be perfected in peace. In particular, the whole subject of Imperial defence must be reviewed in relation to our world responsibilities and to modern weapons. Mutually convenient arrangements must be made to foster Imperial trade.

Movement of men and women within the Empire must be made easier. A two-way traffic should grow. Those who wish to change their homes should be enabled to carry their national insurance rights with them wherever they go. Imperial ties should be knit together by closer personal contacts and understanding.

Our record in colonial government is unsurpassed. Our responsibility to the Colonies is to lead them towards self-governing institutions; to help them to raise their standards of life by agricultural advance, the application of science and the building up of local industries; to improve conditions of labour and of housing, to spread education, to stamp out disease and to sustain health, vigour and happiness. The policy laid down in the Colonial Development and Welfare Acts must be keenly pressed forward. The resources of the Empire need to be developed by the benefit of all its many peoples.

Defence

During a whole year of this great war Britain bore the burden of the struggle alone. She must not lose her position in world affairs now that the war in Europe is won. She cannot afford to break and squander the splendid organisms of defence, Naval, Army and Air, which she has with so much effort brought into existence. Above all the nucleus and special elements of command and research must be kept in the highest position. The three Services must be duly balanced in order to meet all the needs of new weapons and new times. It will not be possible, until a new Parliament has been assembled, to shape in detail the naval, military and air forces under conditions of what we hope will be a lasting peace. There will, first of all be a prolonged occupation of Germany. We have immediately to relieve many of those who have borne the brunt and long burden of the battle by others who have not, so far, had the honour to go to the front.

I am in agreement with Mr Bevin and other Leaders of the Socialist Party that, until the end of the Japanese War and, I hope, until the World Security Organisation has become a reality, all citizens under a democratic government should bear responsibility for defending their Country and its Cause. By a system of national service according to their various aptitudes, our young men must be trained to play their part if danger calls. Only a Britain that is strong and ready to fight in defence of Freedom will count in the high councils of the world and thus safeguard coming generations against the immeasurable horrors of another war.

Four Years' Plan

More than two years ago I made a broadcast to the nation in which I sketched a four years' plan which would cover five or six large measures of a practical character, which must all have been the subject of prolonged, careful and energetic preparation beforehand, and which fitted together into a general scheme.

This plan has now been shaped, and we present it to the country for their approval. Already a beginning has been made in carrying it out and the Education Act for which our new Minister of Labour is greatly respected is already the law of the land.

Back from the War

We welcome the opportunity of fulfilling all obligations of Service men and women. The financial engagements, the provision of opportunities for training for careers, and above all, the plans for treatment and rehabilitation of the disabled will be our duty and our aim.

The broad and properly considered lines of the demobilisation proposals, based on age and length of service, which Mr Bevin has elaborated with much wisdom, will be adhered to, and release will be made as quickly as the condition of the tormented world permits.

Work

In the White Paper presented to Parliament by the late administration are sound plans for avoiding the disastrous slumps and booms from which we used to suffer, but which all are united in being determined to avoid in the future.

The Government accepts as one of its primary aims and responsibilities the maintenance of a high and stable level of employment.

Unless there is steady and ample work, there will not be the happiness, the confidence, or the material resources in the country on which we can all build together the kind of Britain that we want to see.

To find plenty of work with individual liberty to choose one's job, free enterprise must be given the chance and the encouragement to plan ahead. Confidence in sound government – mutual co-operation between industry and the State, rather than control by the State – a lightening of the burden of excessive taxation – these are the first essentials.

Homes

In the first years of peace, the provision of homes will be the greatest domestic task.

An all-out housing policy will not only make a tremendous contribution to family life, but also to steady employment and to the national health. All our energy must be thrown into it. Local authorities and private enterprise must both be given the fullest encouragement to get on with the job.

Price of materials must be controlled as long as supplies are short. Even so, building costs will be high at first. They must be brought down as rapidly as possible. Subsidies will be necessary for local authorities and for private enterprise alike.

We must add to our building labour force as quickly as we can. The strength of the industry was 1,000,000 men before the war. Now it is down to under 400,000. We have already made our plans to expand it as quickly as possible up to and beyond its pre-war strength.

In blitzed areas the repair of war-damaged houses and the rebuilding of those destroyed will be given high priority. In the first two years, as the labour force grows, we intend to build at least 220,000 permanent new houses and have a further 80,000 under way. We hope to increase this still further, but do not intend to make promises we may not be able to fulfil. As a result of intensive research work that has been carried out by many enterprising firms, a number of new types of factory-made permanent houses and housing equipment is being developed. (The erection of these makes smaller demand on scarce building labour than the traditional types.) These will be put into large-scale production with the same energy as was shown in munitions. We must supplement this with at least 150,000 well-equipped temporary houses that can be put up quickly. Our target is 200,000.

So long as there is a serious shortage of houses, rent control must continue on houses controlled at present. The establishment of Tribunals throughout the country to fix fair rents as between landlord and tenant (as recommended by the Ridley Committee) seems to provide the best solution of a long-standing problem.

The rebuilding of badly bombed areas, the general attack on the housing problem and the redistribution of industry demand plans for the use of land which will take into account the needs of each locality and the opportunities offered by national resources. The Government will press forward with the main lines of policy laid down in the Town and Country Planning Acts, including the acquisition of land required in connection with the restoration of blitzed areas on the basis of the 1939 value.

We shall bring forward in the new Parliament proposals for improving the law with regard to compensation and betterment, so as to secure for the future the best use of land in the public interest, including proper reservation of open spaces and the best location of industry and housing.

Food and Agriculture

We must produce a great deal more food than we did before the war, because food is scarce in the world today, and in any case we shall not be able to buy as much imported food as we did.

A healthy and well-balanced agriculture is an essential element in our national life. British agriculture will be maintained in a condition to enable the efficient producer to obtain a reasonable return on the enterprise and the capital invested, and to enable wages to be paid to the worker sufficient to secure him a proper standard of living.

We must maintain the fertility of the soil; we must be skilful in the use and management of our land for the production of the foodstuffs which it is best fitted to provide, and which are most required to satisfy the nutritional needs of our people.

We need imperial cooperation, leading to international cooperation, in the orderly production and marketing of food; and within this country we shall have improved systems of marketing of home products and such other arrangements as may be necessary to maintain stability and avoid the evils of recurring scarcity and gluts. For this purpose each product will be treated on its own merits.

Our policy will be one of stable markets and prices. In return for this all occupiers and owners of agricultural land must maintain a reasonable standard of good husbandry and estate management.

Within these principles the best results will be obtained by restoring the greatest measure of freedom possible, and allowing full scope for each farmer to make the best use of his land.

The war-time directions and controls will be progressively reduced as our food situation improves and consequently the functions of the County Agricultural Executive Committees will be progressively limited to that of affording leadership, help and advice.

Educational facilities will be developed as fast as the necessary teaching staff and buildings can be made available. The extension of agricultural research will continue. The best scientific advice will be made available to all farmers by the new advisory service.

Provision of smallholdings will be resumed as soon as labour and materials can be spared for men who have gained experience as agricultural workers, and allotments will be encouraged by every reasonable means.

The new Forestry Policy will result in far-reaching and permanent programmes of afforestation. We must take care of our big trees, and make provision for their replacement.

Better housing in country districts is a most urgent need. Large numbers of new cottages in rural areas will be provided, as well as greater facilities for bringing existing cottages and farms up to date. A wide extension of electricity supply, water and sanitation will be undertaken for villages, cottages and farms. No less necessary are better communications, better health services and better social facilities for all those who live and work in the countryside.

A policy on these lines will secure a prosperous agriculture. This in its turn will bring benefits to town and country alike and help to provide our people with good food for a steadily improving diet.

Our fishing industry must be restored with intense exertions and at the utmost speed. In war the fishermen have been out after sterner catches, and once again the nation has been well served in danger by their skill and courage.

We must rebuild the industry and make it a way of life which will give attractive employment to the fine men it breeds. What we want now is fish, and this must be tackled by every conceivable method.

National Insurance

National wellbeing is founded on good employment, good housing and good health. But there always remain those personal hazards of fortune, such as illness, accident or loss of a job, or industrial injury, which may leave the individual and his family unexpectedly in distress. In addition, old age, death and childbirth throw heavy burdens upon the family income.

One of our most important tasks will be to pass into law and bring into action as soon as we can a nationwide and compulsory scheme of National Insurance based on the plan announced by the Government of all Parties in 1944.

In return for a single consolidated contribution there will be new and increased benefits, amongst which is to be an old age or retirement pension of 20 shillings for single people and 35 shillings for married couples. Family allowances are one part of the great scheme, and the arrangements made will ensure that men and women serving in the Forces and those disabled will benefit equally with other classes in the community.

The new Ministry of National Insurance has been set up to prepare, administer and control the whole of this great legislation. So massive and complex a task can only be discharged by a large and highly trained staff, which has to be assembled and accommodated. The specialised experience of the Approved Societies will therefore be drawn upon, and their employees, especially those who have served at the front, must have due consideration.

The scheme will not justify itself to the public unless the service given to them in return for their contributions combines human understanding with efficiency. There must be no queuing up for sickness benefits by those who are entitled to them. The same standard of intimacy in personal relationship must be maintained as formerly.

Health

The health services of the country will be made available to all citizens. Everyone will contribute to the cost, and no one will be denied the attention, the treatment or the appliances he requires because he cannot afford them.

We propose to create a comprehensive health service covering the whole range of medical treatment from the general practitioner to the specialist, and from the hospital to convalescence and rehabilitation; and to introduce legislation for this purpose in the new Parliament.

The success of the service will depend on the skill and initiative of doctors, dentists, nurses and other professional people, and in its designing and operation there will be full scope for all the guidance they can give. Wide play must be given to the preferences and enterprise of individuals. Nothing will be done to destroy the close personal relationship between doctor and patient, nor to restrict the patient's free choice of doctor.

The whole service must be so designed that in each area its growth is helped and guided by the influence of a university. Through such a service the medical and allied professions will be enabled to serve the whole nation more effectively than they have yet been able to do. At the same time Medicine will be left to develop along its own lines, and to achieve preventive as well as curative triumphs. Liberty is an essential condition of scientific progress.

The voluntary hospitals which have led the way in the development of hospital technique will remain free. They will play their part in the new service in friendly partnership with local authority hospitals.

Motherhood must be our special care. There must be a large increase of maternity beds and convalescent homes, and they must be provided in the right places. Mothers must be relieved of onerous duties which at such times so easily cause lasting injury to their health. The National Insurance Scheme will make financial provision for these needs. All proper arrangements, both voluntary and State-aided, must be made for the care of other young children in the family, in order that the energies of the male breadwinner or the kindness of neighbours and relations, which nevertheless must be the mainspring, should not be unduly burdened. Nursery schools and nurseries such as have grown up during the war should be encouraged. On the birth, the proper feeding and the healthy upbringing of a substantially increased number of children, depends the life of Britain and her enduring glory.

Education

The Education Act set forth on the 'Four Years' Plan' has already been piloted through Parliament by Mr Butler. Our task in the coming years will be to remodel our education system according to the new law, and a vigorous drive will be needed to supply the teachers and the buildings necessary.

Our object is to provide education which will not produce a standardised or utility child, useful only as a cog in a nationalised and bureaucratic machine, but will enable the child to develop his or her responsible place, first in the world of school, and then as a citizen. Many parents will be able to choose the school they like and to play their part with the educational authorities in the physical and spiritual wellbeing of their children.

Our aim must be to produce the good citizen of tomorrow. Our primary schools call for much encouragement and improvement. Secondary Education for all will have no meaning unless variety, practical training and, above all, quality of standards convince parents that the extra schooling for their children is worthwhile. Technical education, at all levels, must be greatly extended and improved.

No system of education can be complete unless it heightens what is splendid and glorious in life and art. Art, science and learning are the means by which the life of the whole people can be beautified and enriched.

Overseas Trade

Britain relies upon oversea trade for maintaining her people's standard of living. Industry and employment are bound to depend largely on imported raw materials. Even in wartime we have to draw one-third of our food from abroad. Britain's investment overseas and our shipping, which helped to pay for these imports before the war, have been largely sacrificed. In striving for others we have become a debtor nation.

Therefore it is only by greatly increasing our exports and services that we can buy the imports we require, and thus increase the whole vast volume of our internal trade. The exchange of goods and services with Empire countries is our most fertile and natural market.

We must do all we can in various ways to promote international trade, but of course we cannot give up our right to safeguard our balance of payments by whatever means are necessary: in the end the way to sell enough of our exports, both directly and by roundabout trade, is to take full advantage of the great variety of British industry, the inventiveness of British scientists and technicians, the enterprise and experience of British manufacturers and merchants, and the skill of British workpeople and the renowned trustworthiness of their output.

All possible encouragement will be given to the enterprise of individuals and firms to take advantage of export opportunities of all kinds, and nothing must be done to paralyse the spirit of adventure.

Industrial Efficiency

The more efficient British industry is and the fuller the use it makes of modern methods and materials, the higher will be the standard of wellbeing that is possible for our people. We will stimulate scientific research in industry and in the universities, and encourage the scrapping of obsolete plant and methods in every possible way. Taxation must not bear unduly upon new machinery and enterprise.

All that we long to achieve in making good the wartime shortage depends on attaining the highest possible levels of peacetime production as fast as we can. We shall fail in that if the British people, instead of fixing their eyes on production, are led off at this moment into academic and spiteful controversies about Socialism.

We should examine the conditions and the vital needs of every industry on its own merits. We believe in variety, not in standardised and identical structure, still less in bureaucratic torpor. We will not allow drastic changes

233

of ownership to be forced upon industries on no evidence except a political theory, and with no practical regard to the results they may bring. To us the tests will always be – what will conduce most to efficiency, and what will render the greatest service to the community. This is the policy we shall apply, whether it be coal, cotton or the heavy industries.

As against the advocates of State ownership and control, we stand for the fullest opportunity for go and push in all ranks throughout the whole nation. This quality is part of the genius of the British people, who mean to be free to use their own judgment and never intend to be State serfs, nor always to wait for official orders before they can act.

Monopolies

We must guard against abuses to which monopolies may give rise.

It is vital that there should be effective protection of the consumers' interests and of the independent business, whether small or large, against any such abuse. Nationalisation involves a State monopoly, with no protection for anyone against monopoly power. Neither that nor any other form of unfettered monopoly should be allowed to exist in Britain. The right remedy against harmful restrictive practices is to set up an independent tribunal before which charges of monopoly abuse can be laid. Its work and reports should be public, so that any necessary action in restraint of abuse may be taken by Parliament or otherwise.

Controls

We stand for the removal of controls as quickly as the need for them disappears. Control of labour, or materials and of prices, is necessary in war, when we have to give up much of our freedom in order to make sure that the war machine gets all that it requires. Some of these controls will continue to be needed until normal times return. As long as shortage of food remains, rationing must obviously be accepted: the dangers of inflation also must be guarded against.

As long as any wartime controls have to be retained, they must be made subject to strict Parliamentary scrutiny and sanction. We must watch the interest of the consumer always. Controls, originally imposed on his behalf, tend to bind him down and injure him as soon as circumstances change.

We intend to guard the people of this country against those who, under the guise of war necessity, would like to impose upon Britain for their own purposes a permanent system of bureaucratic control, reeking of totalitarianism.

The Small Man in Business

The small man in trade or industry, who adventures all he has in the effort to make a success of the business he undertakes, must be given every chance to make good. His independence of spirit is one of the essential elements that make up the life of a free society. Many thousands of such men have been hit bitterly hard by war. Other men may have jobs to go back to, but the businesses of some of these men are gone, or hanging by a thread.

It will be a definite point in our policy to make certain that the problems of the small man receive special attention. In particular, the returning Service men or women who obtained their livelihood in this way must be given every possible chance to re-establish themselves.

Fuel and Power

Coal is owned by the State, and is a wasting asset. The industry, taken by and large, as the Reid Report shows, has fallen behind some of its competitors overseas.

The industrial activities of this country are principally founded on coal. Adequate supplies, as cheap as possible, must be available for our homes, for our factories and for export. We cannot afford to lose a coal export trade.

Wartime measures are not suited to peacetime conditions. A new, practical start is needed. The position cannot be remedied by mere change of ownership of the collieries. That offers no solution.

A central authority, appointed by the Minister of Fuel and subject to his general direction, will be set up, to insist that the necessary measures are taken and to provide such help and guidance as is useful.

These measures centre upon the proper development and efficient conduct of operations in each coalfield according to the best modern practice. In so far as grouping or amalgamating collieries is necessary for this object, it will be carried through, voluntarily if possible, but otherwise by compulsion.

At the same time in this diversified industry where conditions vary widely, there are often to be found highly efficient undertakings which are sometimes not large: in such cases amalgamation will only be proposed if there are clear advantages to the nation and the industry; we do not propose amalgamation for amalgamation's sake.

The making and carrying out of these plans will be undertaken by the industry itself. The duty of the central authority will be to satisfy itself that the scope and effect of the plans conform to national requirements, and it will have powers of enforcement in reserve.

This policy will preserve the incentives of free enterprise and safeguard the industry from the dead hand of State ownership or political interference in day to day management. It will also provide the necessary sanctions for making sure that the essential improvements recommended in the Reid Report are carried through.

At the same time, increased efficiency must be stimulated in the use and handling of coal and its principal products, electricity and gas. There is room for much greater co-ordination of the local distribution of these services. Opportunities to increase the nation's resources by harnessing water power also will be scientifically investigated and followed up.

Transport

Transport over land and over sea will have to remain under wartime control for a time. We have still to work our detailed plans to meet the new needs of peace. Road and rail, canals and coast-wise shipping, will be encouraged and helped to bring to a successful conclusion plans already under discussion for a transport system of the highest efficiency, in which each method would play its appropriate part, with freedom for the public to choose which one to use, and with protection against any risk of monopoly charges.

New proposals for Civil Aviation, based broadly on the White Paper of 1945, will be adopted and speedily brought into operation.

This policy will ensure the full development of our Commonwealth and Empire services on the partnership lines already established; there will be co-operation with foreign governments on all overseas services linking our country and theirs; we shall at the same time expand our air services within the United Kingdom, aiming at the most complete network of services in and between England and Wales, Scotland and Northern Ireland.

We shall see to it that air transport undertakings are free to manage the services for which they are responsible and that there shall be ample opportunity for development, and for newcomers to enter the lists in the United Kingdom.

It is of course, our intention that British Air Lines shall use British aircraft and we are satisfied that those aircraft in peace as in war will be second to none.

We must ensure the maintenance of a large, modern and highly efficient Merchant Navy. This country must never forget the debt she owes to her merchant seamen. The men who sailed the convoys to Britain, to Malta, to Russia and all over the world must be sure of steady employment. Ships designed to give them good living conditions, good standards of food, and proper provision for their welfare.

There will shortly be a large world surplus of wartime shipping and we shall enter into international consultations for its orderly disposal and for avoiding competitive subsidies after the war.

Money

Our war budget has been rendered possible only by the severest taxation pressing heavily on everybody, by borrowing on a vast scale to meet the pressing crisis, by huge Lend-Lease supplies from the United States and by generous gifts from Canada and elsewhere. All this cannot go on.

The State has no resources of its own. It can only spend what it takes from the people in taxes or borrowing. Britain is now a nation of taxpayers. Its record of providing more than half of the national expenditure during the last years of the war from taxation is unsurpassed. The willingness of this generation to bear their fair share of sacrifice must, though we hope for relief, be continued. Our future needs for the war against Japan, for winding up the German war, and the plans for social progress which we are determined to carry out, cause and require a much higher rate of national expenditure than before the war.

This burden must be borne by all citizens as taxpayers. There is no easy way of one section getting benefits from the State at the expense of another. The nation can have the services it is prepared to pay for. Where all benefit, all will have to contribute. The revenue is not created by waving a magic wand. It is drawn from the fruits of the nation's industry, agriculture and commerce. It is won by work and paid in taxes. The present level of taxation drastically restricts the ability of the ordinary citizen to satisfy his personal desires. It is discouraging to his enterprise and his efforts to better himself by doing the bit extra, for so large a part of anything he gains to be removed by the tax-collector.

It will be our aim and purpose to make an early reduction in taxation in a way that will stimulate energy and permit individual choice. The Government will re-examine the whole structure of taxation in relation to the level at which expenditure will stand after the war, in order to lighten the burden where it presses most, and simplify the tax system.

We will not permit any monkeying with the people's earnings. Our desire is to see property widely spread, and we rejoice that the savings movement, which must go on, has now made almost everyone a property-owner. An object of our financial policy is to keep prices from rising, and make sure that savers do not see the purchasing-power of their savings dwindle.

On a basis of high employment, initiative and hard work on the part of everyone, we can achieve our great Four Years' programme. It is well worth achieving.

Our Purpose

Ours is a great nation and never in its history has it stood in higher repute in the world than today. Its greatness rests not on its material wealth, for that has been poured out in full measure, nor upon its armed might, which other nations surpass. It has its root in the character, the ability and the independence of our people and the magic of this wonderful island. British virtues have been developed under the free institutions which our fathers and forefathers struggled through the centuries to win and to keep. We of this generation are trustees for posterity, and the duty lies upon us to hand down to our children unimpaired the unique heritage that was bequeathed to us.

This is a country built on family life. War and separation have strengthened, not impaired, the love of home. The children must always come first. The Education Act, school meals, family allowances, all show that Parliament is realising that. Family life is a precious asset to be defended at all costs.

We are dedicated to the purpose of helping to rebuild Britain on the sure foundations on which her greatness rests. In recent generations, enormous material progress has been made. That progress must be extended and accelerated not by subordinating the individual to the authority of the State, but by providing the conditions in which no one shall be precluded by poverty, ignorance, insecurity, or the selfishness of others from making the best of the gifts with which Providence has endowed him.

Our programme is not based upon unproved theories or fine phrases, but upon principles that have been tested anew in the fires of war and not found wanting. We commend it to the country not as offering an easy road to the nation's goal but because, while safeguarding our ancient liberties, it tackles practical problems in a practical way.

The Liberal Party Manifesto

The Liberal Party, having for five years formed part of the All-Party Government which has victoriously guided Britain through the dangers of the European war, now appeals with confidence to the new electorate.

The Liberal Party has no responsibility for forcing an early election and, realising that the existing register is imperfect and will disfranchise many thousands of voters, was prepared to continue the Coalition until a new register was ready in October, and had expressed willingness to discuss its continuation until the end of the Japanese war.

Nevertheless now that the decision has been taken, we welcome the opportunity of submitting our programme to the Nation.

From Victory to Peace

Victory in Europe has been won, but the war against Japan calls for unremitting effort. The Liberal Party has pledged itself to support all measures needed to strengthen the arms and shorten the task of our valiant fighting men in the Far East.

The sacrifice and steadfastness of the people of these Islands, the British Commonwealth and Empire – standing alone for a whole year against the insolent might of Germany and her Allies – have saved the world. But victory must be a beginning, not an end – the beginning of a system by which war must be made impossible and through which differences between nations must be settled by just and peaceful means.

We must strive to preserve the common purpose of the United Nations, who have humbled Germany. In particular, the close comradeship in war between Britain, Russia and America must be preserved, fostered and developed in peace. The new World Organisation coming to birth at San Francisco must be supported and strengthened. Nations, like private citizens, must come to acknowledge the rule of law and of impartial arbitration in their dealings with each other. The tasks of peace, like those of war, are too vast for any one nation to accomplish alone. Much patience and self-control will be called for in harmonising various national interests, but the war has taught with tragic clearness that no people can survive in selfish isolation.

The nations determined to preserve peace must have sufficient forces, especially in the air, to crush ruthlessly and immediately any attempt by an aggressive nation to go to war. We ourselves in this country and the Empire must have adequate strength, provided so long as necessary by a system of universal service and with the most modern equipment, to contribute according to our responsibilities as a World Power.

The British Commonwealth

In pursuing this policy we can look with confidence for the sympathy and support of the great self-governing Dominions. The war has brought them together with us in closer consultation and combined action than ever before. The Liberal principle which inspired the creation of the Commonwealth – that of free and independent nations working together in a common loyalty for a common way of life – must be fostered as an element of stability in the world and a practical example of the way in which security can be combined with national freedom.

The Colonies have proved an invaluable source of strength to us in war. It will be our duty, as well as our advantage, to help their development in peace. Basing our rule on the principle of trusteeship, we must consider first the interest of their peoples and encourage economic development and political self-government in association with the Commonwealth.

It will be the object of the Liberal Party to break the deadlock in India, and to bring about a reconciliation between various elements so that Indians themselves may frame a democratic Constitution for complete self-government for India.

Service Men and Women

Victory in total war has been achieved by the common sacrifice of all, by soldiers, sailors and airmen, also by those working in the fields, factories, ships, mines and offices and by the steadfastness of the women in the home. Nevertheless, our first thought at this time must be for those who have been fighting in the Services – cut off for many years at a time from their families, many of them fighting in distant theatres. They have carried the heaviest burden of all. The Liberal Party recognises its duty to safeguard the interest of the Servicemen, their wives and families, and especially those men who are still fighting against Japan. Our influence has been used and will continue to be used to ensure for them the fairest possible conditions of release and rehabilitation; of training for civil life, of gratuities and pensions and of prospects of employment and housing. We are determined to see that no time is lost in providing homes for men returning from the wars. This is the debt the nation owes to its warriors and it must be paid in full.

Social Security

The Liberal Party is fighting independently of all other parties for a radical programme of practical reform.

Though there are brains and hands and resources enough in the world, properly used, to give healthy self-respecting lives to all, mankind is a prey to Fear – fear of poverty and want through unemployment, sickness, accident and old age. With the Beveridge schemes for Social Security and Full Employment, the Liberal Party leads a frontal attack on this Fear.

Freedom from Want can be achieved by Social Security – a defence against unmerited misfortune from sickness, accident or unemployment and from loss of earning power through old age. Social Security is the economics of the good neighbour, and extends and improves the original measures of health and unemployment insurance passed by a Liberal Government.

Full Employment

Full Employment can be maintained in a Free Society. Where there is work to do and men to do it, unemployment is an intolerable waste of wealth, and it imperils healthy family life – basis of the nation's greatness. Our national resources, labour power, and skill of brains, are our most precious national assets, and Government and private initiative alike must ensure that none of them stands needlessly idle.

242

Housing

There is a house famine in the land, Liberals will not be satisfied until there is a separate dwelling for each family at a reasonable rent. This can be achieved only by a completely new approach, applying to housing the same drive as was used to produce aircraft and munitions of war. The responsibility should be placed on a Minister of Housing and no vested interests can be allowed to stand in the way. Local authorities must be enabled to borrow at a low rate of interest, and in no part of the country be allowed to ignore their obligations. Other agencies who are ready and able to provide houses should be encouraged.

We must control the cost of building materials so as to keep down the prices and rents of the houses we build.

In the countryside the problem is no less urgent than in the towns. Farm workers and fishermen must also share the benefits of good houses equipped with water, power and sanitation. The next Parliament must drive forward the new housing programme by every available means.

The Land

Great Britain is a small country with a vast population. It is therefore essential that the best use should be made of its land.

The full development of our national resources; the protection from disfigurement of the countryside; the balanced location of industry, and a successful housing policy all depend upon comprehensive measures of Town and Country planning.

Development rights outside built-up areas should immediately be acquired for the public and there should be a periodic levy on all increases in site values. Every increase in values due to community action should be secured for the community.

The fullest use must be made of agricultural land for food production. The State should, subject to the owner's right of appeal to an impartial tribunal, have the right to take over all land which is badly managed or badly farmed, and any other land which in the interests of good cultivation and of the population on the land should be in its control.

Farming and Fishing

The Liberal Party means to maintain a prosperous and efficient agriculture. The threat of famine in Europe, and our own reduced capacity to pay for imports, mean that more food must be produced at home than before the war. To do this, farmers must have assurance of stable prices, and the advantage of bulk purchase, and cheap transport. Capital must be available on easy terms for drainage, improvements and modern equipment, and science research must be freely at the disposal of the farming community.

Farmers should be free to cultivate their land according to their own judgement and at their own risk, subject only to the maintenance of reasonable standards of farming and meeting the food requirements of the nation.

A prosperous free agriculture demands also the location of light industries in country districts, providing alternative employment and bringing greater purchasing power to the rural population. The distribution of industry is of the first importance to the health, happiness and well-being of our people.

Those who have fought for the country must have the opportunity to live on the land and cultivate it. Land Settlement must therefore be encouraged.

The Ministry of Food must remain to ensure the fair distribution of available supplies to consumers, and to offer long-term contracts assuring farmers of fair prices and guaranteed markets over a period of years.

The wages and housing of farm workers must be comparable with those of skilled workers in other industries.

The need for maximum production of food calls for a flourishing fishing industry, Government assistance will be needed in replacing boats and gear and in providing adequate curing and refrigeration facilities at ports so that fish so badly needed on our tables shall not be thrown back into the sea.

Health

People cannot be happy unless they are healthy. The Liberal aim is a social policy which will help to conquer disease by prevention as well as cure, through good housing, improved nutrition, the lifting of strains and worries caused by fear of unemployment, and through intensified medical research. The Liberal Party's detailed proposals for improved health services would leave patients free to choose their doctor, for the general practitioner is an invaluable asset in our social life.

Education

Liberals supported the recent Education Act, and will do all they can to bring it quickly into operation. Our place in the world will depend on the character of our people and on minds trained to understand and operate the complex technical achievements of the modern world. We cannot afford to neglect talent which lies unused because of poverty of parents. The quality of our teachers must be maintained, but their numbers must be increased so that the school-leaving age can be raised and the size of classes reduced. Day nurseries should be increased and the nursery school system greatly expanded. Playing fields and opportunities for organised games should be normally provided in all schools.

Industry

British Industry will face new and complex problems after the war. If we are to succeed we must sell the goods which the world wants at the price which the world will pay. We can do this only by achieving justice for the three partners in industry – the Manager, the Worker and the Investor.

Of first importance are the status and remuneration of the worker. He has for too long been regarded as a 'hand'. He must become a partner and acquire economic citizenship, through Works Councils set up by law, and through Joint Industrial Councils in every Trade Board Industry. Profit-sharing should be encouraged, and information on the conduct and finance of business should be readily available to assure workers that wages fixed and profit-sharing schemes in operation are fair and just.

Liberals believe the controversy for and against nationalisation is out of date. They approach industrial problems without economic prejudice, and since they represent no vested interest of employers or employed, they alone can plan in the interests of the whole community. They believe in private enterprise and the value of individual effort, experiment, and willingness to take risks. Hence their support of the small trader and their desire to diffuse ownership as widely as possible. Hence also their opposition to cartels and price fixing rings which, often abusing the name of private enterprise, create conditions of monopoly and hold the community to ransom.

But where public ownership is more economic, Liberals will demand it without hesitation. Where there is no further expansion or useful competition in an industry or where an industry or group of industries has become a private monopoly, Liberals say it should become a public utility. Liberals believe in the need for both private enterprise and large scale organisation under government control, and their tests for deciding which form is necessary are the service of the public, the efficiency of production and the well-being of those concerned in the industry in question.

Transport and Power

Railways, with the large part of road transport controlled by them, are clearly in effect a monopoly, and should be treated as a Public Utility on a national plan. Electric power should also be organised as a public utility.

British Civil Aviation must be rapidly expanded both to make consultation and intercourse between all parts of the Commonwealth and Empire swift and easy and to serve the common interest of mankind.

Coal

Coal is our principal mineral wealth, and most of our industry is based on its use. This fact, and the variety and immense potential value of by-products from coal, demand in the interest of the national economy that the Coal Industry shall not be treated merely as a private profit-making concern. It must be regarded not as one industry among many, but as the key to the health of our basic industries and our export trade. Compared with other countries, the British coal-mining industry is inefficient and is losing ground. Since it is apparent that the necessary increase of efficiency cannot be brought about with present organisation, the industry should be a public service, in which the miners can feel that they are working for the benefit of the whole community. But the terms on which the coal-mining industry is made into a public service must be such as to ensure three things:

Decentralisation of operation and freedom to experiment in different coal undertakings.

That the industry pays its way without subsidies from the general tax-payer.

That coal is not made too dear either to industrial or to domestic consumers.

Freedom of Trade

Freedom and expansion of trade are the necessary basis of world prosperity. We can secure the imports needed to maintain our standard of life only by selling our exports in the markets of the world. We should therefore press on vigorously within the conclusion of agreements with America and other countries for the progressive elimination of tariffs, quotas, exchange restrictions and other barriers to trade, on the lines of Article V11 of the Mutual Aid Agreement between Britain and the United States, which implements the Atlantic Charter.

The traditional policy of the Conservative Party to build up a system of economic isolationism within the Empire is inconsistent with world co-operation, and with our obligations under Article V11 of the Lend-Lease Agreement. This policy would not commend itself to the great Dominions; it would be inadequate to maintain the volume of trade needed by Britain, and it would provoke dangerous economic strife.

Taxation

Under the impact of war, ordinary methods of control over expenditure have necessarily been relaxed. The time has now come for strict supervision of national expenditure in order to eliminate waste and to secure a progressive reduction in the burden of taxation, both direct and indirect. In particular, it will be our aim to remove taxes on the prime necessities of life.

The system of taxation must be designed to encourage the re-equipment and modernisation of British industry.

Controls

This war has forced us all to accept many controls which cannot be suddenly relaxed without incurring the dangers of soaring prices and inflation. While Liberals realise this, they are determined that no control shall remain longer than is absolutely necessary for the welfare of the country and the full employment of its people.

247

The Work and Position of Women

The family is the basis of our national life. Liberals were the first to demand family allowances and are determined to secure adequate provision for motherhood and child welfare. They are also determined that the benefits of modern scientific and mechanical development shall be used to eliminate needless drudgery in the home.

In public life, the Liberal Party demands for women equality of opportunity and status; it stands for equal pay for equal work, and for equal opportunity of entry into the public services.

Scotland and Wales

The Liberal Party recognises the desire of the people of Scotland and Wales to assume greater responsibility in the management of their domestic affairs, and has long been in favour of suitable measures of Devolution.

The drift of population from those countries to congested cities in England is unhealthy and should be reversed, by measures for a more balanced distribution of industry throughout these islands and by the full development of the agricultural, fishing, industrial and power resources of Scotland and Wales.

A Better Parliament

Our present system of voting produces Parliaments which are not representative of the people's will. A party with a minority of votes can secure a majority in the House of Commons. Liberals hold that Members of Parliament should be chosen in such a way as to represent fairly the number of votes cast. They would therefore reform the voting system so as to give electors the opportunity of expressing an additional choice or choices, as well as a first choice, when there are more than two candidates for a seat.

In addition, Liberals consider that it is in the interests of democracy that the scales of the electoral system should not be weighed in favour of wealthy candidates, and that Members of Parliament should be chosen for their opinions and qualities, not for their interests. Accordingly, the Liberal Party favours placing the essential costs of elections on the State, subject to suitable safeguards against frivolous candidatures.

The Liberty of the Subject

It is always the task of Liberals to exercise that eternal vigilance which is the price of freedom. Before the war our Members of Parliament challenged every encroachment upon the liberty of the subject. When we joined the Coalition in 1940, Sir Archibald Sinclair obtained a promise from the Prime Minister that it was the Government's intention to preserve in all essentials a free Parliament and a free press and that the Emergency Powers (such as preventive arrest under Regulation 18b and the powers to suppress newspapers) would disappear with the passing of the emergency.

In the next Parliament, whether in or out of office, we shall continue to do our utmost to safeguard and enlarge civil liberties. Power must exist in any modern State. But it need not be arbitrary power. In this country the citizen has two essential safeguards against injustice and oppression, namely: democratic control, through Parliament and elected local authorities, over all those official positions, and the right to appeal to the ordinary Courts of Law whenever a Minister or an official exceeds his authority. Both these safeguards we shall strenuously maintain.

To Sum Up

The Liberal Party submits to the nation the vision of a healthier society in which our people may live full, happy and useful lives and bring up their families in decent homes without the fear of war or of unemployment. At the same time its programme is also a call to hard, strenuous work on the part of all, Government and citizens alike. But the war has shown Britain capable of the task. It has revealed a mighty nation, renewed in its youth, with vast stores of energy and enterprise. It has the skill, the confidence and the determination; what is now needed is a Government wise enough and courageous enough to set the pace of advance.

The People's Choice

MEMBERS OF THE NEW PARLIAMENT

Name	Constituency	Party
Adams, Capt. H. R.	Wandsworth, Balham and Tooting	Lab
Adams, W. T.	Hammersmith South	Lab
Adamson, Mrs J. L.	Bexley	Lab
Agnew, Cdr P. G.	Camborne, Cornwall	Cons
Aitken, Grp-Capt. M.	Holborn	Cons
Alexander, A. V.	Sheffield Hillsborough	Lab
Allen, A. C.	Leicester Bosworth	Lab
Allen, S. S.	Crewe, Cheshire	Lab
Allen, Sir W.	Armagh	Ulster U
Allighan, G.	Gravesend, Kent	Lab
Alpass, J. H.	Thornbury, Glos	Lab
Amory, Lt-Col D. H.	Tiverton, Devon	Cons
Anderson, A.	Motherwell, Lanark	Lab
Anderson, F.	Whitehaven, Cumberland	Lab
Anderson, Sir J.	Scottish Universities	Nat
Astor, Capt. M.	Eastern Surrey	Cons
Attewell, H. C.	Harborough, Leics	Lab
Attlee, C. R.	Stepney, Limehouse	Lab
Austin, Sub-Lt H. L.	Stretford, Lancs	Lab
Awbery, S.	Bristol Central	Lab
Ayles, W. H.	Southall, Middx	Lab

Bacon, Miss A.	Leeds North-East	Lab
Baird, Capt. J.	Wolverhampton East	Lab
Baldwin, A. E.	Leominster, Hereford	Cons
Balfour, A.	Stirling and Clackmannan Western	Lab
Barlow, Sir J.	Eddisbury, Cheshire	Lib Nat
Barnes, A. J.	East Ham South	Lab
Barstow, P. G.	Pontefract, West Riding	Lab
Bartlett, V.	Bridgewater, Somerset	Ind
Barton, C.	Wembley South	Lab
Battley, J. R.	Wandsworth Clapham	Lab
Baxter, A. B.	Wood Green, Middx	Cons
Beamish, Maj. T. V. H.	Lewes, East Sussex	Cons
Beattie, F.	Glasgow Cathcart	Cons
Beattie, John	Belfast West	Irish Lab
Beaumont, H.	Batley and Morley	Lab
Bechervaise, A. E.	Leyton East	Lab
Beechman, A.	St Ives, Cornwall	Lib Nat
Belcher, J. W.	Sowerby, West Riding	Lab
Bellenger, F. J.	Nottingham Bassetlaw	Lab
Bennett, Sir P.	Birmingham Edgbaston	Cons
Benson, G.	Chesterfield, Derby	Lab
Berry, H.	Woolwich West	Lab
Beswick, Flt Lt F.	Uxbridge, Middlesex	Lab
Bevan, A.	Ebbw Vale, Monmouth	Lab
Bevin, E.	Wandsworth Central	Lab
Bing, Capt. G.H. C.	Hornchurch, Essex	Lab
Binns, J.	Rochester Gillingham	Lab
Birch, Lt-Col N.	Flint, Denbighshire	Cons
Blackburn, Capt. A. R.	Birmingham Kings Norton	Lab
Blenkinsop, Lt A.	Newcastle upon Tyne East	Lab
Blyton, W. R.	Houghton-le-Spring, Durham	Lab
Boardman, H.	Leigh	Lab
Boles, Lt-Col D. C.	Wells, Somerset	Cons
Boothby, R.	Aberdeen and Kincardine Eastern	Cons
Bossom, A. C.	Maidstone, Kent	Cons

Bottomley, A. G.	Rochester Chatham	Lab
Bowden, Flg O H. W.	Leicester South	Lab
Bowen, Capt. R.	Cardigan, Carmarthen	Lib
Bower, N.	Harrow West, Middx	Cons
Bowles, F. G.	Nuneaton, Warwickshire	Lab
Boyd-Carpenter, Maj. J. A.	Kingston-upon-Thames	Cons
Braddock, Mrs E.	Liverpool Exchange	Lab
Braddock, T.	Mitcham	Lab
Braithwaite, Lt-Cdr J. G.	Holderness, East Riding	Cons
Broadbridge, Sir G.	City of London	Cons
Bromley-Davenport, Lt-Col W.	Knutsford, Cheshire	Cons
Brook, D.	Halifax	Lab
Brooks, T. J.	Rothwell, West Riding	Lab
Brown, Col D. Clifton	Hexham, Northumberland	Cons
Brown, G. A.	Belper, Derbyshire	Lab
Brown, Lt-Col G. B.	Bury St Edmunds, Suffolk	Cons
Brown, T. J.	Ince, Lancs	Lab
Brown, W. J.	Rugby, Warwickshire	Ind
Bruce, Maj. D. W. T.	Portsmouth North	Lab
Buchanan, G.	Glasgow Gorbals	Lab
Buchan-Hepburn, P. E. G.	Liverpool East Toxteth	Cons
Bullock, Capt. M.	Waterloo,Lancs	Cons
Burden, T. W.	Sheffield Park	Lab
Burke, W. A.	Burnley	Lab
Butcher, H. W.	Holland-with-Boston, Lincoln	
	and Rutland	Lib Nat
Butler, H. W.	Hackney South	Lab
Butler, R. A.	Saffron Walden, Essex	Cons
Byers, Lt-Col F.	Northern Dorset	Lib
Callaghan, Lt J. A.	Cardiff South	Lab
Campbell, Sir E. T.	Bromley	Cons
Carson, Lt E.	Isle of Thanet, Kent	Cons
Castle, Mrs B. A.	Blackburn	Lab
Challen, Flt Lt C.	Hampstead	Cons

Chamberlain, R.	Lambeth Norwood	Lab
Champion, A. J.	Derby Southern	Lab
Channon, H.	Southend-on-Sea	Cons
Chater, D.	Bethnal Green North-East	Lab
Chetwynd, Capt. G. R.	Stockton-on-Tees	Lab
Churchill, W. S.	Woodford, Essex	Cons
Clarke, Col. R. S.	East Grinstead, East Sussex	Cons
Clitherow, R.	Liverpool Edge Hill	Lab
Cluse, W. S.	Islington South	Lab
Cobb, F. A.	Ellands, West Riding	Lab
Cocks, F. S.	Broxtowe, Notts	Lab
Coldrick, W.	Bristol North	Lab
Cole, T. L.	Belfast East	Ulster U
Collick, P.	Birkenhead West	Lab
Collindridge, F.	Barnsley	Lab
Collins, V. J.	Taunton, Somerset	Lab
Coleman, Miss G. M.	Tynemouth	Lab
Comyns, Dr L.	West Ham Silvertown	Lab
Conant, Maj. R. J. E.	Bewdley, Worcestershire	Cons
Cook, T. F.	Dundee	Lab
Cooper, Wg Cdr G.	Middlesbrough West	Lab
Cooper-Key, Maj. E. M.	Hastings	Cons
Corbet, Mrs F.	Camberwell North-West	Lab
Corbett, Lt-Col U.	Ludlow, Shropshire	Cons
Corlett, Dr J.	York	Lab
Corvedale, Maj. Viscount	Paisley	Lab
Cove, W. G.	Aberavon, Glamorgan	Lab
Crawley, Flt Lt A.	Buckingham, Bucks	Lab
Cripps, Sir S.	Bristol East	Lab
Crookshank, Capt. H. F.	Gainsborough, Lincoln and Rutland	Cons
Crossman, R. H. S.	Coventry East	Lab
Crosthwaite-Eyre, Col O. E.	New Forest and Christchurch, Hants	Cons
Crowder, Capt. J. F. E.	Finchley, Middx	Cons

Cunningham, P.	Fermanagh and Tyrone	Irish Nat
Cuthbert, W. N.	Rye, East Sussex	Cons
Daggar G.	Abertillery, Monmoth	Lab
Daines, P.	East Ham North	Lab
Dalton, H.	Bishop Auckland, Durham	Lab
Darling, Sir W.	Edinburgh South	Cons
Davidson, Viscountess	Hemel Hempstead, Herts	Cons
Davies, A. E.	Burslem, Stoke-on-Trent	Lab
Davies, C.	Montgomery	Lib
Davies, E.	Enfield, Middx	Lab
Davies, Harold	Leek, Staffs	Lab
Davies, Haydn	St Pancras South-West	Lab
Davies, R. J.	Westhoughton, Lancs	Lab
Davies, S. O.	Merthyr Tydfil	Lab
Davison, Sir W.	Kensington South	Cons
Deer, G.	Lincoln	Lab
De Freitas, Sqdn Ldr G.	Nottingham Central	Lab
De La Bere, R.	Evesham, Worcs	Cons
Delargy, Capt. H. J.	Manchester Platting	Lab
Diamond, J.	Manchester Blackley	Lab
Digby, Maj. S.	Dorset Western	Cons
Dobbie, W.	Rotherham	Lab
Dobbs, A. J.	Smethwick	Lab
Dodds, N.	Dartford	Lab
Dodds-Parker, Col A. D.	Banbury, Oxon	Cons
Donner, Sqdn Ldr P. W.	Basingstoke, Hants	Cons
Donovan, T.	Leicester East	Lab
Douglas, F. C. R.	Battersea North	Lab
Dower, Lt-Col A. V. G.	Penrith and Cockermouth, Cumberland	Cons
Dower, E. L. G.	Caithness and Sutherland	Cons
Drayson, Capt. G. B.	Skipton, East Riding	Cons
Drewe, C.	Honiton, Devon	Cons
Driberg, T.	Maldon, Essex	Lab

Dugdale, J.	West Bromwich	Lab
Dugdale. Sir T. L.	Richmond, Yorkshire	Cons
Dumpleton, C. W.	St Albans, Herts	Lab
Duncan, Sir A.	City of London	Nat
Duncan, Col. A. G.	Perth	Cons
Durbin, E. F. M.	Edmonton, Middx	Lab
Duthie, W. S.	Banff	Cons
Dye, S.	Norfolk South-Western	Lab
Eccles, D. M.	Chippenham, Wilts	Cons
Ede, J. C.	South Shields	Lab
Edelman, M.	Coventry West	Lab
Eden, A.	Warwick and Leamington	Cons
Edwards, A.	Middlesbrough East	Lab
Edwards, Sir C.	Bedwellty, Monmouth	Lab
Edwards, L. J.	Blackburn	Lab
Edwards, Ness	Caerphilly, Glamorgan	Lab
Edwards, W. J.	Stepney Whitechapel	Lab
Elliot, Capt. W. S.	Accrington	Lab
Erroll, Col F. J.	Altrincham and Sale	Cons
Evans, E.	Lowestoft, Suffolk	Lab
Evans, S. N.	Wednesbury	Lab
Ewart, R.	Sunderland	Lab
Fairhurst, F.	Oldham	Lab
Farthing, W. J.	Frome, Somerset	Lab
Fleming, Sqdn Ldr E. L.	Manchester Withington	Cons
Fletcher, E. G.	Islington East	Lab
Fletcher, W.	Bury	Cons
Follick, M.	Loughborough, Leics	Lab
Foot, M.	Plymouth Devonport	Lab
Forman, J. C.	Glasgow Springburn	Lab
Foster, Brig. J. G.	Northwich, Cheshire	Cons
Foster, W.	Wigan	Lab
Fox, Sir G.	Henley, Oxon	Cons

Frazer, Maj. H. C. F.	Stone, Staffs	Cons
Frazer, Sir I.	Londsdale, Lancs	Cons
Frazer, T.	Hamilton, Lanark	Lab
Freeman, Maj. J.	Watford, Herts	Lab
Freeman, P.	Newport	Lab
Fyffe, Sir D. Maxwell	Liverpool, West Derby	Cons
Gage, Lt-Col	Belfast South	Ulster U
Gaitskell, H. T. N.	Leeds South	Lab
Galbraith, Cdr T. D.	Glasgow Pollok	Cons
Gallacher, W.	Fife West	Comm
Gammans, Capt. L. D.	Hornsey	Cons
Ganley, Mrs C. S.	Battersea South	Lab
Gates, Maj. E. E.	Middleton and Prestwich, Lancs	Cons
Gibbins, J.	Liverpool West Toxteth	Lab
Gibson, C. W.	Lambeth Kennington	Lab
Gilzean, A.	Edinburgh Central	Lab
Glanville, J. E.	Consett, Durham	Lab
Glossop, C. W. H.	Howdenshire, East Riding	Cons
Glyn, Sir R.	Abingdon, Berks	Cons
Gooch, E. G.	Northern Norfolk	Lab
Goodrich, H. E.	Hackney North	Lab
Gould, Mrs B. Ayrton	Hendon North	Lab
Graham-Little, Sir E.	London University	Ind
Granville, E.	Eye, East Suffolk	Lib
Greenwood, A.	Wakefield	Lab
Grenfell, D. R.	Gower, Glamorgan	Lab
Grey, C. F.	Durham	Lab
Gridley, Sir A.	Stockport	Cons
Grierson, E.	Carlisle	Lab
Griffiths, D.	Rother Valley, West Riding	Lab
Griffiths, G.	Hemsworth, West Riding	Lab
Griffiths, J.	Llanelly, Carmarthen	Lab
Griffiths, Capt. W. D.	Manchester Moss Side	Lab
Grimston, R. V.	Westbury, Wilts	Cons

Gruffyd, Prof. W. J.	University of Wales	Lib
Guest, Dr L. Hayden	Islington North	Lab
Gunter, Capt. R. J.	Essex South-Eastern	Lab
Guy, W. H.	Poplar South	Lab
Haire, Flt Lt J.	Wycombe, Bucks	Lab
Hale, C. L.	Oldham	Lab
Hall, G. H.	Aberdare, Merthyr Tydfil	Lab
Hall, W. G.	Colne Valley, West Riding	Lab
Hamilton, Lt-Col R.	Sudbury, West Suffolk	Lab
Hannan, W.	Glasgow Maryhill	Lab
Hannon, Sir P.	Birmingham Moseley	Cons
Hardman, D. R.	Darlington	Lab
Hardy, E. A.	Salford South	Lab
Hare, Lt-Col J.	Woodbridge, East Suffolk	Cons
Harris, H. Wilson	Cambridge University	Ind
Harrison, J.	Nottingham East	Lab
Harvey, Air Cdre A. V.	Macclesfield, Cheshire	Cons
Hastings, Dr Somerville	Barking	Lab
Haughton, Maj. S. G.	Antrim	Ulster U
Hayworth, J.	Liverpool Walton	Lab
Head, Brig. A. H.	Carshalton, Surrey	Cons
Headlam, Sir C.	Newcastle upon Tyne North	Cons
Henderson, Maj. A.	Kingswinford, Staffs	Lab
Henderson, Joseph	Manchester Hardwick	Lab
Herbert, Sir A. P.	Oxford University	Ind
Herbison, Miss M.	Lanark Northern	Lab
Hewitson, Capt. M.	Hull Central	Lab
Hicks, G.	Woolwich East	Lab
Hinchingbrooke, Viscount	Southern Dorset	Cons
Hobson, C. R.	Wembley North	Lab
Hogg, Quintin	Oxford	Cons
Hollis, Sqdn Ldr M. C.	Devizes, Wilts	Cons
Holman, P.	Bethnal Green South-West	Lab
Holmes, Sir J. Stanley	Harwich, Essex	Lib Nat

Holt, Lt-Cdr J. L.	Shrewsbury, Shropshire	Cons
Hope, Lt-Col Lord J.	Midlothian and Peebles	Cons
Horabin, T. L.	Cornwall Northern	Lib
House, G.	St Pancras North	Lab
Howard, A.	Westminster St George	Cons
Hoy, J.	Leith	Lab
Hubbard, T.	Kirkcaldy	Lab
Hudson, J. H.	Ealing West, Middx	Lab
Hudson, R. S.	Southport	Cons
Hughes, H.	Aberdeen North	Lab
Hughes, Lt H. D.	Wolverhampton West	Lab
Hulbert, Wg Cdr N. J.	Stockport	Cons
Hurd, A.	Newbury, Berks	Cons
Hutchinson, H. L.	Manchester Rusholme	Lab
Hutchison, Lt-Cdr G. I.	Edinburgh West	Cons
Hutchison, Lt-Col J. R. H.	Glasgow Central	Cons
Hynd, H.	Hackney Central	Lab
Hynd, J. B.	Sheffield Attercliffe	Lab
Isaacs, G. A.	Southwark North	Lab
Janner, B.	Leicester West	Lab
Jarvis, Sir J.	Guildford, Surrey	Cons
Jeffreys, Sir G.	Petersfield, Hants	Cons
Jeger, Capt. G.	Winchester, Hants	Lab
Jeger, Dr S. W.	St Pancras South-East	Lab
Jenkins, A.	Pontypool, Monmouth	Lab
Jennings, R.	Sheffield Hallam	Cons
John, W.	Rhondda West	Lab
Jones, A. Creech	Shipley, Yorks West Riding	Lab
Jones, D. T.	Hartlepool	Lab
Jones, Maj. F. E.	West Ham Plaistow	Lab
Jones, J. H.	Bolton	Lab
Jones, Maj. P. A.	Hitchin, Herts	Lab
Jowitt, Sir W.	Ashton-under-Lyne	Lab

Joynson-Hicks, Lt-Cdr L. W.	Chichester, Sussex	Cons
Keeling, E. H.	Twickenham	Cons
Keenan, W.	Liverpool Kirkdale	Lab
Kendall, W. D.	Grantham, Lincoln and Rutland	Ind
Kenyon, C.	Chorley, Lancs	Lab
Kerr, Sir J. Graham	Scottish Universities	Cons
Key, C. W.	Poplar, Bow and Bromley	Lab
King, Lt-Col E. M.	Penryn and Falmouth, Cornwall	Lab
Kinghorn, Sqdn Ldr E.	Great Yarmouth	Lab
Kingsmill, Lt-Col W. H.	Yeovil, Somerset	Cons
Kinley, J.	Bootle	Lab
Kirby, Capt. B. V.	Liverpool Everton	Lab
Kirkwood, D.	Dumbarton	Lab
Lambert, Lt-Col G.	South Molton, Devon	Nat Lib
Lancaster, Lt-Col C. G.	Fylde, Lancs	Cons
Lang, Rev. G.	Stalybridge and Hyde, Cheshire	Lab
Lavers, S.	Barnard Castle, Durham	Lab
Lawson, J. J.	Chester-le-Street, Durham	Lab
Lee, F.	Manchester Hulme	Lab
Lee, Miss J.	Cannock, Staffs	Lab
Legge-Bourke, Maj. E. A.	Isle of Ely	Cons
Lennox-Boyd, A. T.	Mid Bedfordshire	Cons
Leonard, W.	Glasgow St Rollox	Lab
Leslie, J. R.	Sedgefield, Durham	Lab
Lever, F. O. N. H.	Manchester Exchange	Lab
Levy, Lt B. W.	Eton and Slough, Bucks	Lab
Lewis, A. W. J.	West Ham Upton	Lab
Lewis, J.	Bolton	Lab
Lewis, T.	Southampton	Lab
Lindgreen, G. S.	Wellingborough, Northants	Lab
Lindsay, K.	Combined Universities	Ind
Lindsay, Lt-Col M.	Solihull, Warickshire	Cons
Linstead, H. N.	Wandsworth Putney	Cons

Lipson, D. L.	Cheltenham	Ind Cons
Lipton, Lt-Col M.	Lambeth Brixton	Lab
Little, Rev. Dr J.	Down, N. Ireland	Ind Ulster U
Lloyd, Maj. E. G. R.	Renfrew Eastern	Cons
Lloyd, Brig. J. S. B.	Wirral, Cheshire	Cons
Lloyd-George, Maj. G.	Pembroke	Lib
Lloyd-George, Lady M.	Anglesey	Lib
Logan, D. G.	Liverpool Scotland	Lab
Longden, F.	Birmingham Deritend	Lab
Low, Brig. A. R. W.	Blackpool North	Cons
Lucas, Sir J.	Portsmouth South	Cons
Lucas-Tooth, Sir H.	Hendon South	Cons
Lyle, Sir L.	Bournemouth	Cons
Lyne, W.	Burton, Staffs	Lab
Lyttelton, O.	Aldershot, Hants	Cons
McAdam, W.	Salford North	Lab
McAllister, G.	Rutherglen, Lanark	Lab
MacAndrew, Sir C.	Ayr and Bute	Cons
McCallum, Maj. D.	Argyll	Cons
Macdonald, Sir M.	Inverness	Lib Nat
Macdonald, Sir P.	Isle of Wight	Cons
McEntee, V. L.	Walthamstow West	Lab
McGhee, H. G.	Penistone, West Riding	Lab
McGovern, J.	Glasgow Shettleston	Ind Lab
Mack, J. D.	Newcastle under Lyme	Lab
McKay, J.	Wallsend	Lab
Mackay, R. W. G.	Hull North-West	Lab
Mackeson, Brig. H. R.	Hythe	Cons
McKie, J. H.	Galloway	Ind Cons
McKinlay, A. S.	Dumbartonshire	Lab
Macklay, J. S.	Montrose	Lib Nat
Maclean, Brig. F. H. R.	Lancaster, Lancs	Cons
Maclean, N.	Glasgow Govan	Lab
McLeavy, F.	Bradford East	Lab

MacLeod, Capt. J.	Ross and Cromarty	Lib Nat
Macmillan, M. K.	Western Isles	Lab
McNeil, H.	Greenock	Lab
Macpherson, Maj. N.	Dumfries	Lib Nat
Macpherson, T.	Romford	Lab
Mainwaring, W. H.	Rhondda West	Lab
Maitland, Cdr J. W.	Horncastle, Lincoln and Rutland	Cons
Mallalieu, Lt J. P. W.	Huddersfield	Lab
Mann, Mrs J.	Coatbridge, Lanark	Lab
Manning, C.	Camberwell North	Lab
Manning, Mrs L.	Epping, Essex	Lab
Manning-Buller, R. E.	Daventry, Northants	Cons
Marlowe, Lt-Col A.	Brighton	Cons
Marples, Capt. A. E.	Wallasey	Cons
Marquand, Prof. H. A.	Cardiff East	Lab
Marsden, Capt. A.	Chertsey, Surrey	Cons
Marshall, Cdr D.	Bodmin, Cornwall	Cons
Marshall, F.	Sheffield Brightside	Lab
Marshall, S. H.	Sutton and Cheam	Cons
Martin, J. H.	Southwark Central	Lab
Mason-Macfarlane, Sir F.	Paddington North	Lab
Mathers, G.	Linlithgow	Lab
Maude, C.	Exeter	Cons
Maxton, J.	Glasgow Bridgeton	Ind Lab
Mayhew, Maj. C. P.	Southern Norfolk	Lab
Medland, H. M.	Plymouth Drake	Lab
Medlicott, Brig. F.	Eastern Norfolk	Lib Nat
Mellor, Sir J.	Sutton Coldfield, Warwickshire	Cons
Messer, F.	Tottenham South	Lab
Middleton, Mrs L.	Plymouth Sutton	Lab
Mikardo, I.	Reading	Lab
Millington, Wg Cdr E. R.	Chelmsford, Essex	C Wealth
Milner, Maj. J.	Leeds South East	Lab
Mitchison Maj. G. R.	Kettering, Northants	Lab
Molson, A. H. E.	High Peak, Derbyshire	Cons

Monslow, W.	Barrow-in-Furness	Lab
Montague, F.	Islington West	Lab
Moody, A. S.	Liverpool Fairfield	Lab
Moore, Sir T.	Ayr	Cons
Morgan, Dr H. B.	Rochdale	Lab
Morley, R.	Southampton	Lab
Morris, Lt-Col H.	Sheffield Central	Lab
Morris, P.	Swansea West	Lab
Morris, R. H.	Carmarthen	Lib
Morris-Jones, Sir H.	Denbigh	Lib Nat
Morrison, H.	Lewisham East	Lab
Morrison, Maj. J. G.	Salisbury, Wilts	Cons
Morrison, R. C.	Tottenham North	Lab
Morrison, W. S.	Cirencester and Tewkesbury	Cons
Mort, D. L.	Swansea East	Lab
Mott-Radclyffe, Maj. C.	Windsor, Berks	Cons
Moyle, A.	Stourbridge, Worcs	Lab
Mulvey, A.	Fermanagh and Tyrone	Irish Nat
Murray, J. D.	Spennymoor, Durham	Lab
Nally, W.	Wolverhampton Bilston	Lab
Naylor, T. E.	Southwark South-East	Lab
Neal, H.	Clay Cross, Derbyshire	Lab
Neill, W. F.	Belfast North	Ulster U
Neven-Spence, Sir B.	Orkney and Shetland	Cons
Nichol, Mrs M. W.	Bradford North	Lab
Nicholls, H. R.	West Ham Stratford	Lab
Nicholson, G.	Farnham, Surrey	Cons
Nield, Maj. B.	Chester	Cons
Noble, Cdr A. H. P.	Chelsea	Cons
Noel-Baker, Capt. F. E.	Brentford and Chiswick, Middx	Lab
Noel-Baker, P. J.	Derby	Lab
Noel-Buxton, Lady	Norwich	Lab
Nutting, A.	Melton, Leics	Cons

O'Brien, T.	Nottingham West	Lab
Oldfield, W. H.	Manchester Gorton	Lab
Oliver, G. H.	Ilkeston, Derbyshire	Lab
O'Neill, Sir H.	Antrim	Ulster U
Orbach, M.	Willesden East, Middx	Lab
Orr, Sir J. Boyd	Scottish Universities	Ind
Orr-Ewing, J. L.	Weston-super-Mare, Somerset	Cons
Osborne, C.	Louth, Lincoln and Rutland	Cons
Paget, R. T.	Northampton	Lab
Paling, W.	Wentworth, West Riding	Lab
Paling, W.	Dewsbury	Lab
Palmer, A. M. F.	Wimbledon	Lab
Pargiter, A. G.	Spelthorne, Middx	Lab
Parker, J.	Dagenham, Essex	Lab
Parkin, Flt Lt B. T.	Stroud, Glos	Lab
Paton, Mrs F.	Rushcliffe, Nottinghamshire	Lab
Paton, J.	Norwich	Lab
Peake, O.	Leeds North	Cons
Pearson, A.	Pontypridd, Glamorgan	Lab
Peart, Capt. T. F.	Workington, Cumberland	Lab
Perrins, W.	Birmingham Yardley	Lab
Pethick-Lawrence, F. W.	Edinburgh East	Lab
Peto, Brig. C. M. H.	Barnstaple, Devon	Cons
Pickthorn, K.	Cambridge University	Cons
Piratin, P.	Stepney Mile End	Comm
Pitman, I. J.	Bath	Cons
Platts-Mills, J. F. F.	Finsbury	Lab
Ponsonby, Col C. E.	Sevenoaks, Kent	Cons
Poole, Capt. C. C.	Lichfield, Staffs	Lab
Poole, Col O. B. S.	Oswestry, Shropshire	Cons
Popplewell, E.	Newcastle upon Tyne West	Lab
Porter, E.	Warrington	Lab
Porter, G.	Leeds Central	Lab
Prescott, Capt. W. R. S.	Darwen, Lancs	Cons

Price, M. P.	Forest of Dean, Glos	Lab
Prior-Palmer, Brig. O.	Worthing West, Sussex	Cons
Pritt, D. N.	Hammersmith North	Ind Lab
Proctor, W. T.	Eccles	Lab
Pryde, D. J.	Peebles and Southern Midlothian	Lab
Pursey, Cdr H.	Hull East	Lab
Pym, L. R.	Monmouth	Cons
Raikes, H. V.	Liverpool Wavertree	Cons
Ramsay, Maj. S.	Forfar	Cons
Randall, H. E.	Clitheroe, Lancs	Lab
Ranger, J.	Ilford South	Lab
Rankin, J.	Glasgow Tradeston	Lab
Rathbone, Miss E.	Combined English Universities	Ind
Rayner, Brig. R.	Totnes, Devon	Cons
Reed, Sir S.	Aylesbury, Bucks	Cons
Rees-Williams, Lt-Col D.	Croydon South	Lab
Reeves, J.	Greenwich	Lab
Reid, J. S. C.	Glasgow Hillhead	Cons
Reid, T.	Swindon, Wilts	Lab
Renton, Maj. D.	Huntingdon	Lib Nat
Richards, R.	Wrexham, Denbighshire	Lab
Ridealgh, Mrs M.	Ilford North	Lab
Robens, A.	Wansbeck, Northumberland	Lab
Roberts, Sqdn Ldr E. O.	Merioneth	Lib
Roberts, G. O.	Caernarvonshire	Lab
Roberts, H.	Birmingham Handsworth	Cons
Roberts, Maj P. G.	Sheffield Ecclesall	Cons
Roberts, W.	Cumberland Northern	Lib
Robertson, D.	Wandsworth Streatham	Cons
Robertson, J. J.	Berwick and Haddington	Lab
Robinson, Wg Cdr J. R.	Blackpool South	Cons
Rogers, G.	Kensington North	Lab
Ropner, Col L.	Barkston Ash, West Riding	Cons
Ross, Sir R.	Londonderry	Ulster U

Royle, C.	Salford West	Lab
Salter, Sir A.	Oxford University	Ind
Sanderson, Sir F.	Ealing East, Middx	Cons
Sargood, R.	Bermondsey West	Lab
Savory, Prof. D. L.	Belfast University	Ulster U
Scollan, T.	Renfrew Western	Lab
Scott, Lt-Col Lord W.	Roxburgh and Selkirk	Cons
Segal, Sqdn Ldr S.	Preston	Lab
Sharp, Lt-Col G. M.	Spen Valley, West Riding	Lab
Shaw, Mrs C. M.	Kilmarnock	Lab
Shawcross, Cdr C. N.	Widnes, Lancs	Lab
Shawcross, H.	St Helens	Lab
Shephard, Lt-Col S.	Newark, Notts	Cons
Shepherd, Lt D. S.	Bucklow, Cheshire	Cons
Shinwell, E.	Seaham, Durham	Lab
Shurmer, P.	Birmingham Sparkbrook	Lab
Silkin, L.	Camberwell Peckham	Lab
Silverman, J.	Birmingham Erdington	Lab
Silverman, S. S.	Nelson and Colne	Lab
Simmons, C. J.	Birmingham West	Lab
Skeffington, A. M.	Lewisham West	Lab
Skeffington-Lodge, Lt T.	Bedford	Lab
Skinnard, F. W.	Harrow East	Lab
Sloan, A.	South Ayrshire	Lab
Smiles, Sir W.	Down, Northern Ireland	Ulster U
Smith, Sir Ben	Bermondsey Rotherhithe	Lab
Smith, Capt. C.	Colchester, Essex	Lab
Smith, Ellis	Stoke, Stoke-on-Trent	Lab
Smith, E. P.	Ashford, Kent	Cons
Smith, H. N.	Nottingham South	Lab
Smith, S. H.	Hull South-West	Lab
Smith, T.	Normanton, West Riding	Lab
Smithers, Sir W.	Orpington, Kent	Cons
Snadden W. M.	Kinross and Western	Cons

Snow, Capt. J. W.	Portsmouth Central	Lab
Solley, L. J.	Thurrock, Essex	Lab
Sorensen, Rev. R. W.	Leyton West	Lab
Soskice, Maj. F.	Birkenhead East	Lab
Southby, Sir A.	Epsom, Surrey	Cons
Sparks, J.	Acton, Middx	Lab
Spearman, A. C. M.	Scarborough and Whitby, North Riding	Cons
Spence, Maj. H. R.	Aberdeen and Kincardine Central	Cons
Stamford, W.	Leeds West	Lab
Stanley, Col O.	Bristol West	Cons
Steele, T.	Lanark	Lab
Stephen, Rev. C.	Glasgow Camlachie	Ind Lab
Stewart, J. Henderson	Fife East	Lib Nat
Stewart, Maj. R. M.	Fulham East	Lab
Stoddart-Scott, Lt-Col. M.	Pudsey and Otley, West Riding	Cons
Stokes, R. R.	Ipswich	Lab
Strachey, Wg Cdr J.	Dundee	Lab
Strauss, G. R.	Lambeth North	Lab
Stross, Dr B.	Hanley, Stoke-on-Trent	Lab
Stuart, J.	Moray and Nairn	Cons
Stubbs, A. E.	Cambridgeshire	Lab
Studholme, Maj. H. G.	Tavistock, Devon	Cons
Summerskill, Dr E.	Fulham West	Lab
Sunderland, J. W.	Preston	Lab
Sutcliffe H.	Royton, Lancs	Cons
Swingler, Capt. S.	Stafford	Lab
Symonds, Maj. A. L.	Cambridge	Lab
Taylor, C. S.	Eastbourne, East Sussex	Cons
Taylor, Vice-Adm. E. A.	Paddington South	Cons
Taylor, H. B.	Mansfield, Notts	Lab
Taylor, R. J.	Morpeth	Lab
Taylor, Dr S.	Barnet, Herts	Lab
Teeling, Flt Lt W.	Brighton	Cons

Thomas, I. O.	The Wrekin, Shropshire	Lab
Thomas, Ivor	Keighley, West Riding	Lab
Thomas, J. P. L.	Hereford	Cons
Thomas, J. R.	Dover, Kent	Lab
Thomas, T. G.	Cardiff Central	Lab
Thomson, Sir D.	Aberdeen South	Cons
Thorneycroft, H.	Manchester Clayton	Lab
Thornton- Kemsley, Col C. N.	Kincardine and Western	Cons
Thorpe, Lt-Col R. A.	Berwick-on-Tweed	Cons
Thurtle, E.	Shoreditch	Lab
Tiffany, S.	Peterborough	Lab
Timmins, J.	Bothwell, Lanark	Lab
Titterington, M. F.	Bradford South	Lab
Tolley, L.	Kidderminster, Worcs	Lab
Tomlinson, G.	Farnworth, Lancs	Lab
Touche, G. C.	Reigate, Surrey	Cons
Turner-Samuels, M.	Gloucester	Lab
Turton, R. H.	Thirsk and Malton, North Riding	Cons
Ungoed-Thomas, Maj. L.	Llandaff and Barry	Lab
Usborne, H. C.	Birmingham Acocks Green	Lab
Vane, Lt-Col W. M. F.	Westmorland	Cons
Vernon, Maj. W.	Camberwell Dulwich	Lab
Viant, S. P.	Willesden West, Middx	Lab
Wadsworth, G.	Buckrose, East Riding	Lib
Wakefield, Sir W. W.	St Marylebone	Cons
Walkden, E.	Doncaster, West Riding	Lab
Walker, G. H.	Rossendale	Lab
Walker-Smith, Lt-Col D.	Hertford	Cons
Wallace, G. D.	Chislehurst, Kent	Lab
Wallace, H. W.	Walthamstow East	Lab
Warbey, W. N.	Luton, Beds	Lab
Ward, Grp-Capt. G. R.	Worcester	Cons

Watkins, T. E.	Brecon and Radnor	Lab
Watson, W. M.	Dunfermline	Lab
Watt, Brig. G. S. Harvie	Richmond, Surrey	Cons
Webb, M.	Bradford Central	Lab
Webbe, Sir H.	Westminster Abbey	Cons
Weitzman, D.	Stoke Newington	Lab
Wells, P. L.	Faversham, Kent	Lab
Wells, Maj. W. T.	Walsall	Lab
Westwood, J.	Stirling and Falkirk	Lab
Wheatley, Lt-Col M. J.	Dorset Eastern	Cons
White, C. F.	Derby Western	Lab
White, Sir D.	Fareham, Hants	Cons
White, Lt-Col D. Price	Caernarvon Boroughs	Cons
White, H.	Derby North-Eastern	Lab
White, Maj. J. B.	Canterbury, Kent	Cons
Whiteley, W.	Blaydon, Durham	Lab
Whittaker, J. E.	Heywood and Radcliffe	Lab
Wigg, Lt-Col G. E.	Dudley	Lab
Wilcock, Grp-Capt. C. A.	Derby	Lab
Wilkes. Maj. L.	Newcastle upon Tyne Central	Lab
Wilkins, W. A.	Bristol South	Lab
Wilkinson, Miss E.	Jarrow, Durham	Lab
Willey, F.	Sunderland	Lab
Willey, O. G.	Cleveland, North Riding	Lab
Williams, C.	Torquay, Devon	Cons
Williams, D. J.	Neath, Glamorgan	Lab
Williams, E. J.	Ogmore, Glamorgan	Lab
Williams, Lt-Cdr G. W.	Tonbridge, Kent	Cons
Williams, J. L.	Glasgow Kelvingrove	Lab
Williams, T.	Don Valley, West Riding	Lab
Williams, W. R.	Heston and Isleworth, Middx	Lab
Williamson, T.	Brigg, Lincoln and Rutland	Lab
Willink, H. U.	Croydon North	Cons
Willis, E.	Edinburgh North	Lab
Willoughby de Eresby, Lord	Rutland and Stamford	Cons

Wills, Mrs E. A.	Birmingham Duddleston	Lab
Wilmot, J.	Deptford	Lab
Wilson, J. H.	Ormskirk, Lancs	Lab
Winterton, Earl	Horsham, West Sussex	Cons
Wise, Maj. F. J.	King's Lynn, Norfolk	Lab
Woodburn, A.	Clackmannan and Eastern	Lab
Woods, Rev. G. S.	Mossley, Lancs	Lab
Wyatt, Maj. W.	Birmingham Aston	Lab
Yates, V.	Birmingham Ladywood	Lab
York, Maj. C.	Ripon, West Riding	Cons
Young, Maj. A. S. L.	Glasgow Partick	Cons
Young, Sir R.	Newton, Lancs	Lab
Younger, Maj. K.	Grimsby	Lab
Zilliacus, K.	Gateshead	Lab

Abbreviations:

Cons	Conservative
Lab	Labour
Lib	Liberal
C/Wealth	Common Wealth
Ulster U	Ulster Unionist
Nat	National
Lib Nat	Liberal National
Irish Nat	Irish Nationalist
Ind	Independent
Nat Lib	National Liberal
Ind Cons	Independent Conservative
Ind Ulster U	Independent Ulster Unionist
Ind Lab	Independent Labour
Ind Cons	Independent Conservative
Irish Nat	Irish Nationalist

Bibliography

Addison, Paul, *The Road to 1945* (Quartet Books 1977)

Alanbrooke, Lord, *War Diaries* (Weidenfeld & Nicolson, 2001)

Ashley, Jack, *Journey into Silence* (The Bodley Head, 1973)

Ashley, Jack, *Act of Defiance* (Reinhardt Books, 1992)

Attlee, C. R., *As it Happened* (Heinemann, 1954)

Attlee, C. R., *The Labour Party in Perspective* (Gollancz, 1937)

Beckett, Francis *Clem Attlee* (Politico's, 2000)

Beckett, Francis, *The Enemy Within* (John Murray, 1995)

Benn, Tony, *Diaries* (Hutchinson, 1994)

Boothby, Robert, *Recollections of a Rebel* (Hutchison, 1978)

Braddock, Bessie, *The Braddocks* (Macdonald, 1963)

Brown, George, *In My Way* (Book Club Associates, 1970)

Bryant, Chris, *Stafford Cripps* (Hodder & Stoughton, 1997)

Bullock, Allan, *Ernest Bevin* (Heinemann, 1967)

Burridge, T. D., *British Labour & Hitler's War* (André Deutsch, 1976)

Callaghan, James, *Time and Chance* (Collins, 1987)

Campbell, John, *Nye Bevan* (Weidenfeld & Nicolson, 1987)

Castle, Barbara, *Fighting All the Way* (Macmillan, 1993)

Colville, John, *Fringes of Power* (Hodder & Stoughton, 1985)

Colville, John, *Footprints in Time* (Collins, 1976)

Cooke, Colin, *Stafford Cripps* (Hodder & Stoughton, 1957)

Donoughue & Jones, *Herbert Morrison* (Weidenfeld & Nicolson, 1973)

Elwyn-Jones, Lord, *In my Times* (Weidenfeld & Nicolson, 1983)

Fisher, Nigel, *Iain Macleod* (André Deutsch, 1973)

Goodman, Geoffrey, *From Bevan to Blair* (Pluto Press, 2003)

Gordon Walker, Patrick, *Political Diaries 1932-1971* (Historians' Press, 1991)

Griffiths, James, *James Griffiths and his Times* (Welsh Labour Party, 1976)

Grimond, Jo, *Memoirs* (Heinemann, 1979)

Harris, Kenneth, *Attlee* (Weidenfeld & Nicolson, 1982)

Harvey, Oliver, *Oliver Harvey Diaries 1941-45* (Collins, 1978)

Haxey, Simon, *Tory MP* (Gollancz, 1939)

Healey, Denis, *The Time of My Life* (Michael Joseph, 1989)

Henderson, Nicholas, *The Private Office* (Weidenfeld & Nicolson, 1984)

Hennessy, Peter, *Never Again* (Vintage 1993)

Hollis, Patricia, *Jennie Lee – a Life* (Oxford University Press, 1997)

Hughes, Emyrs, *Rebel in Parliament* (Charles Skilton, 1969)

Jay, Douglas, *Change and Fortune* (Hutchison, 1980)

Jefferys, Kevin, *Anthony Crosland* (Richard Cohen Books, 1999)

Jenkins, Roy, *Churchill* (Macmillan, 2001)

Jenkins, Roy, *A Life at the Centre* (Macmillan, 1991)

Johnston, Thomas, *Memories* (Collins, 1952)

Jones, Jack, *Union Man* (Collins, 1986)

Jones, Mervyn, *A Radical Life* (Hutchison, 1991)

Kee, Robert, *The World We Fought For* (Guild Publishing, 1985)

Lee, Jennie, *My Life with Nye* (Jonathan Cape, 1980)

Macmillan, Harold, *Tides of Fortune* (Macmillan, 1969)

Martin, Kingsley, *Harold Laski* (Gollancz, 1953)

Mayhew, Christopher, *Time to Explain* (Hutchinson, 1987)

McNair, John, *The Beloved Rebel* (George Allen & Unwin, 1955)

Mikardo, Ian, *Back-Bencher* (Weidenfeld & Nicolson, 1988)

Mitchell, Austin, *Election '45* (Fabian Society, 1995)

Morgan, Kenneth O., *Callaghan – a Life* (Oxford University Press, 1997)

Morrison, Herbert, *Herbert Morrison* (Odhams Press, 1960)

Nicholson, Harold, *Diaries and Letters* (Collins, 1967)

Owen, Frank, *Tempestuous Journey* (Hutchinson, 1954)

Pimlott, Ben, *Harold Wilson* (Harper Collins, 1992)

Pimlott, Ben, *Hugh Dalton* (Jonathan Cape 1986)

Rhodes James, Robert, *Anthony Eden* (Weidenfeld & Nicolson, 1986)

Shinwell, Emmanuel, *Lead with the Left* (Cassell, 1981)

Strauss, Patricia, *Cripps* (Duell, Sloan & Pearce, 1942)

271

Taylor, A. J. P., *A Personal History* (Hodder and Stoughton, 1983)

Taylor of Mansfield, Lord, *Up Hill all the Way* (Sidgwick & Jackson, 1972)

Thomas, George, *George Thomas – Mr Speaker* (Century Publishing, 1985)

Thomas, Hugh, *John Strachey* (Eyre Methuen, 1973)

Turner & Rennell, *When Daddy Came Home* (Hutchison, 1995)

Vernon, Betty D., *Ellen Wilkinson* (Croom Helm, 1982)

Waller, Maureen, *London 1945* (John Murray, 2004)

Wheen, Francis, *Tom Driberg* (Chatto & Windus, 1990)

Williams, Francis, *50 Years' March* (Odhams Press, 1950)

Williams, Francis, *A Prime Minister Remembers* (Heinemann, 1961)

Williams, Philip M., *Hugh Gaitskell Diaries* (Jonathan Cape, 1983)

Williams, Tom, *Digging for Britain* (Hutchison, 1965)

Wyatt, Woodrow, *Confessions of an Optimist* (Collins, 1985)

Index

273